KARAKORAM

"In *Karakoram*, Steve Swenson brings us into the world of alpine climbing with balance and humility. Being able to amass a string of elite ascents while maintaining a full-fledged engineering career at home is rare in the world of alpinists. Steve's dedication to the people in his life, from his family to his expedition teams, is inspirational—and it's in part that dedication that allows him to weave the geopolitical conflicts of the region, and its devastating effects on the people, into this climbing narrative. A fascinating read."

—CONRAD ANKER

Climber and co-founder of the Alex Lowe Charitable Foundation

"The Karakoram is the greatest mountain range on Earth, the ultimate expression of the word 'mountain.' Steve Swenson takes us deep into these amazing peaks, writing in a language that is direct and honest, just like the man himself. His story avoids climbers' jargon and, through intimate firsthand insights, explores how conflict has affected the people of the region over the last thirty-five years. Steve's relationship with Haji Ghulam Rasool proves that trust and friendship trump fear and fanatical fundamentalism every time."

—BARRY BLANCHARD

Mountain guide, author, and winner, 2015 Boardman Tasker Prize for Mountain Literature

KARAKORAM

Climbing Through the Kashmir Conflict

STEVE
SWENSON

MOUNTAINEERS
BOOKS

MOUNTAINEERS BOOKS

Mountaineers Books is the nonprofit publishing division of The Mountaineers, an organization founded in 1906 and dedicated to the exploration, preservation, and enjoyment of outdoor and wilderness areas.

1001 SW Klickitat Way, Suite 201, Seattle, WA 98134
800.553.4453, www.mountaineersbooks.org

Printed in the United States of America
Distributed in the United Kingdom by Cordee, www.cordee.co.uk
20 19 18 17   1 2 3 4 5

Copyeditor: Amy Smith Bell
Design and layout: Kate Basart/Union Pageworks
Cartographer: Bart Wright

All photographs by the author unless credited otherwise
Cover photograph: Colin Prior
Frontispiece: *Greg Child leaving Camp III at 25,000 feet on the north ridge of K2*
Page 12 photograph: *Balti porters on the Baltoro Glacier with Gasherbrum IV in the distance*

A record for this book is available at the Library of Congress.

Mountaineers Books titles may be purchased for corporate, educational, or other promotional sales, and our authors are available for a wide range of events. For information on special discounts or booking an author, contact our customer service at 800-553-4453 or mbooks@mountaineersbooks.org.

♻ Printed on recycled paper

ISBN (hardcover): 978-1-59485-973-1
ISBN (ebook): 978-1-59485-974-8

For Ann, my most steadfast supporter,
and Marty Dahlgren, who first took me to the
mountains and opened the door

CONTENTS

Foreword by Greg Child..9

Author's Note 11

Preface 13

Map Legend 15

Map of the Karakoram Region 16

CHAPTER 1
TO PAKISTAN...19
Gasherbrum IV Southwest Ridge, 1980; East Face, 1980

MAP 2: K-2, Gasherbrum Group, Baltoro Glacier and Environs..........22

CHAPTER 2
ELUSIVE SUMMITS...47
Gasherbrum IV Northwest Ridge, 1983; K2 North Ridge, 1986;
K2 South Face 1987

CHAPTER 3
K2 AT LAST...83
K2 North Ridge, 1990

CHAPTER 4
LIFE AND DEATH..111
Gasherbrum IV Southwest Ridge, 1992

CHAPTER 5
EVEREST...121
Everest Kangshung Face, 1994; North Ridge, 1994

CHAPTER 6
ONE MORE TRY 143
Gasherbrum IV Southwest Ridge, 1999

CHAPTER 7

AFTER 9/11 155

Kondus Valley, 2001; Charakusa Valley: Nayser Brakk, Kapura, and
K7 West Northwest Ridge, 2004

MAP 3: Charakusa and Nangma Valley 170

CHAPTER 8

THE KILLER MOUNTAIN 179

Nanga Parbat Mazeno Ridge, 2004

MAP 4: Nanga Parbat 184

CHAPTER 9

THE WORLD'S HARDEST MOUNTAINS 201

Latok II South Ridge, 2006; Latok I North Ridge, 2007; Choktoi
Spire North Ridge, 2007

MAP 5: The Latok Group 206

CHAPTER 10

THE RISK OF REGRET 231

Saser Kangri II Southwest Face, 2009; Tsok Kangri, 2011;
Saser Kangri II Southwest Face, 2011

MAP 6: Saser Kangri Group 240

CHAPTER 11

ATTACK 265

Nanga Parbat, 2013

CHAPTER 12

PASSING THE TORCH 271

Changi Tower, 2015; K6 Central, 2015

Sources 308
Acknowledgments 309
Index 311

FOREWORD

One thousand two hundred. That is the number of days that Steve Swenson has spent in Pakistan, India, and China during his journeys to the vast Karakoram Range. That's a lot of time spent sweltering in bustling cities like Islamabad where expeditions begin with a whole lot of bureaucratic paperwork, and it's a lot of time spent wearing out the soles of his boots hoofing up river gorges and across the sharp terrain of the glaciers that convey him into the mountains. Steve is a familiar face to village people like the Balti whose hamlets dot the paths into the mountains; they recognize him as a generous friend who leaves more than he takes.

It's been a long time since I traveled with Steve in such places, but I know he has changed little in his affection for the particular ruggedness that the Karakoram Range presents. It's not only the crisp light and jagged skylines that have been drawing him back for four decades; it's also the unique human factors of every expedition that beckons him.

Steve and I shared a couple of trips to K2, one unsuccessful and a second trip on which we got to the summit. On those trips we each learned to appreciate the good camping skills of the other, meaning we developed a mutual appreciation for a shared capacity to go rough for long periods, unwashed, malnourished, uncomfortable, and ragged. These are essential skills for mountaineering trips that are longer than a weekend. It is no beauty contest up there, and we didn't look like the clean-cut studs of ad campaigns now promoting outdoor brands.

Steve had sheer brute strength in spades, and apparently still does. He was always able to punch out more than his share of effort through deep snow, wet porridge snow, terrifying biscuit-crust snow. Whimpering was not one of his foibles; he just shouldered his pack and got the job done, regardless of the wind or cold or heat or the grinding pain of heavy loads.

Being grounded and pragmatic was one of Steve's greatest attributes when hemmed in by mountains. While those around him could get wound up by emotions or possessed by their neuroses, Steve remained calm and objective. He was a bit like a counselor, acting on behalf of the mountain, which needed the climbers to keep sane so they could climb it. Far from his least helluvathing was the way he managed to embark on a major high altitude expedition once a year, all the while holding down an executive position for a serious engineering firm, plus marriage and family, with time on the side to be—for a stretch of years—president of the American Alpine Club. When I used to climb with him in a Seattle climbing gym there were more than a few of us who were awed by all that, because by contrast, we were barely getting by, a bunch of regular guys who were mostly stumped by the machinations of life. One of the group had a great idea: a self-help program with a campaign slogan, BE LIKE STEVE!, on T-shirts and billboards. We chanted it to each other as we tried hard problems in the gym, and it seemed to propel us to new levels. Steve chuckled at this foolishness, then went back to his training.

I saw Steve rattled only once, in Peru, as he and I were trying to climb a horribly corniced ridge on Huascaran. The snow was soft and protruded bulbously over every side of the ridge, and we had to keep climbing up and over house-size blobs of snow. Our belay stations often consisted of holes dug in the snow in which we sat and hoped the snow formations didn't collapse. Alpinists call these sort of formations *gendarmes*, which is a French word for policeman, but I thought they were criminal. We climbed like this for a couple of days, and when a gap in the clouds showed us that we had miles more of this terrain to climb we became discouraged. Steve led one final *gendarme* and when I reached him he said only, "Many thoughts of Lars." He was talking about his son, who at the time, 1984, was a toddler. Steve had been telling me the previous evening about the pleasure he found in taking Lars to the alpine meadows around Mount Rainier where they found a spread of wild berries and grazed until their bellies ached. This ridge was not worth the risk of missing out in participating in his son's life, so we quit the climb and rappelled wildly down the side of the ridge into a verdant valley.

Steve records more than fifteen expeditions in this book. Any career as voluminous as that will include episodes where the climber has teetered on the edge, but Steve has always taken calculated risks rather than roll dice in a crapshoot. Climbing K2 with Steve in 1990 is among the great experiences of my life. Ironically one of the gifts we gave each other on that ascent was the freedom not to worry about each other. By being completely independent up there, completely trusting in one another to make the right decision and not weight the other down with it, we were able to really concentrate on the mountain. To the outsider that might look like every-man-for-himself, but really, we couldn't have gotten any closer.

—GREG CHILD, *Castle Valley, October 2016*

AUTHOR'S NOTE

All descriptions, events, and dialogue described in this book are based on my personal memories, journals, and discussions with other participants. Any errors or misinterpretations are mine alone. In a few instances names have been changed to protect privacy.

PREFACE

I n October 1947, Pashtuns from the Northwest Frontier Province (now called Khyber Pakhtunkhwa, or KPK) in Pakistan, along with soldiers from the newly formed Pakistan Army, crossed into the state of Kashmir. British India had been partitioned into the new independent nations of India and Pakistan on August 15 of that year. During Partition, as this event was known, the Hindu-majority provinces were assigned to India, and the Muslim-majority provinces were incorporated into a geographically divided East and West Pakistan. In the process an estimated one million people were massacred in a wave of intercommunal violence and ethnic cleansing when fourteen million people exchanged geography: Muslims migrated to Pakistan, and Hindus and Sikhs to India. Partition was the largest human migration in history. Both countries had made claims to Kashmir.

As the Pakistanis attempted to take that Muslim-majority state by force, the Hindu maharaja of Kashmir ceded control to India in return for a defense agreement. India promptly sent in its military to confront the Pakistanis, which led to the First Kashmir War (also known as the Indo-Pakistani War of 1947–48). After a year of fighting, the United Nations brokered a cease-fire, leaving the two armies facing off over what has today become known as the Line of Control (LOC) and the Actual Ground Position Line (AGPL). Since the cease-fire of 1949, there have been two more wars, in 1965 and 1971, several localized conflicts, and numerous diplomatic efforts—none of which has resolved the conflict between India and Pakistan. The status of Kashmir became more complicated in 1962, when China prevailed over India in a border war and took a portion of Kashmir that is still claimed by India.

The Karakoram Range and the Western Himalayas are located within this disputed region of Kashmir, and they create a natural barrier between these antagonists. Four of the world's fourteen mountains higher than 8,000 meters (26,247 feet) are located in the Karakoram, including K2 (8,611 meters, or 28,251 feet), the second highest peak after Mount Everest (8,872 meters, or 29,108 feet). Kashmir also includes Nanga Parbat (8,126 meters, or 26,660 feet), the world's ninth highest mountain and the westernmost 8,000-meter peak of the fifteen-hundred-mile-long Himalayan Range. Before World War II and the subsequent partition of India, expeditions from all over the world had explored, mapped, and climbed in these mountains. The First Kashmir War closed that region to climbing and trekking, but just a few years later and throughout most of the 1950s, Pakistan reopened much of the Karakoram and the western Himalayas under its control. During that decade, K2, the three other 8,000-meter Karakoram peaks (Broad Peak, Gasherbrum I, and Gasherbrum II), Nanga Parbat (part of the Himalayan Range), and a number of significant smaller peaks were climbed for the first time. But tensions in Kashmir between India and Pakistan and a border dispute between India and China led to reclosure in 1961.

For the next thirteen years, the Karakoram and the western Himalayas were off-limits to climbers. During that period mountaineering proliferated in other parts of the Himalayas and high mountain regions of the world. In 1974, however, Pakistan reopened most of the Karakoram and the western Himalayas it administered, making available to a new generation of alpinists a trove of mountains that had been locked away in a "political wilderness," most still unclimbed. Subsequent conflicts and skirmishes along the LOC and the AGPL in the intervening decades resulted in a cycle of reclosing and reopening many of these mountains. Throughout this book I explain how the Kashmir conflict has affected climbing in the Karakoram and the western Himalayas. After the terror attacks of 9/11, political violence resulting from the ongoing conflict between the militants and security forces in northwestern Pakistan has further increased security issues for climbers. I've suggested ways to minimize risk.

In 1980, six years after these mountains were reopened, I organized my first expedition to Pakistan to attempt a new route on one of the most difficult mountains in the Karakoram. My partners and I had climbed big mountains throughout North and South America, but we'd only read about the scale and magnitude of the peaks in South Asia. In addition to breathtaking landscapes, that expedition revealed a part of the world to me populated by rugged and independent people. I was captivated. That trip, thirty-seven years ago, began an ongoing journey that fulfills my childhood dreams of exploration and discovery in the natural world.

An odyssey begun out of pure ambition to climb the great Karakoram mountains and reach their elusive summits redefined my personal values. On my fifteen expeditions to that region, the meaning and importance of partnership, fortitude, personal responsibility, and compassion has been clarified. This book offers those stories, set within the context of complex international conflict.

Map Legend

⚊	Camp	··················	Route/Trail
☐	Town/City	▬▬▬▬▬	Road
○	Village	——————	River/Stream
▪	Other location	▬·▬··▬··▬··	National border
▲	Mountain		Ridgeline
⟨⟩	Pass		

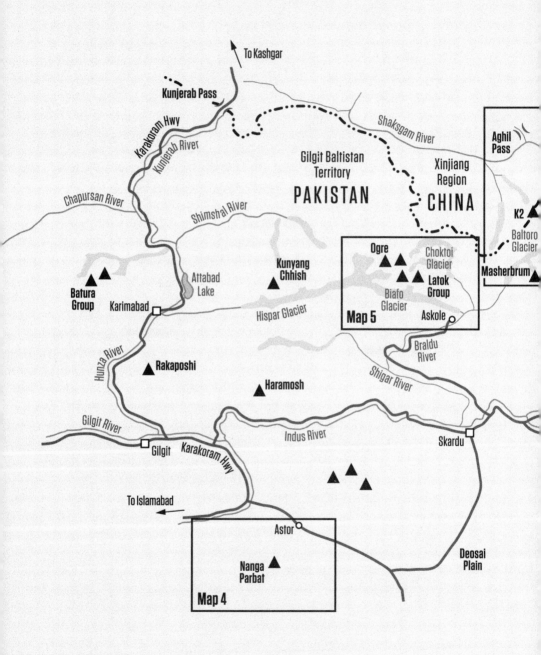

MAP 1: *The Karakoram Range*

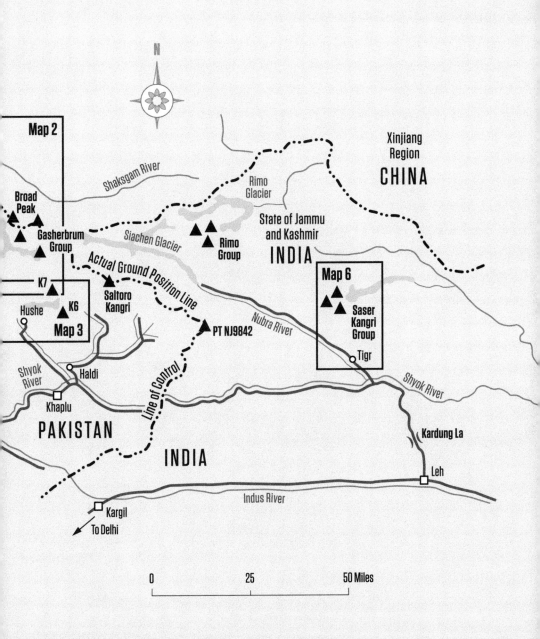

A seriously ill Jim Nelson is carried by Balti porters to Concordia. (Photo by Charlie Schertz)

CHAPTER 1

TO PAKISTAN

GASHERBRUM IV SOUTHWEST RIDGE, 1980
EAST FACE, 1980

The aging British Airways Lockheed L-1011 rattled and shook as it banked sharply on its approach to the runway in Islamabad, Pakistan. Leaning over from my cramped seat, I looked down through the scratched window and caught my first vision of the immense and rugged Karakoram Range that occupies the far western part of the Greater Himalayas. The view from 30,000 feet was both intimidating and exciting, and I tried to identify some of the famous peaks I'd only seen in photographs. It was May 1980, and at age twenty-six I was about to embark on the ultimate climbing adventure on Gasherbrum IV (7,925 meters, or 26,001 feet)—one of the world's steepest, highest, and most difficult mountains. It stood among other Karakoram Himalayan giants such as K2, Broad Peak, and Gasherbrum I. American climber Galen Rowell referred to this range as "the Throne Room of the Mountain Gods." Gasherbrum IV had only been climbed once before, by an Italian expedition in 1958. The summit was reached by mountaineers Carlo Mauri and Walter Bonatti.

The massive west face of Gasherbrum IV towers above Concordia, where several glaciers converge to form the Baltoro Glacier (63 kilometers, or 39 miles, in length), the approach route for all the Karakoram 8,000-meter peaks. With steep rock and ice on all sides, Gasherbrum IV doesn't have any easy stretches or flat places to camp. Our team consisted of my friends and climbing partners from Seattle: Todd Bibler, Don Fredrickson, Matt Kerns, Craig McKibben, and Jim Nelson. I had taken on much of the trip organization, so the role of expedition leader fell to me. We had also recruited a doctor, Charlie Schertz, to join us. Having studied the account of the first ascent of Gasherbrum IV, the team was compelled by the peak's size, beauty, and technical climbing difficulty. This mountain would be more challenging than anything we had ever climbed, and our plan was to ascend by a new route: the southwest ridge. We knew each other well, and everyone had worked hard to get this far.

The plane landed, marking the culmination of two years of work: to secure special climbing permits, visas, and regulations from the Pakistan government; to prepare budgets; to obtain equipment, baggage, and financial sponsors; and to gather and pack our supplies. To prepare physically, each of us had followed a rigorous workout regimen to give us the strength to climb steep ice and rock at extreme altitude. As we gathered our many bags and boxes in the Islamabad terminal, I felt confident about the challenges ahead. Stepping outside the airport, however, I was completely unprepared for the heat and the crushing mass of people wanting to carry our bags, offer us rides, sell us trinkets, and beg us for money. We had hired a local adventure tour company to help us with logistics and the government bureaucracy, and fortunately several of its employees were waiting for us. Together, we carried everything to their small bus and headed toward our hotel.

The roads were as chaotic as the airport. Pedestrians, ox carts, three-wheeled motorized scooters belching blue smoke, rickshaws, buses, trucks, and automobiles all jockeyed for position—it was a total free-for-all. In this British Commonwealth country traffic flows on the left side of the road, but that basic rule was frequently violated. And then there was the noise—poorly muffled engines, the loud tinkling of elaborate ornaments swinging from trucks, the *clip clop* of animal hooves on pavement, and the relentless honking, which seemed to be the music this procession danced to. The roadway's edges were packed with impoverished-looking people, bearded men in unkempt shalwar kameez—the traditional loose pajama-like trousers and long, collared shirts. Most of the few women out in public also wore this kind of clothing, but theirs was more colorful or embroidered; their matching scarves covered their heads and shoulders. Some women were completely hidden under flowing burkas that had a rectangle of openwork fabric over the eyes.

Jet lag caught up with us in our air-conditioned hotel rooms, and we slept for the first time in several days. Out of that stupor inherent to crossing a dozen time zones, I woke at first light to loud chanting coming from a loudspeaker mounted on the minaret of a nearby mosque. "Allahu Akbar, Ash-hadu an-la ilaha illa llah" (God is great. I bear witness that there is none worthy of worship other than Allah). At first I thought the muezzin's call to prayer was part of an exotic dream I was having, but as reality came into focus, I jumped out of bed and pulled back the shades to see the sun, barely discernible through the ruddy haze hovering over the city.

The team still had several tasks to complete before heading to the mountains. Provisioning and arranging travel were bewildering but easily tackled. Failing to comply properly with the climbing permit the Pakistan government had issued could cause such long delays we could be forced to go home without ever having set foot in the mountains.

Our destination, Gasherbrum IV, was on the Pakistan border with China, just a few miles from the Line of Control (LOC) with India. Given the government's security concerns over Kashmir and their archenemy India, it was no surprise that our climbing permit was full of security-related rules and regulations. But despite periodic closures as a result of fighting and border tensions, these ruggedly beautiful mountains have been highly sought after by climbers and trekkers. When we arrived in 1980, most of the Pakistani Karakoram had been recently reopened. I assumed the main reason the government had started issuing permits to foreigners again was to help justify their territorial claims.

As part of the permitting process, Pakistan's Inter-Services Intelligence (ISI) agency did a routine security check of all the expeditions. Everyone on our team had to be vetted by the ISI before we left the United States and before the government would issue the permit and visas to enter Pakistan. Throughout Islamabad we noticed police and soldiers armed with automatic weapons stationed at key intersections and buildings. Pakistan

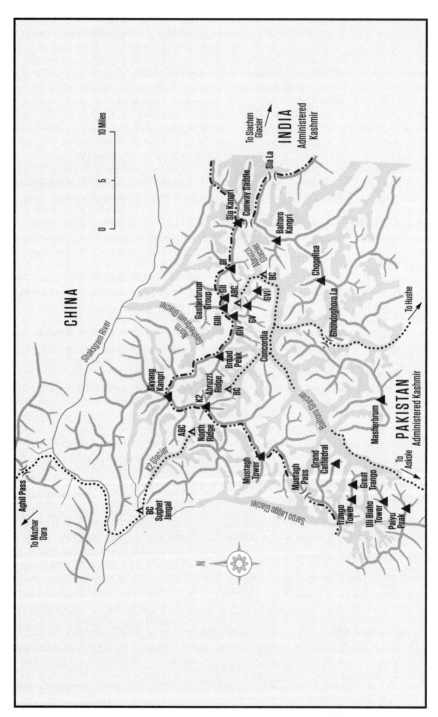

MAP 2: *K-2, Gasherbrum Group, Baltoro Glacier and Environs*

suffered from its birth trauma and the fear of Hindu domination that had been the impetus for Partition. Its conflicts with India over Kashmir and the politics of successive military governments had created an atmosphere of perpetual readiness to defend the country.

On our flight from London to Islamabad, I met an American named Mike Sheldon, who was with the US State Department and lived in Islamabad. He told me that six months earlier, the US embassy there had been attacked and burned by militants. Because of this, combined with the ongoing hostage crisis with American diplomatic personnel in Tehran following Iran's Islamic Revolution, the State Department had sent all nonessential personnel back to the United States. Mike was returning to his job in Islamabad after a visit with his family in Maryland. Having left his wife and children behind, he seemed lonely, and as we got off the plane, Mike offered our team a place to stay.

After a couple of nights in a hotel, I thought we could use a home away from home, so I gave Mike a call. Soon we were settled in a quiet neighborhood in his big, empty house. That comfortable, friendly, and supportive environment made it easier to endure the numerous meetings with government officials to fill out seemingly endless and pointless paperwork. It was also a good opportunity to learn more about Pakistan from someone who had been there for a few years. I understood the dangers we faced when climbing, but what kinds of security dangers did we face in this country? Why had the embassy been burned? Mike answered our questions and helped us stay out of trouble.

We thought completing our bureaucratic chores would take about three days, but for Craig and me these tasks wore on for eleven long days. Frustrated and stuck in Islamabad's oppressive 110°F heat, we argued over how we were spending our money. Ours was a small expedition on a tight budget, mostly self-financed with a few private donations. The bureaucratic roadblocks took more than just time; they involved paying additional fees we hadn't anticipated. The constant negotiations to minimize these extra costs infuriated Don, the most frugal among us. Craig proved himself to be a steadfast voice of reason. As our skilled treasurer, he somehow found creative ways to shift money around so we didn't have to put more into the pot.

The team was required to register with the police. All seven of us had to be present when registering, and we made several trips to the nearby old city of Rawalpindi before we found the office open. We waited in line for hours in a cramped, hot, dimly lit room, cooled only by a slow fan, before submitting our paperwork to a thin bearded man in a skullcap and shalwar kameez. With slow, mechanical movements that must have been performed thousands of times, he stamped our forms, tied them together with string, and tossed them onto a dusty pile of similar bundles. Piles of these papers (that had probably never been looked at again) were stacked to the ceiling around the room's periphery.

Provisioning in the bazaars for our expedition purchases was nothing like a visit to Costco or an American mall. The commercial areas in Islamabad were arranged according to items of a similar nature, so some streets had shops that sold produce and dry goods; elsewhere we found shops selling household products for our field kitchen. The stalls abutted each other, each about the size of a single-car garage with a corrugated-metal rollup door facing the street. How each shop stayed in business was a mystery, because they all sold exactly the same items for similar prices.

Each morning, the team divided into pairs—usually Todd and Don, Matt and Jim, and Craig and I—each with a different assignment. Charlie set out on his own to round up the remaining medical supplies. Todd and Don collected equipment, such as fuel containers and stoves that our porters would need on the trek to base camp. Matt and Jim shopped for food we wouldn't be able to get in the mountains (high-quality pasta and candy bars). Craig and I took care of banking and insurance and assisted the others where we could. To get from one shopping area to another, we rode in old yellow and black British Morris Minor taxis. Once out of the shelter of the car, we were pressed into a flood of people and traffic. The locals seemed comfortable bobbing around vehicles in the street, but I wasn't used to such maneuvering and often forgot to look the other way for cars driving on the left side. I followed one of the locals and hoped for the best. Some of the side streets were calm, with beautiful food stalls full of fresh produce and colorful piles of red, yellow, and green spices. But our excitement over such novel experiences was short-lived each day as the afternoon temperatures rose, draining our energy and our resolve. I thought of Noel Coward's poem from the days of India's British Empire with the refrain: "Mad dogs and Englishmen go out in the midday sun."

From Islamabad, we traveled to Skardu, the Kashmiri town that is the jumping-off point for expeditions to the Greater Karakoram. After the wars between India and Pakistan over the region, Skardu and most of the range ended up on the Pakistani side of the Line of Control. But the only road to Skardu came from the Indian side of the LOC, which was blocked. Similar to West Berlin at the start of the Cold War, Skardu was cut off from the rest of Pakistan. A road to Skardu was being built along the Indus River gorge on the Pakistani side of the LOC, but when we arrived the road had not yet been completed. All the troops, supplies, and—in our case—climbers had to be airlifted in. The commercial turboprop plane from Islamabad to Skardu would take off only if the weather was perfect: these planes flew between mountains along the way that were up to 26,000 feet high. Flights to Skardu were often canceled and seats were hard to come by; some expeditions had waited for weeks to get there. By June 5, six days after arriving in Pakistan, Charlie, Don, Jim, Matt, and Todd got a flight to Skardu, where they could get out of the heat and purchase our remaining supplies there.

Craig had been an invaluable asset in patiently dealing with all the red tape, so I asked him to stay behind with me for a few more days to have our final briefing with the Ministry of Tourism, the government agency that issued our permit. There we were assigned a liaison officer (LO), who would accompany us on our expedition. The Himalayan countries customarily appointed an LO for climbing expeditions. The LO's duties vary: in a high-security region like the Karakoram, the LO is usually a military officer whose main purpose is to ensure that the expedition travels only to places allowed in its permit and complies with all rules and regulations. LOs are supposed to help interpret and facilitate logistics, but they are often unfamiliar with the area and don't speak the local languages, so the adventure tour staff assumes responsibility for these issues. Paying for the LO is a financial burden that generally adds little value, but it is part of the price of admission.

In Pakistan the LO is typically an army captain, a high-status profession. A Muslim expression says it all: "Guarding the nation's borders for one night is worth a thousand nights of prayer." In a place where most people bow toward Mecca six times a day, this means a lot. Many Pakistani officers come from elite or upper-middle-class families. In the patriarchal society, women serve the men, and the boys receive extra care compared with their female siblings. In the Pakistan Army, young officers, who grew up being waited on, are assigned a batman (a personal servant). Unfortunately, many of the army officers assigned to expeditions as LOs have little or no experience in the mountains and are used to having others prepare their meals and do their household chores. An LO can thus be a burden to an expedition if he expects to be served in the way he is accustomed. Experienced Himalayan climbers told me that it is the luck of the draw whether our LO would be a prima donna or a team player.

Things did not start out well with our assigned liaison officer, Captain Noor Alam. Our expedition was required to supply the LO with the same type of clothing and equipment that we had brought for ourselves. But the Ministry of Tourism had neglected to send us Captain Noor's sizes while we were still in the United States, so we had brought average-size clothing and boots. Captain Noor was short and stocky, however, and the clothing didn't fit. He had to approve his clothing and equipment before the expedition was allowed to go into the mountains. As we drove to numerous shops around Islamabad, Craig remarked, "How is it possible that climbing Gasherbrum IV depends on us finding a pair of jeans that fit?"

With the rest of the team off to Skardu, Craig and I tended to the final details. Each evening Mike took us to the US embassy swimming pool to cool off. After the embassy had been burned a few months earlier, it was relocated to a temporary compound several miles away, but the pool and a few recreational facilities were reopened at the old site. After showing our ID to the US Marine guard, we walked past the ruins of the embassy buildings on our way to the pool. The three- and four-story brick and concrete buildings still stood, but above the broken-out windows, blackened walls recalled the flames that covered them with soot. The interiors were charred beyond recognition.

On November 22, 1979, Mike had been at his embassy desk, working as a commercial attaché responsible for facilitating exports from the United States to Pakistan. He heard a small demonstration outside the walls grow into a large, noisy crowd. He wasn't that concerned until he heard gunshots and saw that the demonstrators had overwhelmed the small contingent of marines and climbed over the walls. The embassy staff moved to the relative safety of a secure vault within the complex, where they locked themselves in to wait for rescue by the host country, as dictated by diplomatic rules.

A marine guard had been shot and seriously wounded as he tried to defend the embassy, and he was brought into the vault with the rest of the staff. The heat inside the vault became increasingly intolerable as the embassy buildings burned. Terrified, the 140 personnel waited in vain for hours, hoping the Pakistani security forces would rescue them. Mike told me that his shoes had started to melt to the floor. Without proper medical attention, and despite their efforts to save him, the marine guard died. Above them the vault had a hatch that opened onto the roof of the building, and at one point the demonstrators beat on it to get at the staff they knew were inside. When the noise on the roof quieted down, the group tried to escape from the heat of the burning building. Peeking out from the roof hatch, they discovered it was dusk and the angry mob had dispersed. As Mike and his coworkers climbed onto the roof, Pakistani military helicopters swooped in to evacuate them from the still burning building. In addition to the marine who had died in the vault, an army warrant officer and two Pakistani staff members were killed in the attack.

The enraged mob of Pakistani students and religious fundamentalists had attacked the embassy because Iran's Ayatollah Khomeini had accused the United States and Israel of being behind an attack on Islam's holy site at Mecca. The Ayatollah's report was false, however; in reality, a Saudi Arabian group of Islamic zealots had led a takeover of the mosque that was eventually suppressed by Saudi soldiers and French commandos. The government of Pakistan had done nothing to protect the embassy staff. The reaction of the United States was restrained, apparently because the Carter administration didn't want this incident to detract from efforts to resolve larger strategic issues between the two countries. Still angry, Mike told us that the official US response to the embassy attack was "shameful." They had been left to die in the embassy vault. If it weren't for a bit of luck, he remembered, the incident could have been one of the most devastating losses of diplomats in American history.

With Mike's story on my mind as I walked toward the tranquil pool, past buildings gutted by the violent attack, it was a disturbing contrast. Each evening, the destruction filled me with a sense of foreboding. I felt an urge to escape to the beauty and safety of the mountains as quickly as possible, to leave the chaos of politics behind. It was the first time that a climbing trip had exposed me to the drama of something other than the challenge of the climb itself. Our stay in Islamabad dragged on for five more days. Mike introduced us to some members of the Western diplomatic community. We were invited to their small evening parties, where the conversation was often about politics in South Asia. Craig and I learned that the Cold War had spread to this part of Asia because the United States was supporting the Pakistan-backed mujahideen fighting the Russians who had invaded Afghanistan six months earlier. One of the US diplomats was a former teacher with the Peace Corps in Kabul, and he believed that most of his former students had probably been killed by the Soviets.

With all the paperwork taken care of and the logistics arranged, Craig and I, relieved and excited, finally boarded the Pakistan International Airways (PIA) Fokker F27 turboprop for Skardu with our LO, Captain Noor. The 1950s-era aircraft had a cruising altitude of 20,000 feet. Our flight followed the Indus River gorge into the mountains and past one of the world's highest peaks, Nanga Parbat (8,126 meters, or 26,660 feet). Although PIA was disparagingly known as "Perhaps I Arrive," our pilot flew carefully past the icy flanks of spectacular mountains. I was thrilled to see their majesty up close for the first time. On the approach to Skardu, the Indus River wound through a brown, dry landscape below the peaks' snowy ridges. Snowmelt cascaded down thousands of feet into rivers and creeks in the valley, feeding a complex irrigation system that created a green oasis around the town. The pilot announced that the aircraft's wingtips would be close to the mountainsides as the plane circled to land on the runway. "Do not be alarmed," he told us.

After landing in Skardu, the three of us were driven to our hotel in an open-air jeep. Brown mud-brick houses dotted the poplar-lined streets. The K2 Hotel was located in a beautiful spot overlooking the Indus River below the ancient Kharpocho Fort. The fort was rebuilt after the Mughal conquest of Kashmir in the sixteenth century, when the population converted from Tibetan Buddhism to Islam. Tourism had only just begun to reach Skardu again after the closure of the Karakoram to foreigners between 1962 and 1974. The rundown hotel, with its lackadaisical staff, did not have hot water and offered only simple meals. Craig and I found the rest of our team sitting with the hotel manager in an office so thick with hashish smoke I could hardly make out their faces. With eyes barely open, they greeted us. "Welcome to Skardu," Charlie said.

The word got out that there was an expedition in town that would be hiring porters, so the next morning we found a throng of mostly barefoot men in tattered clothing in the hotel courtyard. The team needed about a hundred porters to carry our supplies, and Nazir Sabir, of the adventure tour company we'd hired in Islamabad, told us that it was customary to select half of them in Skardu and the other half fifty miles later, at the end of a jeep road where we would start our trek to base camp. Nazir was a young man from the Hunza region north of Gilgit (besides Skardu, Gilgit was the other main town in the mountains of northern Pakistan). As a young boy, Nazir had been inspired to climb by the belief that he could see America from the top of the high mountains surrounding his village. He made a name for himself after doing the first ascent of Paiyu Peak in 1976 with several other Pakistanis. Nazir had been assigned to our expedition to help with logistics in Skardu.

The area's Balti people were very poor, and for many of them the only source of income was working for expeditions like ours. Jobs were scarce in 1980; with all the bureaucratic hurdles and lack of tourist infrastructure, only the most ardent climbers and trekkers trickled into the area. When three hundred young men showed up at our hotel, Matt said, "These guys look desperate." He worried it would be difficult to control the crowd if we hired only a fraction of them. Nazir tried to manage the current situation by having all the men sit in rows according to their village, but we didn't know that we were expected to hire a few porters from each of the villages. We had been told by some Americans living in Skardu that Hushe men were friendly and strong, so we made the mistake of hiring too many porters from that village. This caused a mini riot.

As the opportunity for employment faded, the porters who had not been hired rushed toward us in desperation, shouting words in their local Balti language and waving identity cards in our faces. Many of them shoved scraps of paper at us with testimonials from previous expeditions that said things like "Hassan was a very strong porter" or "Mohammed carried a load for us to K2 base camp." About a dozen local police gathered around, and in an attempt to control the crowd, they pushed and hit the porters with heavy sticks, which only added to the chaos. Shocked by this sudden turn of events, we shouted at the police, "Stop!" Our shouting was lost in the din, so we entered the fray to physically separate the police from the crowd. That seemed to calm the situation, and we promised to hire more porters from different villages.

The next morning, we left Skardu in a caravan of jeeps and tractors pulling trailers full of porters and our equipment and other supplies. Driving along the Shigar River on a rough, narrow road with steep drop-offs, rickety bridges, and creek crossings, we cleared occasional blockages from small landslides with picks and shovels. The valley's barren rocky landscape was interrupted every few miles by villages green with fields of wheat, peas, and barley that were irrigated from side streams diverted into a labyrinth of channels. Several of our jeeps had large cargo beds in the back like a pickup truck. To save on the number of passenger jeeps we hired, we rode in the cargo bed on top of our food and equipment. Sitting up high on the loads with the wind in my face, I enjoyed unobstructed views of the surrounding mountains. I ducked under low-hanging wires and trees whenever the jeep drove through villages.

The jeeps stopped at Bongla, where the Braldu River flowed out of the mountains into the Shigar River. Here we would start our trek. In a more orderly process we hired the remaining fifty porters. Sitting in the shade of a lone tree in the barren landscape, we assigned a number to each fifty-pound load and recorded the name and village of the porter who would be responsible for delivering it to our stopping point each day. The loads were picked up, lashed to the porters' backs, and they disappeared up the trail in a cloud of dust. I didn't know whether I should laugh, cry, or shout. After months of planning and days of traveling and bureaucratic haggling, it felt so good to be walking among these great mountains and focusing on what we had come here for: climbing Gasherbrum IV.

I enjoyed the next few hours walking alone along the river valley. Steep brown hillsides soared up thousands of feet on both sides. I crossed a bridge over the river and entered the village of Dassu, where we would camp our first night. As I followed the porters down the trail, I wondered what lie ahead. I trusted that we could depend on each other to stay safe, remain friends, and hopefully summit the mountain. But for the two weeks it would take to hike to base camp, our primary responsibility would be to manage the porters as we moved through the treacherous mountain environment, making sure they stayed safe, healthy, and willing to carry loads. After paying off the porters, we intended to spend six or seven weeks at or above base camp trying to climb Gasherbrum IV, and our porters would return to carry loads out.

Our Balti porters came from remote, isolated high-altitude villages. They subsist on chickens and their eggs, dairy products (and occasionally meat) from grazing goats, and the small patches of wheat and barley that they farm. The growing season is brief in the cold, arid environment, so these commodities are in short supply and many villagers suffer from malnutrition. Medical care is almost nonexistent, and most injuries and ailments go untreated. Infant mortality under age one is more than 30 percent. The Balti people, like the Sherpas in Nepal, originated in Tibet. Thin and wiry, they look like the Sherpas, but their dress and grooming is different. The men are bearded and wear the traditional shalwar kameez or, in the case of some poorer villagers, layers of brown woolen homespun in different stages of disrepair. Nearly all of the men wear a soft, round woolen hat rolled up around the edge to form a brim. In 1980, when we arrived, there were no schools in the villages so these people were mostly illiterate. They were, however, skilled in their age-old traditions of tending the fields and caring for chickens, goats, and yaks.

That evening, after dinner, Charlie began what became a daily practice administering to porters and villagers who took advantage of this rare opportunity to see a medical professional. The porters typically had complaints related to their work, such as blistered feet and headaches. The villagers' medical problems were often more serious, like a child with a cleft palate or a baby with severe burns as a result of crawling into a cooking fire inside the family hut. Charlie had recently completed a surgery residency back in the United States and did what he could, but he faced some impossible situations. One evening, for example, he was led to a hut where the husband in one room explained the gynecological problems his wife was experiencing after childbirth. He wanted Charlie to help, but the woman was in a different room and Charlie wasn't allowed to examine her.

Government rules required us to provide each porter with shoes, socks, sunglasses, and a plastic raincoat and, for each group of ten, a large reinforced plastic tarp for shelter plus a kerosene stove for cooking. We had issued each porter his personal equipment when hired, but after beginning our trek, we discovered they had sold or left behind most of what we had given them. Many porters brought only the clothes on their backs, a thin wool blanket, and a pair of floppy rubber shoes with no socks. Somehow we had been savvy enough to not give them their sunglasses at the start of the trek, which within a few days were needed to keep them from becoming snowblind. Daily living was a hardship for these men, and the contrast with our own lives was uncomfortably apparent. We had modern tents, clothing, and sleeping bags, but our porters were only lightly equipped for such a difficult trek over long glaciers to base camp at 17,000 feet.

Back in Skardu, we had hired Muhammad Hussein as our sirdar—the person in charge of the porters, the man responsible for ensuring that all our loads got to base camp. Most of the porters were in their teens or twenties, not old enough to have worked for expeditions in the 1950s and early 1960s, before the Karakoram had been closed to foreigners for more than a decade. Muhammad Hussein had worked for expeditions before the closure, which meant he was at least in his fifties—his face was deeply lined, his hair was thinning, and he had a gray beard. A tall, powerful man, he held a commanding presence among the porters.

When Nazir introduced him and suggested we hire him, I remembered that Muhammad Hussein had been mentioned in a book about a tragic American expedition trying to make the first ascent of K2 in 1953. The American climbers had descended from high on the peak in a storm while trying to bring down one of their members who was ill. They all made it back to base camp except for the sick climber, who was swept away by an avalanche. The Americans were in bad physical condition after their ordeal. One of them, George Bell, had frostbitten feet and couldn't walk out. This was before helicopter rescues. Muhammad Hussein carried George Bell for ten days from K2 base camp to Skardu. It was pure luck that we found him for our expedition, and a great honor to have him accompany us.

Given our shoestring budget, we economized on everything except things that were safety related or enabled us to comply with government regulations. We couldn't afford to pay the tour company for a guide to man-age the trek to base camp, so we were doing it ourselves. To keep the car-avan moving, we coordinated closely with Muhammad Hussein to resolve such daily issues with the porters as wage disputes, food distribution, health problems, and struggles with individual loads. He helped us to enforce environmental protections like not littering and bans on wood burning, to repair broken equipment, and to ensure the group's safety. These concerns occupied our every waking moment. To further save costs, we initially assumed we would do our own cooking on the trek. Each of us had been on several expeditions to Alaska and other mountains in North America without relying on the assistance of paid staff. But here we were relying on local food we didn't know how to prepare, and we had to feed our LO, who certainly wasn't going to do any cooking or cleanup. It became obvious that managing the porters would consume all of our time, so we hired as cook Muhammad Taki, a lively man from the village of Haldi, about a four-hour jeep ride from Skardu. Taki had been a cook on a large French K2 expedition the previous year, and he became indispensable at keeping us fed and acting as an interpreter. Our porters spoke only their local Balti language; to communicate with us, they spoke to Taki, who translated Balti into Urdu for Captain Noor, the LO, who translated Urdu into English for us. Compared to more experienced and well funded expeditions, we must have seemed like a ragtag group to Taki.

By running the expedition ourselves, we assumed some jobs concerning the porters that were unpleasant. Walking with no socks in their rubber shoes, their feet were rubbed raw. Every evening Charlie patiently cleaned and bandaged some of the ugliest foot sores I have ever seen. A few days into the trek, as I headed to the mess tent for dinner, I spotted Craig standing in the river with a bar of soap, scrubbing the back of a porter whose skin had been irritated from kerosene leaking from his load. We had been cheated by the man in the auto repair shop in Islamabad, who had given us faulty containers.

These more intimate interactions gave us the opportunity to build personal relationships with the people who were helping us and to make sure they were treated fairly. On the trail I noticed Jim chatting with one of the porters, inquiring with hand signs and a few common words about how many children he had. Matt sat with them one evening, reading aloud letters of recommendation they had recently gotten from expedition leaders. Don often stopped at the top of a steep hill or a rugged section of the trail to say "Shabash" (meaning "bravo") to the porters as they passed. Most important, when it came time to pay them, Craig calculated the exact wage, added a tip, and personally handed the cash to each porter to make sure he wasn't cheated by an intermediary. We didn't have any of the porter strikes or unanticipated demands that other climbers had warned us about.

The scale of the lower Braldu River valley was larger than anything I had ever seen. The river was a mass of churning brown water, and beneath the rushing roar came an ominous, deep *whump-whump*—the sound of boulders moving along the riverbed by the powerful current. The arid landscape was periodically interrupted by green villages that hung on the hillsides surrounded by a network of cultivated terraces. Above the valley, rocky slopes climbed thousands of feet to snowy peaks, which seemed like respectable climbing objectives but would be dwarfed by the mountains farther up the valley.

The first four nights of the trek, we camped next to villages along the river. The wood and mud huts were snugly clustered to preserve scarce arable land. The villagers had seen very few outsiders. The women seemed either afraid of us or had been told to hide. As we walked by, I could see someone watching us from the corner of a window or the edge of a door. Each evening, village men and children gathered around to watch as we set up our tents and sat down for meals. One morning, I woke up to find an older man in my tent inspecting my gear and silently staring at me. After that curious incident we stretched a rope around the perimeter of our camp for privacy and to keep the locals from interfering with our duties. The villagers never took anything; they only seemed inquisitive.

While still walking between villages on the third day, the route passed through a narrow gorge. There, the trail traversed above the river for several miles on steep sandy slopes that extended several thousand feet up a mountainside. The river washed away and undercut the sand at the bottom of the gorge, causing the entire slope to slowly move downward, making it impossible to maintain a trail. The loose sand made footing difficult, and a slip could result in a fall into the torrent below. Both foreigners and local porters had been killed in this gorge between the villages of Chakpo and Chongo. The risk was even greater when it rained, because water loosened the boulders embedded in the sand and they came careening down the hillside at travelers below.

On the morning we walked through the gorge, it was cloudy but not raining. But it was Friday, June 13—an unlucky day. Just as we headed into the steepest part of the gorge, rain began. The porters stopped, put down their loads and, kneeling down toward Mecca, bowed and prayed aloud, asking Allah to keep them safe. While the porters were praying, Muhammed Hussein and a couple of Hushe men helped us carve a rudimentary trail with ice axes and shovels to improve the footing along this perilous track. We did our best to keep the porters moving quickly, to minimize their time in the gorge and exposure to falling rocks. In places we had to pull the porters up nearly vertical dirt slopes that were running with mud from the pouring rain. Miraculously, we all arrived in Chongo—muddy and exhausted from the stress—but unharmed and relieved.

We left the final village of Askole on June 15. Over the remaining ten-day walk to base camp, we got into a routine of sorts. The porters rose at daylight and completed as much of the day's walk as possible while it was still cool. By late morning, they stopped to make tea and eat their tortilla-like flatbread (chapatis) they'd prepared earlier. By early afternoon, we arrived at the predetermined campsite for the night. While we were trekking through the villages, food for the porters had been available locally. Beyond the last village, we had to distribute rations to them from our food supply. Our base camp was so far beyond Askole that we needed fifty porters just to carry food for the fifty porters who carried *our* food and equipment. Each evening, we measured the amount of rations we gave to head porters, who distributed the food to their group (usually porters from the same village cooked, camped, and worked together). Our expedition consumed about 250 pounds of food daily, and the five porters carrying that weight were paid off and sent back.

One evening a porter came forward, saying he didn't receive any food. We went through our calculations and established that we had indeed handed out the right amount. As expedition leader, I called the head porters forward and learned that one group didn't receive enough food for one of its members. I discovered that one porter had managed to get his name on two of the group lists so that he could collect double rations. It was easy for us to have made this mistake because so many of the porters have the same name. I called the offending porter forward, and he eventually admitted that he had been stealing an extra ration that belonged to someone else. Noticing the commotion, Muhammed Hussein came over. He didn't understand English, so one of the group leaders explained to him in Balti what had happened.

As Muhammed listened, I watched his calm expression turn to fury when he realized one of his porters had been stealing food. He lifted a walking stick in anger, intending to beat the porter with it. We did not want to hurt anyone, and having an injured porter would only create problems for us. I reached up and grabbed the stick midswing to prevent Muhammad from hitting the porter. It wasn't easy for me to restrain him. In these harsh places, where food was scarce, the law of the land for stealing was severe. With this one exception the porters were scrupulously honest. To pay them, we carried huge rucksacks filled with local currency—something everyone knew, but we were never robbed.

Four days after leaving the village of Askole, we arrived at a place called Paiyu that overlooked the snout of the Baltoro Glacier. We spent two nights there so the porters could cook a supply of chapatis in advance in a comfortable place. Camping on the glacier was more of a hardship for them because of the greater exposure to the wind and cold. This precooked bread was their version of an energy bar; pulling out a hunk to eat with their tea made life on the ice simpler.

After leaving Paiyu, we approached the Baltoro Glacier, which is what scientists call a valley glacier in a wet snow zone. To create this kind of glacier, avalanches from the surrounding mountains move ice and rock to where it accumulates in the valley. The winter snow deposited on the surface melts in the summer. The mountains surrounding the Baltoro Glacier are so large and extensive, they generate enough ice to form a thirty-nine-mile-long, three-mile-wide river of ice and rock—one of the longest glaciers in the world outside of the polar regions. Our group planned to climb onto the glacier and walk the rest of the way to base camp across rubble-strewn ice thousands of feet thick in places. Because the glacier is constantly moving, it creates a hilly, jumbled mess of loose rock over treacherous ice that is difficult to walk on. As the glacier rolls over the underlying bedrock, or where a tributary glacier joins in from the side, the ice cracks to form crevasses and sometimes gets tossed up into a mass of unstable towers.

The group usually found a route around these obstacles, but periodically we stopped to help the porters balance their way across a crevasse on a narrow bridge of ice. The greatest concern was the weather. The porters in their floppy, smooth-soled rubber shoes were lightly equipped, and our food supply for them was limited, so their comfort and safety depended on getting to base camp and sending them home as quickly as possible. If we were hit by a severe storm on the upper glacier, we might have to send the porters back before reaching our base. In that event, transporting all loads to base camp might take weeks, giving us a lot less time to actually climb Gasherbrum IV.

The porters understood the hazards of traveling on the glacier, and when we first got onto the ice, they stopped and prayed like they had several days earlier. Once we resumed walking, our human train meandered through the ice towers on the glacier, dwarfed by huge mountains that rose on either side—Paiyu Peak (6,660 meters, or 21,850 feet), Uli Biaho Tower (6,109 meters, 20,043 feet), the Trango Towers (the highest point in the group is 6,286 meters, or 20,608 feet), Grand Cathedral (5,828 meters, or 19,120 feet), Masherbrum (7,821 meters, or 25,659 feet), and Mustagh Tower (7,276 meters, or 23,871 feet). At night we slept in down bags inside nylon tents while each porter group rebuilt rock shelters left by other expeditions. The shelters consisted of a circular rock wall, ten feet in diameter and four feet high, lined on the bottom with flat rocks to insulate them from the ice and covered with the large blue tarp we gave them propped up in the middle with a stick. Crowded together inside to stay warm, the porters wrapped themselves in thin homespun wool blankets and cooked on kerosene stoves that we also provided. I enjoyed getting to know many of the porters by name and made the rounds each evening to their improvised shelters to check on them. Full of smiles, they invited me inside, where it was pleasantly warm. They offered to share a cup of their "salt tea," a greasy-looking concoction of tea, ghee, and salt; I usually declined, politely.

After two days walking on the ice, we rounded a bend in the glacier and far ahead, barely visible through the morning haze, we caught our first glimpse of Gasherbrum IV. What had been an abstract notion for over a year was now frighteningly real. I was stunned by the peak's beauty and compelled by the prospect of climbing it. Yet, when faced with the actual danger and difficulty of such an ascent, I was scared. I seriously questioned what I had gotten myself into.

For the next several days the huge trapezoidal west face of Gasherbrum IV dominated our view as we walked up the Baltoro Glacier. The wall reflected the light at sunset with a yellow glow so bright the vision was called "the shining wall." Four days after leaving Paiyu, we reached Concordia. To the north, up the Godwin Austen Glacier, stood the iconic pyramid of K2 (8,611 meters, or 28,251 feet), the world's second highest mountain. South of K2 was Broad Peak (8,051 meters, or 26,414 feet), a big snowy double-summited peak less difficult to climb than K2 but still a considerable effort as the world's twelfth highest mountain. Gasherbrum IV rose straight above us at the head of the glacier.

I understood then why its name is derived from the Balti words *gasher* (meaning "beautiful") and *brum* (meaning "mountain"). The name given to Gasherbrum IV was extended to the other five mountains that comprise the Gasherbrum group. The peaks are arranged in a giant upside-down U, numbered in order of their height, with Gasherbrum I being the highest (because only a very small part of the summit is visible from the Baltoro Glacier, Gasherbrum I is also called Hidden Peak). Gasherbrum IV is situated to the north at the closed end of the U, with Gasherbrum V and VI along the west leg and Gasherbrum I, II, and III on the east leg. The South Gasherbrum Glacier sits inside this U and drains the ice from the surrounding peaks through the opening to the south. There, two days after leaving Concordia, we established our base camp at 17,000 feet on rocky glacial debris above the confluence with the Abruzzi Glacier. It was June 24 and we had been in Pakistan for twenty-five days.

A Japanese expedition trying to climb Gasherbrum II was already there, and more expeditions attempting that peak and Gasherbrum I would arrive later on. We paid off the porters, and they quickly disappeared down the glacier. Jim was sick so he had stopped to rest. Charlie, Todd, and Matt ran back to help him up the few miles, and he seemed okay after he arrived. It was an abrupt transition for our group, from managing the large caravan to being left alone for the next forty-five days.

That evening, I sat behind our cooking shelter and ate my lentils and rice, thankful for the simple meal that seemed like a feast. Surrounded by the daunting mountain landscape, I was grateful for all the support that got us to that spot. I wondered what was in store for us. Our expedition would depend on the weather. Above his tent, Todd had set up Buddhist prayer flags that fluttered in the breeze. They read: "Let the longtime sun shine upon you, all love surround you, and the pure light within you guide your way on."

To allow our bodies to acclimatize, we would need to gain elevation in stages. As we climb higher, the atmospheric pressure decreases, which means there is less oxygen in every breath we take. On our trek to base camp we had to breathe faster than normal to get enough oxygen in what many climbers refer to as "thin air." Acclimatizing gave our blood greater oxygen-carrying capacity and made us less susceptible to altitude-related sickness. Without taking the necessary weeks to acclimatize properly, we would be at greater risk of life-threatening ailments such as high-altitude pulmonary edema (HAPE) and high-altitude cerebral edema (HACE). We were not using supplemental oxygen on this climb, which is common for mountains of this size. Almost all expeditions to Mount Everest, for example, breathe supplemental oxygen to reduce the physical stress and make climbing easier at extreme altitude. For myself, I consider the use of supplemental oxygen by modern climbers to be cheating—not like blood doping or steroid use, but an unwillingness to climb the mountain on its own terms. If a climber isn't able to reach the top without supplemental oxygen, it would be better to climb a smaller mountain. Plus, for our smaller expedition, the equipment and transport costs for using bottled oxygen were a significant added expense.

The team planned to spend several days at base camp, then move up to advance base camp (ABC) at about 20,000 feet before making attempts on Gasherbrum IV. We wanted a well-stocked ABC with plenty of food and fuel, because Gasherbrum IV was over six miles of difficult glacier climbing up the South Gasherbrum Glacier from base camp. We needed a safe and comfortable place to operate from that was closer to the mountain. Our first day at base camp we organized food and equipment. Then we started to move supplies up the glacier. We hoped to take four or five days to ferry loads up before occupying ABC. After another four or five days acclimatizing there and above, we thought the actual summit climb might take four or five more days. This left us with over a month of slack in our schedule to wait out bad weather. If storms or climbing difficulties ate up too much of this time, it might not be enough.

The South Gasherbrum Glacier flows over two precipitous drops in the underlying rock as it extends down to our base camp. Similar to rapids in a river, the relatively smooth glacier is broken up into a chaotic jumble of tottering ice towers and deep crevasses. We had two options for finding a safe way through these icefalls that spanned the width of the glacial valley. We could go up the middle of the glacier, climbing through them and exposing ourselves to falling ice and hidden crevasses. Or we could skirt the icefalls by climbing up onto the steep, avalanche-prone snow slopes on either side of the glacier. Since we couldn't inspect the slopes that reached thousands of feet above us, and conditions could change every time it snowed, we decided to take the middle of the glacier. Our route avoided the most dangerous-looking towers and crevasses. In such icefalls, deep crevasses can be hidden by a thin veneer of snow that might look safe to cross but could collapse, sending us plunging into icy, dark depths. So we climbed roped together, testing the snow ahead of us with our ski poles before stepping forward.

Because of poor weather and the time-consuming task of finding a safe route through the icefalls, it took us fifteen days to move our loads of food and equipment to advance base camp by July 9. There, the 6,000-foot-high south face of Gasherbrum IV towered above us. Steep on all sides, it is the most difficult peak in the group to climb. At 26,001 feet, it was nearly 6,000 feet higher than any of us had climbed before. To reach the summit, technical mixed rock and ice climbing at extreme altitude lay ahead. Back at base camp, Jim had been sick on and off, sometimes with a high fever, and Charlie was having a hard time acclimatizing. After spending several weeks there with a very bored Captain Noor, they finally felt well enough to join us at ABC on July 17. Craig, Todd, Don, Matt, and I had been stuck there because of bad weather.

From photographs obtained earlier, we had pieced together a route that followed a relatively easy snow slope on the south face to a short rocky section up to the crest of the southwest ridge at 23,000 feet. We could follow this to the summit. After an initial reconnaissance from ABC, we decided to stick with that plan. The weather improved, and we split into two groups: Craig, Don, and Todd started up the south face on the same day Jim and Charlie reached ABC, while Matt and I climbed up in support with additional supplies the next day. The first group reached 22,800 feet—the rocky section above the snow slope—and ran into dangerously loose rock. They decided to abandon the route and came down to where Matt and I were waiting. We descended to ABC together to choose a different route up the mountain.

After spending weeks getting to where we started the actual climbing on Gasherbrum IV, it was discouraging to be turned back so quickly. We had time and resources to attempt a different route, but it was hard to regroup and get the team excited about a new plan. We agreed to focus our efforts on the unclimbed east face. Craig, Matt, and Jim seemed committed to this plan, but I later discovered that Todd and Don were not sold on the idea. To get to the base of the east face, we had to climb up through the Italian Icefall, which drains the glacier separating Gasherbrum IV from Gasherbrum III. It was named after the expedition that climbed up through it on their way to the northeast ridge, where they made the first ascent of the mountain in 1958.

On July 22, as I led the way through the icefall roped together with Matt who was followed by Craig roped with Jim. I unwittingly stepped through a fragile snow crust that hid a crevasse and took a thirty-foot free fall. The sudden yank launched Matt, who was second on the rope, several feet into the air. Upon landing, he dug his ice axe into the snow to avert being dragged into the crevasse after me, and the rope stopped me with a jerk. Dangling head-down in an icy cavern, I felt my forty-pound pack compressed against my chest and head, making it difficult to breathe. I was hanging only about ten feet above the bottom of the crevasse. To relieve the pressure, I unclipped my pack and dropped it. I yelled up to Matt, saying I was okay and asked him to lower me to the bottom of the crevasse. Matt hauled my pack up on a loop of rope, then I clawed my way up the side of the crevasse into the sunlight. I was grateful Matt had reacted so quickly; if I had fallen a bit farther, I would have hit head-first.

The four of us climbed through the rest of the icefall without incident. Craig and I pitched our bivouac tent on the glacier below the east face at around 22,500 feet. With supplies running short, Matt and Jim decided that Craig and I were climbing stronger than they were, and our team had a better chance of success if they sacrificed their attempt and headed back down after giving us the food and fuel they had brought up. Don and Todd had left ABC after the rest of us and arrived at our camp a few hours later. They announced to Craig and me that they didn't want to climb the east face; they had decided to try to repeat the Italian route on the northeast ridge that started at a high pass, or col, between Gasherbrum III and IV farther up the glacier. They didn't explain their decision, however, and I never knew if they thought the east face was unsafe or too difficult, or if they thought there was simply a much better chance of getting to the top by attempting the original route.

I was disappointed to see the team split up like this. I thought our discussion the previous day would have brought out any concerns or differing opinions. We had all agreed to work together on the same route; we would be weaker by splitting up. Don and Todd spent a couple of days exploring the northeast ridge before determining that it was too difficult to climb with the minimal gear they had brought. They headed down to base camp, foregoing any chance of summiting Gasherbrum IV.

On July 24, Craig and I made our first attempt on the east face, which has two large triangular snowfields positioned one above the other in the shape of a giant hourglass. At the neck of the hourglass is a band of rock about two hundred feet high. The two snowfields looked like straightforward climbing—but only if the snow conditions were firm and we weren't wallowing in deep, avalanche-prone unstable fluff. We would encounter our main difficulties at the rock band. The rock forming the upper portion of the mountain was hard, smooth, compact marble, making it hard to find handholds and footholds and cracks to place pitons for protection. Our plan was to bivouac just below the rock band, climb the rock early the next morning, and then move on to the upper snowfield. We would follow the upper snowfield to the summit and then descend back to our camp that night.

Unfortunately we encountered deep snow, and breaking trail up the steep slope with forty-pound packs was challenging. By midday we finally reached the top of the lower snowfield below the rock band at around 23,800 feet, but the snow was thin over the rock so we couldn't dig a snow platform wide enough for our tent. It started to snow, and the small trenchlike runnels carved into the upper snowfield funneled large spindrift avalanches down onto us. Even if we had managed to set up our tent, we would have been buried by new snow. We were forced to retreat back to our camp on the glacier. To move up this route, we would need several days of good weather to consolidate the snow.

Craig and I had enough food and fuel to wait three days on the glacier for weather and conditions to improve and still have four days of supplies for the climb. Snowfall kept us cramped inside our tent the next three days. We bemoaned the lack of "real" climbing, instead having simply walked around on glaciers, fallen in crevasses, and rested in our tents. On July 28 the weather was clear, so we made one more desperate attempt, moving our camp up to the base of the east face to save time if the conditions were good the next day. But at 1:00 in the morning it started snowing, and by daylight our tent was half buried in spindrift. With our hopes dashed, we packed up and headed down to ABC, where we had more food and fuel. When we got there, everyone else was gone, probably to base camp. The difficulty of finding a suitable route had taken its toll. Being surrounded by the Gasherbrum peaks was breathtaking, but we were lonely, just the two of us, far from base camp at the bottom of the glacier. For the next two days, Craig and I were stuck at ABC in stormy weather.

On August 1 the skies cleared. Rather than descend to base camp, we decided to make one more attempt on Gasherbrum IV's east face. The debilitating effects of spending almost a month at over 20,000 feet coupled with the unlikely chance of success made me feel weak and discouraged. On August 2 we left the tent at 7:00 a.m. on a beautiful morning. After climbing about a thousand feet, we encountered snow conditions that were deeper and even less stable than before. Fearing that the slope might avalanche, Craig and I made the heartbreaking and difficult decision to end the expedition.

Jim had felt sick most of the time we were on the mountain, but in his stoic manner he didn't want to give up. He dealt with the discomfort but eventually realized he needed to go down to base camp. I had last seen him on July 23, when he and Matt left Craig and me at the base of the east face. Back at base camp, Jim's condition had worsened and he wasn't able to keep any food down. He didn't have symptoms of HAPE or HACE (gurgling from fluid in the lungs or a severe headache), so he thought it was a form of acute mountain sickness (AMS) that comes with a milder headache, nausea, and fatigue. The main treatment for these altitude-related ailments is to get the patient to a lower elevation, where the air is thicker. After descending 3,000 feet from ABC to base camp at 17,000 feet—still not an oxygen-rich environment—Jim didn't feel any better. Our expedition doctor, Charlie, was there to take care of Jim, but without better diagnostic tools he couldn't figure out what was wrong. Jim became gravely ill. To keep him alive, all Charlie could do was administer the two bags of intravenous fluid he had, but those wouldn't last long. Jim needed to get to a hospital. Arranging an evacuation out of these rugged mountains was not going to be easy—and time was a matter of life or death.

In 1980, nearly two decades before the commonplace use of satellite telephones on such expeditions, we didn't have equipment capable of communicating with civilization. On July 29, while Craig and I were still struggling on Gasherbrum IV's east face, Matt and our cook, Muhammad Taki, ran for help with a letter from Captain Noor explaining Jim's condition and asking the Pakistan Army for a helicopter evacuation. On the hike in, our expedition had waded the Dumordu River where it entered the Braldu, but when Matt and Taki reached that spot it was too deep from summer runoff to cross. They had to hike ten miles up to where the Dumordu River flowed out from under the Panmah Glacier and cross the

ice above the water to get to the other side. While running across the glacier, Matt slipped. As he was falling toward the raging torrent, Taki grabbed
his wrist and pulled him to safety. Including this twenty-mile detour, Matt
and Taki traveled day and night for seventy-two hours to reach Skardu—a
trek that had taken us fourteen days on the hike in.

In the meantime, Jim needed to be moved to lower elevation at Concordia, which at 15,000 feet, was as high as the Pakistan Army was willing
to fly its helicopters at that time. The local Balti base camp staff for the
Japanese and recently arrived Spanish Gasherbrum II expeditions made a
litter out of ski poles and blankets and carried Jim down the glacier for two
days to reach the evacuation site. I later approached these men and tried to
pay them for their assistance. Speaking only basic English, they pushed my
handful of rupees away, saying, "Steve, sahib, this is a human payload and we
cannot accept payment for that."

When Matt and Taki delivered Captain Noor's letter, the Pakistan Army
mobilized quickly to evacuate Jim. It was a dangerous mission flying a pair
of helicopters close to the mountains on either side of the Braldu River
valley and the Baltoro Glacier to reach the elevation of Concordia (near the
maximum altitude the aircraft could fly). By the time the helicopter flew
Jim, Matt, Charlie, and Captain Noor to Skardu on August 6, Jim's condition was critical. His kidneys had shut down, and treating him was more
than Skardu could handle in its small hospital. Fortunately the weather
was good, and the passenger flight from Islamabad was sitting on the tarmac ready to return. Through Captain Noor's insistence, they rushed Jim
onto the plane along with Charlie. As soon as Jim reached the hospital in
Islamabad, he was taken into surgery. The doctors discovered that Jim had
a total bowel obstruction caused by scar tissue from a previous operation.
Charlie assisted in the operation. When they administered the anesthesia,
Jim's blood pressure dropped to almost zero. The surgeons managed to
revive him and perform a successful operation. Jim survived.

With the 1980 expedition over, it was time to return home. As our plane
lifted off the tarmac in Islamabad, I thought about my overall experience
in Pakistan. Initially intimidated by the recent attack on the US embassy
and the rising tide of anti-Western religious extremism I had seen in Islamabad, I was also captivated by the mountains and the devoted treatment by

our local Balti porters, staff, and liaison officer. If it weren't for the sincere dedication of all these people, Jim would not be alive. These contradictory experiences made me realize that to stay safe, it is important to understand the mind-set of the local people wherever one travels.

CHAPTER 2

ELUSIVE SUMMITS

GASHERBRUM IV NORTHWEST RIDGE, 1983
K2 NORTH RIDGE, 1986
K2 SOUTH FACE, 1987

I returned from Pakistan in mid-August to the small but comfortable apartment I shared with my girlfriend, Alice. Back home in my "normal" life, it felt like I had never been away, and my recent experiences seemed surreal. Although coming home was an adjustment, I enjoyed my work arrangement, which allowed me to balance my professional life with my climbing. As a student, I had interned for an engineering consulting firm, which hired me after I graduated. I was fortunate: I'd been working there for the past three years. I helped the project managers meet their schedules and budgets. They trusted my work, and in return, they put up with my disappearing each year to go climbing. When I felt cooped up in the office, I took an extra hour at lunch to run and work out, then I put in an extra hour at the end of the day. I had a steady reliable income and no intention of abandoning my engineering career to try to make a living as a climber, either guiding or in the outdoor recreation industry. A couple of months after I returned from the Gasherbrum IV expedition, Alice became pregnant. We were happy about the baby and decided to get married that fall. We felt good about our decision. Alice knew that serious climbing was important to me and would always be a part of my life.

An American expedition had recently obtained permission from the Chinese Communist government to attempt the first ascent of the Kangshung (East) Face of Mount Everest in the fall of 1981. The team was made up of many of the country's most experienced Himalayan climbers, and nine months before their departure, I wrote the organizers asking if I could join them.

The Chinese government, which had taken control of Tibet (including the north and east sides of Everest) shortly after World War II, had closed access to foreigners. But China was gradually opening to the outside world after President Nixon had visited Beijing in 1972, and these massive faces on Everest had opened for the first time since the 1930s. I didn't know any of the climbers, and I didn't think my climbing résumé would be strong enough to warrant an invitation. It seemed like such a stretch that I didn't mention the letter to Alice. To my surprise, Lou Reichardt, one of the climbers who had made the first American ascent and first ascent of K2 without supplemental oxygen in 1978, wrote back. He said I was just the sort of person they were looking for and asked me to join the expedition.

Understandably, my pregnant wife was angry that I hadn't talked to her about this possibility earlier. The timing was bad: the expedition was leaving the following August, which was only six weeks after Alice was due to deliver. I ultimately declined the offer. While the reality of family life meant that I couldn't do everything I wanted, it was hard to pass up this once-in-a-lifetime opportunity to prove myself with such an elite group. They were attempting an original route up a mountain I had read about since grade school. It meant a lot just to be asked, though, which was encouraging.

Lars Swenson was born on June 25, 1981. The love I felt holding my infant son was new and intense. Our lives suddenly revolved around his needs and kept us busy: feeding the baby, interrupted sleep, and child-rearing decisions. Within the first year, Alice and I realized that we dealt with issues differently. The things I tried to do to resolve our disagreements didn't seem to work and only led to frustration and confusion. I fell into a pattern of working harder, thinking that would make everything okay. It was a perfect storm of misunderstanding. By early 1983, when Lars was not yet two years old, we decided to separate. At the time, I recalled a college climbing trip, trying for a winter ascent of Mount Rainier. We had spent a couple of days in the hut at Camp Muir waiting for the weather to clear with an older climber. He gave us some advice: "Never let anyone take this away from you. You will have parents, employers, girlfriends, wives, and others who will try and talk you out of this. Never let them do that."

Not long after saying no to the Everest trip, I found Gasherbrum IV entering my thoughts. By the spring of 1982, I had planned another expedition to the mountain for 1983. I'd seen a photo of the north side of Gasherbrum IV taken from the top of Broad Peak. The unclimbed northwest ridge looked like a more feasible route than the one we had tried in 1980. Above 22,000 feet, steep snow slopes on the north (Chinese) side of the ridge led to a short but nearly vertical rock band below the north summit. I couldn't see in the photo whether there was a way to climb up onto the ridge, but not knowing everything was part of the adventure when trying first ascents.

I immediately spoke to Craig McKibben, one of the strongest and most determined and reliable climbers from the 1980 expedition, about returning to Gasherbrum IV. Unfortunately he wasn't able to join us. Matt Kerns, who had run with our cook, Muhammad Taki, in 1980 to initiate the rescue for Jim Nelson, was able to go. To complete the team, I recruited several other climbers from the Pacific Northwest. I had known Carlos Buhler, an active alpine climber who lived in Bellingham, for several years. We had only climbed together on some day trips, but Carlos had an impressive résumé of expeditions to Nepal and the Pamir Mountains in what at that time was still called the Soviet Union. He agreed to join us. Jack Lewis, part of Washington's alpine climbing community, had been on expeditions to Alaska. We had been on some rock climbing trips together, and with Jack's easygoing demeanor, I thought he would be a strong team member. Tom Bowman, from Oregon, found out about our trip and wrote to me expressing interest. Gary Lee, an oncologist, completed the team as the expedition doctor.

During the expedition planning stage, Coloradan Michael Kennedy, editor of *Climbing* magazine (the preeminent periodical for the sport in the

United States), contacted me. He and Mugs Stump wanted to accompany our team and share our base camp. They wanted to attempt a two-person lightweight-style ascent of the 9,000-foot unclimbed west face of Gasherbrum IV. Michael and Mugs had more technical climbing experience than the rest of us, and the west face would be a steeper and more difficult route than our proposed line. Michael had recently completed several difficult routes in Alaska and a significant attempt on the north ridge of Latok I in Pakistan. Mugs had completed some technically difficult new routes in Alaska as well.

The group arrived in Islamabad on May 2, 1983, and registered that day with the police in Rawalpindi, as we had in 1980. For an unknown reason the police said to come back the next day, so we returned to Islamabad. When we tried to buy insurance for the liaison officer and porters, the insurance company requested more cash, so we had to get additional money exchanged first. We tried to get rupees by cashing in travelers checks at the National Bank of Pakistan and also make a cash deposit while we were there for a helicopter rescue if we needed it. But the bank said we had to cash our traveler's checks at the American Express office, which we needed to do before we could make the rescue deposit. By the time we got to the American Express office, it had closed for the day. The next day, we were able to complete all these bureaucratic tasks easily. I guess we just needed to pick the right day.

More expeditions were climbing mountains in the Pakistan-administered Karakoram than when I had been there in 1980. Once we arrived in Skardu we discovered many of the men working as porters were already busy helping other groups. There wasn't a shortage of opportunities, so we didn't cause a mini-riot this time. After the jeep ride to the road head, the team began the familiar trek to base camp. On our way to Askole we traveled a different way than in 1980, this time on the south side of the Braldu River. We crossed a rickety bridge made from logs and sticks propped onto boulders in the water—a temporary bridge used by the locals when the river was low. In a few weeks the bridge would be removed before it washed away when summer snowmelt caused the river to rise. By traveling on this seldom-visited side of the river, we were able to see how Balti villagers lived who had rarely, if ever, encountered foreigners. At one village a man brought a two- or three-year-old boy who had a bloated stomach to visit Gary. Gary had no means to determine what was wrong, so he assumed the toddler had giardia. He prescribed an antibiotic that I pulverized, dissolved in water, and spoon-fed to the child. The little guy threw up most of it which made our efforts seem pretty ineffective since we were only passing through.

After several days of walking, I could feel myself relaxing from the stress of the past months. Trekking with porters meant we were done each day by early afternoon and then could rest while our cook, Ali Murad, prepared our meals. Captain Gorsi, our Pakistan Army liaison officer, was from a well-educated family in Peshawar, near the border with Afghanistan; he seemed willing to help and I enjoyed his company. As our expedition got under way, Gorsi started feeling quite homesick, so I spent the afternoons with him, calculating porter loads, porter layoffs, food distribution, and dealing with various daily problems. As we approached the mountain, I felt stronger as I mentally switched gears to prepare for what I came here to do.

When we reached base camp at just under 16,000 feet on May 19, Ali sprang into action, building a rock wall to house our kitchen and dining space. He was very modest, polite, and one of the most selfless men I have ever met. After he prepared a meal for the group, he would give all the food to us and never eat. The porters had gone, and Ali, Gorsi, and our climbing team had to adjust to a different pace. Our lives would be full of hard work when the weather was good, and hopefully a patient acceptance of what Mother Nature dished out would prevail when the weather was bad. Most of us were hard-wired to seek the former and struggled with the latter. As I set up my tent and established my new home for the next six to eight weeks to acclimate, I reminded myself that I needed to unwind and enjoy the journey. Happiness, success, and ultimately my survival depended on being able to focus on the challenge in front of me.

Unlike our expedition to Gasherbrum IV in 1980, our base camp on the West Gasherbrum Glacier was very close to the mountain. Because of this, we could start climbing and establishing camps on the mountain right out of base camp. Carlos and Jack forged a route up the glacier and over a small col onto a small glacier beneath the northwest ridge. They were pleased to report that a steep but straightforward snow and ice couloir (gully) led from the glacier all the way to the crest of the northwest ridge. Matt and Tom helped carry supplies up onto this small glacier, and after several days of bad weather, Gary and I moved up there to spend the night and establish Camp I at 18,000 feet. The plan was to fix rope up the couloir and place Camp II on the ridge, which would give us a chance to acclimatize. The snow slopes above Camp II, which I had seen in the photo from Broad Peak, led to where we planned to dig a snow cave for Camp III. We wouldn't fix any more rope above Camp III and would carry everything we needed above there to a small high camp below the final rock band that led to the north summit.

On June 7, after nearly two weeks of bad weather, we reached the site for Camp II at around 21,000 feet at the top of the couloir. Michael and Mugs were acclimatizing on our route in preparation for their attempt on the west face, and together with Carlos, Gary, and me, it took us three hours to dig a narrow snow ledge against a rock wall for two small tents pitched end to end. Everyone but Carlos and I descended, and the two of us shared one of the tents perched on the edge of the 3,000-foot couloir.

We slept poorly. It was stormy and cold, and our breath condensed on the interior tent walls, creating frost that fell on us when the wind shook the tent. This, combined with snow blowing in the door when one of us came in or out, made it hard to stay dry. With the weather so foul, it was a problem to relieve ourselves. We had to be careful when we stepped outside the tent because a slip could send you on quite a ride. To avoid getting out, Carlos peed into an empty freeze-dried dinner foil bag and handed it to me to set in the snow outside the door. Unfortunately the bag had a small hole, so it dripped.

Carlos, Matt, Jack, and I spent the next week traversing a steep narrow band of snow out of Camp II and fixing the last of our rope to a gully that took us up onto the snowfield on the ridge. Partway up that snowfield at 23,000 feet, we dug the snow cave for Camp III. On June 14, Carlos and I stayed after carrying a load there with Matt and Jack, and they descended to Camp II. That afternoon, the sky showed all the usual signs of an approaching storm with a halo around the sun and large hat-like lenticular clouds forming on the summits. In the morning, the weather was poor but Carlos and I headed up with enough supplies for a multiple-day summit attempt, with the intention of turning around if conditions didn't improve. The weather continued to deteriorate, and soon we were engulfed in the wind and clouds with little visibility.

Given that we were still a long way from the summit, I suggested that we go down and return when conditions improved. Carlos wanted to continue, but I forced the issue by refusing to go on, and we headed down. When we returned to Camp III, Gary and Tom were there, determined to wait out the storm in the snow cave and scout the route ahead. Carlos and I headed all the way down to base camp to wait for better weather.

Four days later, on June 19, the skies cleared after dumping three feet of fresh snow at base camp. Michael and Mugs had made an attempt on the west face and tried to wait out the recent storm high on the route. That morning, Ali spotted them rappelling down, and after several days of no visibility or communication during the storm, we were relieved. By dinner, we saw Michael and Mugs coming down the glacier and we lit the lantern and made extra food. They were exhausted and told horror stories about poor rock and a lot of new snow from the storm. They were done with their climb on the west face.

The next morning the weather was good again, so Jack, Matt, Carlos, and I decided to go back up. Although we were in regular radio contact, we were concerned about Gary and Tom, who had been stuck in the snow cave at 23,000 feet for five days during the storm. Tom had been feeling poorly, and they were both exhausted from that ordeal. They came down as we headed up. I was worried about Jack, who had repeatedly tried to go above Camp II, but each time he was struck with a lack of energy and appetite. He headed up to try again with Matt, Carlos, and me. At Camp II, Jack didn't feel any better, unfortunately, so he headed back down, discouraged. Altitude sickness can strike anyone, even great climbers, no matter how skilled and experienced. The only way to feel better is to descend. Although Jack wouldn't return to the Greater Ranges, he would go on to make a number of first ascents in Alaska with Tom; they had become close friends on the expedition.

With Tom, Gary, and Jack on their way down to base camp, the team was coming apart in a disturbing replay of what happened on Gasherbrum IV in 1980. On June 24, Matt, Carlos, and I, occupied the snow cave at Camp III. With all the new snow that had fallen, I had to crawl through a four-foot-long tunnel entrance that was initially half that long to the room deep inside the snow slope. Tom and Gary had enlarged it during their stay the previous week, so there was plenty of space. Other than the light on the snow at the entrance that illuminated the cave, we were completely isolated from the weather and conditions outside. The next morning it was Lars's second birthday. I wished I could be with him to celebrate. It was an important moment in his life, and I felt conflicted about what I was doing, knowing the event would come and go without me.

After downing a cup of tea and a granola bar, I emerged from the snow cave to discover that the weather was perfect. From our vantage point high on Gasherbrum IV, we were surrounded by spectacular views of the Karakoram. We were strategically located on the crest of the northwest ridge, about three thousand feet below the summit, without any wind or a cloud in the sky. It was the moment I'd been anticipating for three years. Up to this point we had placed fixed ropes on all the steep climbing, which made for a quick, easy descent. But from here on, we were committing ourselves to several days of climbing up new technical ground at extreme altitude with the limited supplies and equipment we could carry with us.

As we headed up, the snowfield that straddled the ridge got steeper and ended at a rock buttress not far above us. I detected a lack of enthusiasm from my partners, but for different reasons. It seemed that after two trips to Gasherbrum IV, Matt, who was the youngest and had less experience than Carlos and I, realized that the risk and commitment involved in this kind of technically difficult high-altitude climbing was not what he wanted to do. I guessed that his longtime friendship and loyalty to our partnership made it hard for him to talk about his feelings: he didn't want to disappoint me. In retrospect, I should have assured Matt that he should do what was right for him, but at the time I didn't have that insight.

The snow surface was firm for walking, but as the angle steepened, my footsteps began to make a hollow sound that reverberated down into the snowpack. I was afraid that the wind from the previous storm had created a dangerous snow slab that could fracture and start an avalanche, taking us with it. To get off the slope, I traversed left about a hundred feet to below the east side of the buttress, where the slope was less exposed to the wind. The snow was safer there. Looking up, I noticed a climbable-looking couloir-chimney system that cut through the rock buttress and led to the crest of the ridge above. I told Carlos and Matt that I had found a better way, and they reluctantly agreed to check it out. But after the three of us followed my footsteps back to the base of the couloir-chimney, both of them refused to continue. Carlos thought we would probably find more wind slabs on the snow slopes higher up, and Matt simply seemed exhausted and discouraged.

I couldn't believe it! I wanted to climb as high as possible until we either reached the summit or encountered something too dangerous or too difficult. Carlos was a serious Himalayan climber. Why didn't he want to keep climbing? High on Gasherbrum IV, Carlos may have noticed Matt's lack of enthusiasm and realized it was down to him and me. Perhaps he had decided there was little point continuing without a larger and more experienced team. Turning back in perfect weather was devastating, but without a willing partner, there was no other choice.

Carlos, Matt, and I reached base camp on June 26, and Gary, Michael, and Mugs had already left. Carlos and Ali departed early the next day to find porters, leaving Matt, Tom, Jack, and me behind. While waiting for porters at base camp, the weather remained perfect for another seven days. It tortured me to sit there staring up at Gasherbrum IV during the longest spell of good weather that I had seen on both trips to the Karakoram. On July 3, when Ali returned with our porters, it began to snow, just in time for our walk out.

Back in Skardu, flights to Islamabad weren't running because it was still cloudy. We ran into two climbers from a large British expedition, Don Whillans and Greg Child, who were returning to the United Kingdom to inform the family and friends of Pete Thexton that he had died of high-altitude pulmonary edema (HAPE) while descending with them on Broad Peak. Don and Greg needed to convey their tragic news before Pete's family found out from another source. They joined us in our search for transportation, and we eventually found a vehicle and driver willing to take all of us to Islamabad.

I enjoyed meeting Don, a colorful and iconic British climber. When I was a teenager, I'd read about his first ascents of the Central Pillar of Freney route on Mont Blanc (1961), Patagonia's Central Tower of Paine (1963), and Annapurna's south face in Nepal (1970). Greg was a young climber from Australia living in the United States. He had just found out that his American wife had moved them from San Francisco to Seattle while he was in Pakistan. He seemed disturbed by this news, but I was pleased at the prospect of having a new potential climbing partner in Seattle with similar interests.

After reaching Islamabad, Captain Gorsi insisted we visit his home, Peshawar, near the Khyber Pass and the Afghan border, before we flew home. We agreed. After my first trip to Pakistan in 1980, I had read up on the country's history and current events. I learned that the country's military dictator, General Muhammad Zia-ul-Haq, and the Pakistan Army continued to exert strong control over the country, much of it because of international support for the general's efforts to oppose the Soviet occupation next door in Afghanistan. Superpower rivalry outweighed any concerns over regional conflicts. At the time the United States was providing tremendous financial and weapons resources (matched dollar for dollar by Saudi Arabia) to the Pakistani Inter-Services Intelligence (ISI) agency for their covert operation to support the mujahideen in their war against the Russians. General Zia's goal was to evict the Soviet-supported regime in Afghanistan, which wasn't beholden to Pakistan and might be sympathetic to their archrival, India.

To garner popular support for this effort, the general partnered with religious conservatives to portray the Russian occupation as an attack on Islam. Muslim leaders declared a number of fatwas (religious edicts) that ordered the faithful to participate in a jihad (religious war). General Zia knew that spiritual zeal would incite fighters more than anything else, and soon the mujahideen became a battle-hardened force of fifty thousand from all over the Muslim world. I was aware that Peshawar served as the political, arms-dealing, training, and financial center for the ISI-trained mujahideen currently fighting the Soviets in Afghanistan, but I was not prepared for what I saw there.

Matt, Tom, Jack, and I drove with Captain Gorsi to Peshawar from Islamabad. As we entered the city, I saw that every kind of portable weapon, with maybe the exception of Stinger missiles and launchers, was displayed for sale in the bazaar. In the wartime realm of friend or foe, I should have been among friends, since the CIA was providing much of the funding and weapons for the mujahideen. But the situation didn't feel safe. There were anti-American slogans painted on the walls along with appeals to the faithful to fight against the opponents of Islam. I slid a bit farther down in my seat and was glad when we arrived at our hotel. Like most covert wars, there wasn't a clear distinction between the good guys and the bad guys, and although the mujahideen were fighting our proxy war against the Soviets, it was clear they weren't our friends.

General Zia would later be referred to as the grandfather of the global Islamic jihad because his efforts to influence Afghan politics in favor of Pakistan's conflict with India would unleash a powerful new force of Islamic fundamentalists upon the world. Their agenda would eventually expand beyond Afghanistan and promote a global jihad to impose Sharia (sacred law in Islam). US foreign policy was driven then by Cold War politics, and the opportunity to hurt the Russians in Afghanistan trumped any concerns for delivering money and arms to the groups referred to by American politicians as "freedom fighters." The difference between how the mujahideen were depicted in the United States and what I observed was an eye-opening experience.

Coming home after this second expedition to Gasherbrum IV, I experienced the same time warp as three years earlier. My life felt like it comprised two parallel but separate realities. The expedition soon faded in my memory, and my life picked up right where it had left off. Since Alice and I were separated, I was apprehensive about homecoming—except for seeing Lars. At two years old, he had changed a lot while I was gone. He was cautious but remembered me, and it didn't take long before we were having fun again together. The issues with my marriage were still there with no resolution, so Alice and I decided to divorce. We didn't own anything except a couple of beat-up Volkswagens; we only needed to agree on how we wanted to raise Lars. Fortunately our split was amicable enough that we negotiated a joint custody arrangement in everyone's best interest.

My life in Seattle settled into a new routine. Lars was with me every other week, and those days I had the responsibilities of single parenthood. On work days when Lars was with me, I took him to daycare in the morning, headed to work, trained at lunch with my running friends, picked up Lars before daycare closed, fixed dinner, gave him a bath, read a bedtime story, and put him to sleep. On weekends we did typical dad-kid things, like going to the zoo or the park, catching up on household chores, and making occasional visits to my parents and siblings who lived nearby. When Lars was with his mother, I stayed late at work to catch up and went climbing on those weekends.

I spent time at various crags in British Columbia and in the Cascade Mountains east of Seattle. Greg Child had become part of the Seattle climbing community after we both returned from Pakistan and I had gotten to know him better. A compact, powerful climber with dark curly hair and an irreverent sense of humor, Greg had a lifelong passion for the outdoors that inspired his interest in climbing. We became regular climbing partners and spent several weeks climbing together in the Cordillera Blanca in Peru in June 1984. After a couple of failed attempts on other peaks,

Greg and I managed to climb the west rib of Huascarán (in the Cordillera Blanca range). A memorable moment on that trip was when Greg scooped up a small lizard with his hand on our way to meeting some friends for dinner in Huaraz. Before heading into the restaurant, Greg put the lizard in his mouth, and after we sat down, he occasionally let it pop its head out between his pursed lips and it flicked its tongue at the people on the other side of the table. Greg repeated this a few times before our friends realized they weren't imagining things. We had a good laugh over it.

He was witty, which was reflected in his work to build a career as a writer. We shared stories about our families and I learned that as a teenager, Greg found that climbing helped him escape from a challenging family situation. He grew up in Sydney, and after spending time on the local Australian crags, he journeyed to the rock-climbing mecca of Yosemite and had been living in the United States ever since. Most of the time Greg was taking the piss out of one of us or the situation, but he had his darker moments that seemed to harken back to experiences he didn't talk much about. He had made the journey to America with literally only the pack on his back. The unflappable determination he applied to the things he cared about had already resulted in significant climbing success.

In late 1984 a friend invited me to a party at her house. Since it was my week with Lars and she was a single mom with two small children, I brought him with me. I didn't know most of her guests, so I volunteered to take care of all the kids and put them to bed. As I was reading a story in their bedroom, another outsider, Ann Dalton, came in and sat by me to watch and chat. I didn't realize that Ann was a children's librarian at the local public library, but my story time made an impression.

Ann called me a few days later, and we started spending time together. I liked her unpretentious, kind manner and commitment to family, friends, and the community. We had a lot of fun and more than a few adventures while hiking, biking, and sea kayaking. Lars was only three and a half, and we agreed not to bring him into our relationship until it became serious, so we took our time getting to know each other. By the summer of 1985 we felt it was time to include Lars in our time together. Ann loved working with children, so it was no surprise that she viewed having Lars around as an added benefit to the relationship. Like most children, Lars had a natural curiosity and enthusiasm for the world around him. Ann spent hours planning and doing kid things with Lars and me that I otherwise wouldn't have thought of or had the patience for. After I returned from a six-week climbing trip to the Alps in late September, Ann and I felt the time was right to move in together. Combining our households turned out to be a wonderful decision for all of us.

I was still drawn to the big mountains, but it was difficult to assemble a team well suited for the task. I knew Greg Child well enough to know that he would be a great partner for this kind of climbing. I suggested we put together a team to complete the route on the northwest ridge of Gasherbrum IV that I'd attempted in 1983. Although Greg hadn't been to Gasherbrum IV, he was attracted to the mountain for the same reasons I was. We agreed to go there together. I applied and received permission from the Pakistan government for another attempt on the mountain in 1986.

In 1985, a full year before Greg and I were scheduled to leave for Pakistan, I received an invitation from Lance Owens to join a large American expedition he was organizing to K2's north ridge in 1986. An eccentric emergency room doctor who didn't have the climbing experience to attempt a mountain like K2 himself, Lance was organized and determined to attract several experienced members from the American Everest Kangshung Face Expedition that had been successful on their second attempt in 1983.

At 28,251 feet (8,611 meters), K2 is the world's second highest mountain and straddles the international border, with China on the north and Pakistan to the south. K2 is 777 feet lower than Mount Everest, but it is much steeper, has only a few small flat places for campsites, and lacks nearby communities with an abundance of well-trained high-altitude workers (like the Sherpas in Nepal). These differences make K2 harder to climb than the world's highest mountain. The mountain requires the willingness and the experience to meet sustained difficulties, inspiring climbers to call it "the mountaineer's mountain." Steep on every side, K2's difficulty and architecture had attracted me since I was a child. By the end of 1985, 39 different climbers had reached the summit of K2, while 186 had climbed Mount Everest. Early expeditions to K2 read like grand adventures, with weeks-long approaches up rugged mountain valleys and climbers relying on inflatable goatskin rafts and flimsy woven vine bridges to cross treacherous rivers.

Almost all ascents of K2 had been made from the mountain's southern side in Pakistan. Few foreigners had visited the northern side since the region was mapped in 1937. During the 1954 Italian K2 expedition that climbed the mountain for the first time from the south, the Pakistani Air Force took their leader, Ardito Desio, on a reconnaissance flight around the mountain. He became intrigued with a ridge that split the huge north face in a continuous, steep line, dropping nearly twelve thousand feet from the summit to the glacier. For decades, Desio's published images of that side of the mountain had sparked climbers' imaginations.

In 1963, however, the Pakistani government gave the entire Shaksgam River basin, including K2's northern slopes, to China as part of an agreement that established the border between the two countries in northern Kashmir. After that, this sensitive border area was closed to the outside world until restrictions began to loosen and climbing permits became available along the Chinese borders with Nepal and Pakistan in the early 1980s. The Chinese knew these permits to do first ascents of routes on the north sides of major peaks like K2 and Everest would be highly sought after, so they offered them to the highest bidder. In 1980 the Japanese Alpine Club succeeded in obtaining a 150 million yen package (then about $600,000) for the sole rights to produce a television program on the ancient Silk Road, a climbing permit to the north side of K2, and newspaper coverage of these events. A large forty-four-member national Japanese expedition made the first ascent of K2's north ridge in August 1982.

After two unsuccessful expeditions to Gasherbrum IV, I wasn't getting it right with the teams I was assembling. I might have better luck not taking on the organizational responsibilities myself and going with this large team of experienced climbers to K2. Making this decision was difficult, but approaching K2 from the north on the other side of the Karakoram from Gasherbrum IV would be a completely new experience for me. This approach was seldom visited. Only the Japanese in 1982 and an Italian group who climbed it the following year had done it. Chinese permitting and logistics were much more bureaucratic and expensive than the process was in Pakistan, making it a trip that would be difficult to organize and finance on my own. For these reasons I decided to go on the K2 trip. But it was hard for me to tell Greg that I was dropping out of our Gasherbrum IV expedition. Disappointed, he was determined to proceed with the rest of the team.

Ann drove me to the Seattle airport on May 18 along with Catherine Freer, a longtime Seattle friend I had helped get onto the K2 trip. Short and powerfully built, Catherine—one of the leading female alpinists in the country—was serious, contemplative, and independent. At the airport we met one of our teammates, Dave Cheesmond, who had emigrated from South Africa to Canada and lived in Calgary. Thin and wiry with dark hair, he had a reputation for not taking himself or those around him too seriously. He had made first ascents of several difficult alpine routes in the Canadian Rockies and although he had not summited he had been an integral part of the successful 1983 Everest Kangshung Face Expedition. Dave noticed the three huge duffels of personal gear Catherine had brought. Despite her experience, she had a difficult time limiting herself to only the essentials. Transporting our gear was a significant expedition cost, and most of us had limited ourselves to about half that amount. In an authoritative but lighthearted manner, Dave tore into Catherine's bags in the airport departure lounge, and the two of them argued over items Dave said she didn't need. Gregg Cronn, another expedition member who had climbed Rakaposhi (7,788 meters, or 25,551 feet) in Pakistan a few years earlier with Dave, stood back. As takeoff approached, Catherine acquiesced and left behind a pile of portable exercise equipment and extra clothes. We almost missed our plane, and I had to run past my family waiting out at the gate to see me off. (In 1986, security regulations still allowed that.)

Our first stop was San Francisco. Knowing this trip would be a long separation for five-year-old Lars, I had made or purchased enough small presents for him to open one each day I was gone. I sent my last batch from the airport. Once we left the United States, communication would be difficult. I called my family because of the hurried good-bye in Seattle. George Lowe, a North American alpine climbing icon, joined the rest of the team in San Francisco for the flight to Beijing. George had passed up many world famous climbing objectives for little-known mountains with cutting-edge technical climbing objectives, but he had also reached the summit on the 1983 Everest Kangshung Face Expedition. About ten years older than I, with a thick head of graying hair, George was on my top ten list of climbing heroes and one of the main reasons I had been drawn to the trip. I was excited to climb with him but also afraid that I might not measure up. His legendary mild western drawl rose in pitch when he was emphatic.

After landing in Beijing, I realized that the logistics of running a climbing expedition in China were indeed very different from one in Pakistan. Our permit was issued by the Chinese Mountaineering Association (CMA), a government-run adventure tour organization that had a monopoly on arranging all expedition travel and accommodations at greatly inflated prices. Before the CMA would issue our visas, we were required to wire the estimated cost of the entire trip ahead of time. During several meetings with the CMA director, Mr. Ying, all he wanted to talk about was our budget. The CMA would keep meticulous records of our actual expenditures during the expedition, and then they would reconcile the amount we deposited initially with our actual costs. Our activities were organized for us, much like a tour group. We didn't have any opportunity to interact with the local people who were selling supplies or providing services that we needed for our expedition because the CMA did all of that for us. I missed Pakistan and the freedom (and frustration) of running our expedition like a small business. We were paying extra money to the CMA that wasn't all going to local businesses and service providers. George and Dave, who had been to Beijing on their way to the Kangshung Face on Everest, assured us this was the price of admission.

The team flew to Urumchi, the capital of the far-flung western Chinese province officially known as the Xinjiang Uyghur Autonomous Region. Xinjiang, as it is commonly called, is a large dry province. Historically it was sparsely populated, mostly by Uyghurs, a Muslim Turkic people. In the past fifty years there has been an infusion of Han Chinese into Xinjiang, which has created ethnic tensions in the region. The Uyghurs' complaints about their treatment by the Chinese government are similar to those made by the Tibetans, who claim they are victims of cultural prejudices and political and economic domination by the Chinese. The tension has resulted in small but sometimes violent Uyghur nationalist movements, some of which are linked to other fundamentalist Islamic movements in South Asia. Rather than addressing the Uyghurs' concerns, the Chinese have used repressive tactics, which they claim are necessary to crack down on any unrest that they label as separatist aspirations. Unfortunately, this has only made the situation worse.

From Urumchi, Lance, Gregg, Dave, Catherine, George, and I flew farther south to Kashgar, since K2 is located on the border between Xinjiang and the Pakistan province of Gilgit-Baltistan. Kashgar participated in what historians refer to as "The Great Game," a clandestine conflict in the late nineteenth and early twentieth centuries between the British and Russian Empires for control of Central Asia. British explorers who traveled, climbed, and mapped large areas in the Karakoram played a role in this conflict by establishing a presence for Queen Victoria in these rugged border areas. British explorer Eric Shipton is considered by modern climbers as one of the earliest proponents of small Himalayan expeditions unburdened by high-altitude porters and excessive equipment. He was stationed at the British consulate in Kashgar that supported the Crown's interests during that period. Given the historic contribution that Shipton made to modern climbing, we considered the former consulate to be like our version of Graceland. Before leaving Kashgar, Dave, Gregg, and I visited the consulate to pay homage, only to discover it was an abandoned, dusty, single-story stucco building on the edge of town.

The CMA hired a bus to take us to Yecheng, the last major town, where we got into four-wheel-drive jeeps and trucks and traveled up over the Kunlun Mountains. Outside the cities we stayed in Chinese Army barracks and shared meals with the young soldiers in their mess hall. It was a desolate, dry, rocky landscape, and for these young soldiers it must have seemed like the middle of nowhere. At one outpost, Lance, Gregg, Dave, and I had a four-on-four basketball game of Americans versus Chinese, which gathered a lot of spectators. Several inches over six feet, Gregg was taller than everyone and a pretty good shot. With typical overenthusiasm, Lance kept fouling. Dave and I tried to pass the ball, avoid the fray, and not get injured. We managed to win by a couple of shots despite the altitude, which left us totally out of breath.

Snow was falling when we crossed over a 16,000-foot pass. The road continued down to Mazar, a small military outpost west of the Tibetan plateau, where we left the main road and drove west to Mazhar Dara, where we got dropped off. There we would begin our trek to base camp.

The north side of K2 is such a desolate, mountainous landscape, no one lives there. Without a local population nearby to serve as porters, the Chinese had arranged for camel drivers to bring their animals from faraway villages to carry our supplies to base camp. Of the two species of camels, our drivers used the hairy two-humped Bactrian camels that are native to the Central Asian steppe as opposed to the more common Dromedary or Arabian camel that lives in North Africa and the Middle East. These domesticated camels had been used as pack animals in this part of the world since ancient times because of their ability to withstand cold, heat, drought, and high altitude.

Sturdy but ornery creatures, the camels bit, spat, and kicked, so we were told to keep our distance and let the drivers take care of getting the loads on and off the animals. With the onset of warmer weather, the camels were shedding their long woolly winter hair in large mats, leaving them with a shaggy rock star–like mop on the top of their heads. Each driver was responsible for four to six camels. He loaded each by pulling down on the halter attached to a wooden spike driven through the camel's nose, forcing it to kneel down, front legs first, in a slow forward motion. The camels were equipped with crude wooden saddles wedged between their humps. They snorted and grunted in displeasure but submitted to having our supplies slung over the saddles and tied down with ropes around their torsos.

On May 29 we began our trek to base camp. We started out at about 12,000 feet along the Yarkand River on an abandoned road, which the Chinese probably built sometime in the 1960s for border access. Fortunately, China and Pakistan are allies; their shared border had been established peacefully by the 1963 Sino–Pakistan Agreement. To the east, along the border with India, the Chinese had taken over a fourteen-thousand-square-mile area called the Aksai Chin in the 1962 Sino–Indian War. India claims that this area was historically part of Kashmir and therefore it belongs to them. The Chinese and Indians have occasional border incursions into each other's territory in the Aksai Chin, but here along the Pakistani border, it was peaceful. On either side of the river valley where we walked, purple and gray slopes of sand and loose rock rose several thousand feet to the craggy ridges above.

The team camped the first night at a place called Yilike, where the Zug Shaksgam River came in from the south and joined the Yarkand. In the morning, we followed the Zug Shaksgam for half a day until we reached the confluence with the Suruquat River, which we hiked along for the rest of our second day. On June 1 we continued up the Suruquat to reach the nearly 16,000-foot Aghil Pass, the northern gateway to the Karakoram. We gazed far below at the first significant obstacle between us and the base of K2: the Shaksgam River gorge. We had planned our trip to arrive before warm summer temperatures melted the winter snows and turned the river into a raging torrent, making it too deep for the camels to wade. We had to walk down the river gorge for three days.

The river meandered between rock walls on both sides of the gorge, forcing several crossings each day. Shortly after reaching base camp, we knew we would be trapped in the event of an emergency by the floodwaters until late summer, when the water levels dropped again. In this remote part of China, there were no helicopters, making a rescue impossible. Little had changed since 1887, when Sir Francis Younghusband became the first Westerner to cross Aghil Pass. Like him, we were completely isolated and on our own. It was just the kind of adventure I was looking for.

The track down the south side of the pass was steep and rocky, and once we arrived at the Shaksgam, we discovered that we had arrived early enough in the year and there was no surface water flowing in the riverbed. Two days later, we turned left up the Sarpo Laggo valley and ascended a short rise. From there, the north face of K2 blazed before us—a massive pyramid that dominated the surrounding peaks. The weather was so clear that the contrast between the bright mountain and the dark sky had an edge I felt I could reach out and grasp. I thought of Eric Shipton, who first surveyed this area in 1937. When faced with this same view, he wrote in *Blank on the Map*: "The cliffs and ridges of K2 rose out of the glacier in one stupendous sweep to the summit of the mountain, 12,000 feet above. The sight was beyond my comprehension. . . . I saw ice avalanches, weighing perhaps hundreds of tons, break off from a hanging glacier, nearly two miles above my head; the ice was ground to a fine powder and drifted away in the breeze long before it reached the foot of the precipice, nor did any sound reach my ears."

K2 base camp on the south, or Pakistan, side is situated at the base of the peak, and climbing the mountain starts from there. It is possible to locate the base camp close to the mountain because the porters who carry loads on the south side can walk up the long Baltoro Glacier that flows from the bottom of the mountain. But on K2's north side, our camels could not walk up the long North K2 Glacier to the base of the mountain because the rocky rubble and ice would cut their feet. This presented a major logistical problem because our base camp was located where the camel drivers were going to drop their loads at a place called Sughet Jangal—seventeen miles from the mountain. It would be impossible for us to climb K2 unless we could relocate most of these supplies from base camp to our advance base camp close to the base of the mountain. ABC would serve as our base of operations while climbing on the peak.

To move all our supplies from Sughet Jangal to ABC, Lance had recruited sixteen Americans to serve as a support team that would accomplish this work before the rest of us arrived. This arrangement was used by the large, regimented Japanese expedition that had made the first ascent by this route four years earlier, so Lance thought it would work for us. I had some misgivings as to whether it would work with our group of independent-minded Americans. Lance, Gregg, Dave, Catherine, George, and I arrived at base camp on June 3 and found the support team camped there. It was a windy place, and sand blew into everything, destroying tent zippers, filling sleeping bags, and covering everything with grit.

There I met the two remaining members of our expedition, Alex Lowe and Choc Quinn, who had volunteered to hike in with the American support team to manage their work. Alex (no relation to George) from Montana, was one of the strongest young alpine climbers in the United States. Tall with sandy brown hair and a powerful chest, he had legs seemingly too skinny to propel him uphill at the speed he was known for. Choc was a cheerful and sturdy Canadian, originally from Ireland, who had been a last-minute addition. The original team had included a Spokane climber, Kim Momb, who had been on the Everest trip with George Lowe and Dave Cheesmond. But Kim had been killed in an avalanche working as a heli-skiing guide the previous winter. So Dave had recruited Choc, his Canadian Rockies partner, to be our eighth member.

Covered in grime, Alex and Choc seemed burned out from their work over the past three weeks. When the support team volunteered for this job six months earlier, it might have sounded like a fun and exotic opportunity to visit western China and trek to the base of the north side of K2. In reality they had signed up for three weeks of hard labor, moving about three thousand pounds of food and equipment seventeen miles up a nasty, rubble-covered glacier. They had established two camps on the glacier that they used to ferry loads up to ABC. Very little of the supplies had actually made it all the way there. After a few carries, many on the support team lost their enthusiasm for the job, even with plenty of encouragement and help from Alex and Choc. I could tell it had been a frustrating and exhausting experience, but they were excited about our arrival and getting onto the mountain soon.

It was strange to watch the camels and support team leave. We would be isolated there for at least ten weeks, with no communication with the outside world. It looked like we still needed to do a lot of load carrying on the glacier before we could occupy ABC and start climbing on the mountain. We rested and organized loads at base camp for a couple of days and then, like almost everyone else on the team, I carried four loads of fifty pounds or more to glacier camp I, three loads to glacier camp II, and one load to ABC over the next eight days. On June 13 we moved up to advance base camp at over 16,000 feet, tired but happy to be camped beneath the 12,000-foot-high north face of K2.

The expedition planned to climb the mountain in traditional expedition style by placing fixed ropes and fixed camps all the way up the mountain. Without local high-altitude porters (like Sherpas in Nepal) to help us, it was going to be a herculean task to carry and install over 10,000 feet of seven-millimeter rope, plus equip four camps on the mountain with tents, sleeping bags, stoves, fuel, and food. Everyone would pitch in, but we knew the physical strain of doing this work at elevations between 16,000 feet and the highest camp at over 26,000 feet would take its toll. When all was done and it was time to make a summit attempt, it was likely that only a few of us, if any, would be healthy enough to try. This is the process that George and Dave had used on their successful ascent of the Kangshung Face on Everest three years earlier. By the time I joined the expedition, it had been decided this was how we were approaching the climb.

Lance had done a good job assembling a group of experienced, compatible climbers. Since most of us had never climbed with each other before, there was a pecking order based on experience, strength, and ability that was typical in expedition-style climbing. George was so accomplished, and he had such intense focus and strong opinions, that we acquiesced to his decision making early on. George felt he could rely on Dave, whom he knew from Everest, and Alex, one of his strongest climbing partners in North America. Those three were our lead climbers, and Gregg, Choc, Catherine, and I had to prove ourselves. Our performance fixing rope and establishing camps reshuffled this hierarchy and determined the composition of the first summit attempt.

The seven-millimeter rope we were fixing up the mountain came in thousand-foot lengths, wound onto twenty-five-pound spools. Following George and Dave's Everest system, the lead climber tied into one of the rope ends and those following fed it out as the leader climbed up. The leader placed intermediate anchors in the ice or rock along the way and a double anchor when the spool ran out. We had to be careful; the small diameter low-stretch nylon rope we employed was intended for use as fixed rope—it wasn't an elastic lead rope designed to withstand a fall. The person going first couldn't take a leader fall onto the rope because it might break. Once the leader fixed the end of the rope, the followers climbed up using a pair of mechanical ascenders attached to the rope, one for each hand. Each ascender had a sling attached to the climber's harness, and with a rhythmic motion they alternately slid them up the rope that the ascenders would grip when they pulled down. The followers kicked their crampons into the ice and stepped up each time they slid the ascender up the rope.

I shared in the work to break trail through steep snow, fix rope, and dig tent platforms for Camp I at 19,000 feet. After that, George and Dave asked me to assist them in placing the fixed rope to Camp II, which was a nice vote of confidence. On June 16 the three of us occupied Camp I. It was exhausting to work at elevations we were not yet acclimatized to, but especially for the lead climber, so we alternated who went first.

Climbing above Camp I was going to be a calf-burning rising traverse to the right along a sixty- to seventy-degree slope of hard ice (imagine climbing a frozen lake tilted at that sharp angle). I led first from Camp I and made progress kicking in my front points, swinging my tools, and placing ice screws along the way. After every ten steps I panted for air. When my spool ran out, I anchored the rope so my partners could come up. After joining me, George fed rope off a spool to Dave, who then started leading. George wanted to fix more rope when they were finished, so he sent me back to Camp I to bring up two more spools. As I climbed back up, I could hardly manage such a heavy pack at 21,000 feet. Later, as we rappelled back to Camp I, Dave advised me, "You don't always have to do everything George says."

On June 19, Alex, Catherine, and Choc finished placing ropes up similar terrain to Camp II at 22,000 feet. George, Dave, Gregg, and I carried loads there and moved in to do several days of work above. By June 24, George and I finished fixing rope through mixed rock and ice along the crest of the north ridge to 24,000 feet before the weather deteriorated and we headed down for a much-needed rest. I stopped at Camp I for the night and enjoyed sharing a tent with Lance, who asked me if I thought there was a God. Catherine, also in the tent, asked me to help her make a camera case out of a stove bag.

I descended to ABC on June 25, Lars's fifth birthday. I had been absent for three of his birthdays. Although I was in Seattle for most of the year, I was often gone in June, a prime time for climbing in the Karakoram. It wasn't ideal, but it was how I tried to balance the different aspects of my life. Although it was wonderful (and safer) to focus solely on climbing while on expeditions, being separated from my family was always difficult. When home, I was careful to prioritize them over work or business travel. As night came on, a snowstorm unleashed its fury on my tent. I listened to an audio tape Ann had made of her reading a story to Lars. She had coaxed Lars into saying hi and wishing me good luck on K2. In the darkness with the tent flapping in the wind, I felt a deep loneliness, hearing the voices of the people I loved most. Ann's story was set in a beautiful Pacific Northwest rainforest—a further reminder that home was far away. But accompanying my loneliness was a deep appreciation for this opportunity to be fully engaged in such a wild and rugged landscape.

Our good weather spell had ended, and I was tired. There is a delicate balance between getting the hard load work done on the mountain and resting enough to have the energy to make a summit attempt when the time comes. The work/rest cycle needs to be managed on a daily basis. The weather looked like it would be bad for several days, so there was time to walk down to Sughet Jangal for a rest and to visit our base camp staff. Descending to 12,000 feet sped up my recovery with fresh food and thicker air.

The weather improved in early July, and I returned to ABC. By July 6, George, Alex, and I fixed rope above Camp II, along more mixed ice and rock terrain to within a few hundred feet of Camp III at 25,000 feet. Our team's attrition rate from working at these elevations was significant. Lance admitted that he was the least experienced and didn't have the strength to contribute much to the work higher on the mountain. Jovial Choc was fun to hang out with, but this was his first experience at high altitude, and the physical and emotional strain held him back. Dave's hard work early on had taken its toll, and he was either sick or couldn't keep up. Catherine suffered from chronic headaches up high that didn't prevent her from contributing above Camp II, but she was inconsistent. A few years earlier Gregg had suffered from high-altitude cerebral edema on an expedition to Kangchenjunga (at 8,586 meters, or 28,169 feet, it is the world's third highest mountain, straddling Nepal and India). Concerned about a recurrence, he cautiously contributed to the work above Camp II.

Most of the effort at that point was falling on Alex, George, and me. Alex was a high-energy guy. His strength and systematic way of resolving problems made him a tremendous force on the mountain. But he had an emotional sensitivity that contrasted with his overt physical prowess. He threw himself into a project like this so completely that I wondered how long he could keep it up. George intimidated me at first with his apparent unbreakable determination and singular focus. It seemed hard for him to relax. My body was so compromised at these elevations without supplemental oxygen that I never felt that good. I had a terrible dry, cracked, sore throat. I wondered if I should ignore it, or if that would backfire on me higher up and I would get really sick. At night, in the delirium of interrupted sleep, my health became a constant worry.

On July 8, George, Alex, and I went up to finish fixing rope and occupy Camp III. Gregg came with us to carry a load of supplies and got to within three hundred feet of the camp before returning to Camp II. He told us later he experienced a severe headache and associated grogginess that felt like the onset of HACE. Given what had happened during his Kangchenjunga expedition, these symptoms were understandably frightening, so he decided to limit his activity to Camp II and below.

I chopped the tent platforms out of the snow and ice for Camp III, while George and Alex went down to pick up Gregg's load. I had a miserable night sleeping at this altitude for the first time. It was bitterly cold, and I couldn't stay warm. With no appetite, I forced down several hot drinks. It snowed that night, and conditions were so poor in the morning that we decided to go down to ABC. It was extremely cold on the descent, and rappelling down the fixed ropes wore holes in my gloves. After several hundred feet I realized my thumb was sticking out of one of the holes—it was so numb I couldn't feel it. I stopped to warm it up and experienced a severe case of what we call the "screaming barfies"—so named for the usual expletives and potential for vomiting when an afflicted appendage throbs with pain as it thaws. But this was a good thing in my situation, because that meant my thumb wasn't frostbitten. Confused and exhausted, I continued my cold descent in a maelstrom of blinding wind and snow. When we got to the rocky moraine above ABC, exhaustion forced me to stop for a rest. Time slowed down as I watched the mountain disappear and reappear out of the clouds. I stumbled into camp on the thin layer of rock that slid over the ice below, nearly sending me sprawling.

A series of storms punctuated by brief periods of clearing fooled us into making several abortive trips up to Camps I and II. By July 22 a large amount of new snow had fallen on the mountain, and with no end in sight I headed down with Gregg, Lance, Dave, and Choc to Sughet Jangal for some R&R. Staying at ABC at 17,000 feet was causing us to slowly deteriorate, and there was no advantage to being there now that we were acclimatized. I wasn't concerned about being too far away from the mountain when the weather improved because I knew I could get back to ABC in one day. During this extended period of bad weather, George, Catherine, and Alex stayed at ABC, ready to go back up at a moment's notice if the weather improved. But the living conditions there were poor, mostly because our food was not varied and appealing enough for us to consume the five thousand to seven thousand calories per day of the carbohydrates, protein, and fat we needed to recuperate and prepare for the next climb above 23,000 feet.

George was especially determined. He spent days in the tent waiting for the moment the weather cleared. After working together for weeks now, George and I came to rely on each other. We had developed a mutual respect for each other's abilities. He revealed more about his life as a family man and a scientist; instead of ordering me around, he embodied a more collaborative spirit that enabled us to take better care of each other. These kinds of partnerships were as important, maybe even more important, than the climb we were on. Although I admired his discipline and determination, these characteristics sometimes expressed themselves as counterproductive stubbornness. Was it humanly possible for George to work so hard on the mountain and then recover adequately without a break from the conditions at ABC? George, Alex, and I had begun to discuss strategy since we were doing most of the work up high. I argued that descending to base camp would make us stronger when the weather improved and we made a summit attempt. But both of them, along with Catherine, decided to remain poised at ABC.

On July 28 the sky cleared. Gregg, Lance, Dave, Choc, and I hurried back up to ABC. George, Alex, and Catherine had headed up to Camp I late that sunny morning. After all the new snow, I was concerned: the slopes above and below Camp I regularly avalanched when the sun came around and baked that part of the mountain in the afternoon. Fortunately they were all at Camp I, which was protected under an overhanging visor of ice, when the surrounding slopes cut loose. They watched, frightened, when tons of wet snow poured over the camp just a few feet out from the tents. I caught up with George and Alex at Camp III three days later. We had wasted a lot of effort by not coordinating our movements on the mountain. George and Alex had to break trail all the way to Camp III without my help. Because windblown snow filled in their track each night, I had to break trail by myself most of the way up to Camp III.

By the time I got to Camp III on July 31, I was completely done in. George and Alex were busy fixing rope to Camp IV and arrived back at Camp III soon after my arrival with discouraging news. The snow to Camp IV was deep and unconsolidated, which meant there was a good chance the summit snow slopes would be similar. George and Alex went down to Camp II to rest, and I waited at Camp III until they returned a couple of days later.

Using the fixed rope George and Alex had placed three days earlier, the three of us plus Catherine climbed a short snow slope above Camp III to a small notch that moved us off the ridge onto the north face. From there we plowed through more steep snow interspersed with short rock steps. The route took us left to a spectacular rock platform on the crest of the north ridge, where we pitched two small bivy tents for Camp IV (at 25,800 feet). The place was aptly named the Eagle's Nest by the two earlier expeditions. Catherine didn't feel well enough to continue and descended back to Camp III. The plan for the rest of us was to make a summit attempt the next day. That afternoon George volunteered to fix our last three hundred feet of rope up a steep, exposed snow ramp above the camp before returning to the tents for the night. Our plan for the morning was to quickly reach the end of George's fixed rope, then climb about two thousand feet up a hanging glacier and upper couloir to the summit ridge. It was only a short walk from there to the top.

At 2:00 a.m. George woke us saying he had a faint gurgling in his chest—a sign of HAPE. He insisted on descending to Camp III on his own, where Catherine could help him. "You guys need to go for the summit today," he said to Alex and me. By the time Catherine radioed us that George had safely arrived, Alex had a headache, and he was unsettled by the abrupt exit of his main partner. He delayed making a decision, and by 5:00 a.m. as the sun started to light the sky, it was getting late for a summit attempt. "What do you want to do?" I asked. "Let's go up," Alex said, but his usual ragged smile was gone.

We struggled through deep drifts onto the steep north face, taking time to follow small snow ribs and avoid wind-loaded pockets where we might trigger an avalanche. High clouds obscured the sun. In the distance beyond the rocky northwest ridge, where Nanga Parbat should have appeared, we saw a storm rapidly approaching. Alex and I stopped to discuss our situation less than a thousand feet from the summit. If we continued, we'd reach the top near dark and in a blizzard. The slopes were loaded with loose, unconsolidated snow that Alex believed was hazardous because of avalanche danger. The risks seemed too great, so we reluctantly turned around.

Alex and I descended to ABC, the weather closed in, and the next morning it was snowing heavily. All eight of us had a meeting about what to do. I presented a plan to have another attempt. With fixed ropes to 26,000 feet and camps stocked with food and fuel, we had a chance to reach the top. But it kept snowing for five days, and on August 10 our camel drivers showed up at Sughet Jangal. Everyone except Dave, Catherine, and I decided to leave. Each member of the team had their personal reasons to stay or go. Serious high altitude–related illnesses like what George and Gregg had experienced require weeks of recovery at much lower elevations before a climber can go back up to extreme altitude. Alex and Choc felt the need to return home after being gone for nearly four months (including the extra time they spent with the support team). Lance had succeeded in getting all of us to the mountain, and there wasn't a lot more he could do to help.

With only the three of us, our chance of success was extremely low. After all the work I had put into the expedition, and with all our supplies and equipment still up on the mountain, I wanted to make at least one more summit attempt. If that failed, we could at least clean up the mountain and bring everything down. At ABC on August 12, at 5:30 a.m., I received the final radio call from George, Alex, Lance, Gregg, and Choc, who were leaving Sughet Jangal for home.

Two days later, I woke up to absolutely clear skies. The next day, Dave, Catherine, and I set out for Camp I. It would take incredible good luck for the weather, snow conditions, and everyone's good health to line up and enable us to reach the top. But despite discouraging prospects, the atmosphere of the expedition had changed completely—our little group seemed much happier than the angst-ridden larger team. The relaxed smaller group was full of humor, thrilled to be sharing such an amazing place.

After reaching Camp I, the plan was to keep moving up, camp by camp, until we made the summit, encountered bad weather, or someone had a health problem. We moved to Camp II on August 16, where the snow conditions were firmer than on any of our previous attempts. If we were looking for a miracle to get us to the top of K2, this was it. I started hoping. Two days later, we moved up to Camp III, but at 2:00 a.m. it started to snow heavily, and by the next morning the tent was nearly buried. It was depressing to have been doing so well, needing only two more days of good weather to summit. We spent the next day at Camp III, waiting for the weather to improve, but it snowed again all night. It wasn't happening.

The best thing we could do was to bring down our equipment and clean up the mountain. Dave and I went up to Camp IV in the storm for the tents and equipment. David, Catherine, and I were able to bring everything we had at Camp III down to Camp II. But together with everything we had at Camp II, we had accumulated too much to carry down ourselves. We decided to put everything into a couple of heavy duffel bags, drop them about five thousand feet down the north face, and pick them up at the bottom. I stayed at Camp II to pack everything in the duffels and hauled them three hundred feet up the ridge to a spot where the duffels could fall freely down the face to the glacier. Several hours later, Catherine and Dave radioed they were at the bottom of the face, so I tossed the bags. They saw them fall to the bottom and collected them. I headed down and reached ABC after dark.

It took us four days of heavy load carrying to bring the most valuable equipment down to Sughet Jangal. A Chinese scientific expedition was going to come there the following year, so we left a well-protected cache of equipment under heavy tarps for them at ABC. The camel drivers had come back for us, and on August 27 we left Sughet Jangal in rain that later turned to snow. It felt good to have such a light pack and to feel the big heavy flakes hit my face as we walked into the wind. With nothing to be anxious about now, I calmly walked out and enjoyed my surroundings. The camel drivers took care of us at all the river crossings, and our interpreter did all the cooking.

A couple of days later, I walked with Catherine over Aghil Pass while Dave accompanied the camel drivers behind us. The stone and mud-walled

Kurghitz summer dwellings there were occupied by women and children herding goats. As we passed one of the buildings, a young woman who looked to be in her mid-teens hurried out to show us the small bundle in her arms. She opened up a well-worn homespun blanket, and inside was an infant so new that the shiny afterbirth mucus still coated its face. The new mother was proudly beaming. Our angst over K2 seemed very far away.

After reaching the road, Dave, Catherine, and I regained the ability to communicate with the outside world. While we were climbing on the Chinese side of the mountain, thirteen climbers from different expeditions had been killed throughout the season on the Pakistan side of K2. This made 1986 the most disastrous year in the mountain's history. Five of the fatalities had occurred when climbers pressed on toward the summit despite a gathering storm, which trapped them in their high camp—the same storm that had caused Alex and me to retreat near the top. We had been so close to those climbers. Despite our disappointment, we had trusted our instincts about going down.

Nonetheless, I was discouraged to be coming home yet again without a summit. Those feelings were temporarily worsened when I learned that while I was on K2, Greg Child and his team had made the first ascent of the Gasherbrum IV's northwest ridge, on the route I had pioneered partway. Although I was disappointed to not have been a part of it, I was glad for Greg and his partners. My prior frustrations on Gasherbrum IV obscured the fact that I was gradually getting better at what was most important: putting together a group of friends who had the skill, strength, and disposition for climbing big mountains. By going to K2, I had made the mistake of trading a strong group of friends for an expedition that looked good on paper but was full of people I didn't know well enough. I had developed a deep love of the sport that was only possible if I embraced the process of self-discovery. That was the beauty—and also the difficulty—of these experiences.

In the fall of 1986, back in Seattle, Greg Child mentioned that he was part of an expedition that was going to the Pakistan side of K2 the following year. The expedition would be led by Doug Scott, the British climber best known for being the first to climb the difficult southwest face of Mount Everest with Dougal Haston in 1975. Doug's Everest climb was a huge affair, with twenty-three British climbers and a large contingent of high-altitude Sherpas. The team had climbed in traditional expedition style, using fixed rope up to 27,500 feet, and eventually put a total of five climbers on top. After that, Doug had quit participating in large, logistically complex expedition-style trips and had become one of the early advocates of climbing big Himalayan peaks in the self-sufficient manner called alpine style.

Alpine-style climbers carry all their own food, fuel, and equipment as they move up a mountain. The style doesn't use fixed ropes, stocked camps, high-altitude porters, and supplemental oxygen. Doug had written about his experience on Everest, where he realized that even the most difficult climbs at extreme altitude could be beaten into submission with modern equipment and enough labor. Commitment, fortitude, skill, and strength are prerequisites for alpine-style climbing, commonly used on smaller peaks. Doug and several of his peers wanted to apply these principles in a much larger and challenging Himalayan arena. Climbing alpine style, he had made the first ascent of the Ogre (1977), the north ridge of Kangchenjunga (1979), the south face of Denali (North America's highest mountain, 1976), and the East Pillar of Shivling in India (1981, with a team that included Greg Child).

Greg put in a good word for me, and I was invited to join the team. Doug was leader, and we would be climbing alpine style. So far, all my expeditions to the Great Ranges had been done expedition style, but without the use of high-altitude porters. On my recent attempt on K2, it had been a grueling and self-defeating effort fixing rope and stocking camps high on the mountain when most of our team had succumbed to various health problems. I looked forward to learning from an expert how to climb light and fast on a big and difficult mountain like K2.

I left Seattle for Islamabad on June 14, 1987, with Greg and another team member, Phil Ershler. Short and muscular, Phil had a pleasant, no-nonsense personality. He was a well-established guide on bigger mountains in the Western Hemisphere like Denali, Aconcagua, and Mount Rainier. He had also climbed the north face of Everest on a solo summit bid in 1985. When we arrived in Pakistan, I met Doug, whom I had only seen previously on his lecture tours. Doug's tall, stout appearance seemed diminished, and we learned that just before leaving England he had broken several ribs falling off a horse. He had also brought his twenty-three-year-old son, Michael, who was built like his father and had a lot of energy and enthusiasm.

Doug and Michael had a warm, close relationship, and although Lars was only six, I liked thinking that I might have a similar rapport with him when he became a young adult. Another team member, Tim Macartney-Snape, flew in from Australia. Tall, lanky, and sporting a bowl haircut, Tim had climbed a new route on the north side of Everest in 1984 and had climbed Gasherbrum IV with Greg the previous year. He seemed wonderfully low-key—a good indicator that he would remain calm in tough situations. We were also fortunate to have Carolyn Gunn, a cheerful and understanding veterinarian, as the medical person on the expedition.

The approach to K2 in Pakistan is the same one we had used for Gasherbrum IV in 1980 and 1983. It had been four years since I had trekked up the Braldu valley and the Baltoro Glacier. Since then, the security situation had changed significantly. Pakistan was involved in a conflict with India over the Siachen Glacier as part of the Kashmir dispute. The largest in the Karakoram, the Siachen Glacier is forty-seven miles long and drains a 270-square-mile area just on the other side of a 20,000-foot pass at the head of the Baltoro Glacier. The Pakistan military was using the Baltoro Glacier to approach their battlefront.

Changes to the route as a result of the conflict were immediately apparent. On my previous trips it had been a difficult four-day trek over the Chongo La (la means "pass" in Tibetan) and up the Chakpo-Chongo gorge to the village of Askole. But to facilitate the movement of military personnel and supplies, the trail had been replaced by a road that was extended from Dasso to Askole. Beyond Askole, we found a much larger military presence, with new Pakistan Army outposts at regular intervals along the glacier and mule trains supplying the troops.

In a previous treaty with India, Pakistan had accepted a delineation of the Line of Control (LOC) in disputed Kashmir. But in the agreement, the north end of the LOC ended at a coordinate point called NJ9842 that was more than fifty miles south of the Chinese border. This prompted a dispute because it was unclear which country was entitled to about two thousand square miles of mostly ice and rock. In the mid-1970s Pakistan staked its claim to this area by issuing climbing permits for expeditions to peaks along the vast and tentacled Siachen Glacier. India launched Operation Meghdoot on April 13, 1984, and used special helicopters to land Indian

Army units at the nearly 20,000-foot passes along the Saltoro Ridge just west of the Siachen Glacier. In response, Pakistan rushed its troops up to these heights, only to find the Indian soldiers already entrenched along the high ground. The two sides engaged in World War I–type trench warfare, in a rugged, cold, extreme altitude mountain environment along a new front called the Actual Ground Position Line (AGPL).

Walking up the glacier, the team camped for the night near one of several outposts located along the Baltoro Glacier. Our liaison officer said it would be courteous to stop by for a visit. Each outpost had about a half dozen soldiers who slept in tents and cooked, ate, and hung out in a fiberglass dome enclosure about the size of a garden shed. The blanket of winter snow had melted in the summer sun, exposing rubble-covered ice that slowly sinks as it starts melting. The glacial surface had receded faster around the large rocks lying on the surface of the ice, leaving them suspended several feet in the air by columns of ice. The rocks balanced on these ice pedestals created formations known as glacier tables. The tents and fiberglass dome at the outpost were similarly suspended, and the sun's UV, especially at this altitude, had broken down the nylon rain covers on the tents, leaving them badly torn and flapping in the wind as they drooped over the top of dirty mounds of ice like an oversize hat.

No one was in the tents, so the team walked past what looked like several years of accumulated garbage to the fiberglass dome that was supported on its ice pedestal. The perimeter was hanging in space, making the normal entrance inaccessible. We looked inside by poking our heads up through a hatch in the floor. Inside we found the soldiers lying around in the dark interior, and they sat up slowly to greet us. They were making tea on a kerosene stove that emitted a sooty exhaust into the poorly ventilated shelter. Overcome by the fumes, we retreated outside and asked the soldiers to join us.

Dropping out of the dome, they squinted in the sunlight, perking up after escaping the toxic air inside. Their sun-darkened faces were framed with bushy black beards, and they wore down parkas that used to be white, now blackened from the soot that covered the dome's interior. The soldiers served us tea as we sat outside talking. They appeared to be in their late teens or early twenties. Most were from lowland areas in Pakistan like the Punjab, still learning how to take care of themselves in the mountains.

Lacking experience, they had an abundance of enthusiasm to fight the enemy. It was unlikely that any of these soldiers would get hurt or killed in action, however—most of the casualties were from natural hazards like avalanches, frostbite, hypothermia, falling, and altitude sickness.

That evening our porters gathered in a big circle, singing and dancing to the beat of hands pounding on five-gallon plastic kerosene jugs. Rasool, one of the cooks Doug hired, was dancing in the center of the circle. Small and wiry, Rasool had a closely cropped beard and his hair was thinning. His vivid dance told a story about a devious woman trying to lure a young man into her bed. This was hot stuff for these young men who were lonely and afraid of the dangers they faced on the glacier. It was a good release for them to cut loose, hooting and hollering over such racy entertainment far away from the watchful eyes of the village mullah.

As his dance progressed, Rasool spun and flailed his arms wildly and worked himself into a frenzy. Eventually he reached a point of total exhaustion, collapsed on the ground, and like some kind of whirling dervish, he lay there panting with his eyes staring up into the sky in a dazed way. I ran over and nudged him gently with my hand to see if he was responsive. After several minutes, Rasool started to recover. I gave him a sip of water and asked if he was okay. He eventually got up, dusted himself off, and said, "Steve, sahib, it is no problem, I am fine."

The porters continued singing. I wondered what these songs were about. Shahid was one of the Pakistani members of a film crew accompanying us to get location shots for a Hollywood feature film about K2. I asked him what they were singing about. "These are very sad love songs," he said. "The lyrics are things like, 'I made a home for you in my heart, but now that I can't have you, my heart will stop.'" I asked Shahid why all the love songs were sad. "Since all the marriages are arranged, the courtship begins after couples are married," he said. "Often love doesn't come, or it comes with a person to whom they are not married—hence the tragic songs." The conversation had been about these desperately poor mountain villagers who served as our porters. But then Shahid, a middle-class professional living in Islamabad, said that at home he would often hear a man ask his friend, "How in love are you," and the friend would answer, "I'm so in love that I cry every night."

We reached base camp on June 30. The plan was to climb a new route on the east face of K2. First we needed to acclimatize, so over the next three weeks we climbed partway up Peak 6880 and Skyang Kangri (7,545 meters, or 24,754 feet) northeast of K2 and to over 22,000 feet on Broad Peak (8,051 meters, or 26,414 feet), across the glacier from base camp. Those explorations gave us ample time to examine potential climbing lines on the mountain's east side, which led us to conclude that it was too avalanche prone. We decided to try a different route.

In 1987 the only means of communication was regular mail, delivered to base camp periodically the old-fashioned way—via runner. I received a letter on July 20 from Ann telling me that Dave Cheesmond and Catherine Freer had disappeared on Hummingbird Ridge on Mount Logan, Canada's highest peak. They were presumed dead. Climbing big mountains is inherently dangerous, but losing these two friends felt like someone had ripped a hole in my heart. I sat below K2—the mountain that Dave, Catherine, and I had shared so happily just a year earlier—and recalled my last phone conversation with Dave. In his usual straightforward manner, he had encouraged me to go back to K2 again that year. "You should go for it, man," he had said, "and just get up the thing."

Tim had also received a troubling message from his girlfriend: "Family emergency, please contact me as soon as possible." This cryptic note left Tim very worried and unsure about what to do. Doug and Michael were experiencing health problems. Doug's ribs had refused to heal at this altitude, and Michael was having difficulty acclimatizing. By the end of July, Doug, Michael and Tim decided to drop out of the expedition.

For our final acclimatization trip, Phil, Greg, and I climbed up to Camp II at 22,000 feet on K2's standard Abruzzi Ridge Route, the southeast ridge route named after the Duke of Abruzzi, who made the first attempt to climb the peak in 1909. Given the long history of climbing on this route, there were plenty of old pitons, cable ladders, bits of fixed rope, and tent platforms along the way—some of which looked to be from attempts made between World War I and World War II. The Abruzzi Route is not a continuous prominent ridge but rather a series of ribs connected by gullies. The rock is loose; fortunately we had good snow cover. In warm temperatures on a dry year the route looked like it would be subject to serious rockfall problems.

After a couple of nights at Camp II, we returned to base camp to rest before making a summit attempt. The weather was consistently poor, however, and we spent most of the first three weeks of August waiting. During this period the three of us made two attempts up mostly snow and ice climbing on the south face, but we were turned back by the same frustrating weather pattern. It would be clear in the morning, but by the afternoon when we reached around 23,000 feet, it clouded over and began snowing and blowing. Both times we decided to bivouac on a tiny ledge hacked out of the slope, hoping the weather would clear during the night. But in the morning it was still snowing and blowing, so we decided to descend.

I was very disappointed by another failure, but I felt better that it was completely caused by weather. I found out later that no one made a successful ascent of K2 that year. My disappointment was tempered by enjoying the freedom of movement I had experienced climbing alpine style.

CHAPTER 3

K2 AT LAST

K2 NORTH RIDGE, 1990

O n the flight back from K2 in 1987, I had said to Greg and Phil, "We need to go back." Phil laughed. "We aren't even home from this trip yet and you're asking us if we want to go back?" he said. I thought we should go to the mountain's north side, where I had been in 1986. "The north side is a beautiful route in a very remote place that hasn't changed much since the early explorers like Younghusband and Shipton were there," I said, referring to Sir Francis Younghusband, who made the first crossing of the Aghil and Mustagh passes from Xinjiang to India in 1887, and Eric Shipton, whose team first mapped K2's north side in 1937.

We had just experienced the craziness on the Pakistan side of K2, I argued, where everyone converges on the Abruzzi Ridge and it's every man for himself. I had nearly gotten to the summit with Alex Lowe on the north side the previous year, and I knew Greg and Phil were the perfect partners to succeed on my next attempt. "I know how we can get up it this time,"

I insisted. I knew they wouldn't be able to resist. We looked at each other and said, "Let's do it."

When we returned home and started talking it over in earnest, we realized that the soonest we could all go was almost three years away, in 1990. In early 1988, I wrote to the Chinese Mountaineering Association asking for a permit for that year. They sent me a telegram denying my request, saying they had already issued a permit to a Polish expedition for 1990. I suspected that the real reason for their refusal was the financial dispute I had with the CMA when I had left Beijing in 1986. When we left China that year after our K2 expedition, Lance Owens had given me the responsibility for reconciling all our final expenses with the CMA (Dave, Catherine, and I had been the last ones to leave the country). While we had been on the mountain, the CMA had increased the unit costs for camels, jeeps, hotels, airline flights, transporting cargo, meals, and things like liaison officer and interpreter costs. Before the three of us had left China, the Chinese demanded an additional several thousand dollars beyond our original agreed-upon budget.

I refused to pay the extra amount, arguing that this retroactive escalation was unfair. The CMA director, Mr. Ying, insisted that the amounts in the original budget were only estimates and that the association had the right to increase costs at any time. The discussion devolved into name calling, and we reached an impasse. Mr. Ying threatened to prevent me from boarding my flight home the following morning if I didn't pay up, but he backed down when I threatened to call the US Embassy if the CMA attempted to hold me against my will. I finally walked out of the meeting late that evening and went to bed. At 2:00 a.m. the CMA rousted me out of bed and started up another round of negotiations. We finally agreed to split the difference, and after I paid the final bill, Mr. Ying's disposition flipped 180 degrees. He was effusive about our wonderful friendship and said that we were welcome in China. Mr. Ying was still in charge two years later. Despite his seeming goodwill in 1986, I sensed that the CMA's refusal to give me a permit for a 1990 expedition was in retaliation.

For advice, I called Nick Clinch, former president of the American Alpine Club, a national advocacy organization for climbers. He was also America's most experienced Karakoram expedition leader and had successfully led the expeditions that made the first ascents of Gasherbrum I in 1958 and Masherbrum in 1960. Nick suggested that I try to get a permit through the back door by contacting the local Xinjiang Mountaineering Association (XMA) in Urumchi and ask for a permit. "In China, there is competition for power and authority between the provincial and national state-run enterprises," he said. "If the pendulum has swung in favor of the local mountaineering associations, then the national CMA may not be able to do anything about it." He gave me a contact name, and I sent a request to the XMA. A couple of months later, I received a response from the XMA: they would grant us permission to climb K2's north ridge in 1990.

I discussed our plans for K2 with another Seattle climber, Jim Wickwire, who had climbed K2 from the Pakistan side in 1978. He and three of his teammates were the first Americans to reach the summit. Jim was planning a climbing expedition to China in 1989 to attempt the first ascent of Menlungtse (7,181 meters, or 23,560 feet), just inside Tibet near the Nepalese border. He was arranging his travel to Beijing to do the negotiations for his trip and mentioned to the CMA that I was going to accompany him to negotiate the budget for K2 with the XMA at the same time. Jim and I had worked out this strategy to test which mountaineering association was really in charge, to try to force either the XMA or the CMA to do the negotiations with me and issue my team the actual permit as a way to prove it. Jim got a letter from the CMA welcoming him to come for his negotiations and informing him that the XMA did not in fact have the authority to issue a K2 permit for my team. The CMA itself would do the negotiations with me. The strategy seemed to work, so I wrote back to both the XMA and the CMA, informing them that I would come to negotiate the details of our K2 expedition. I figured that the organization with the power to issue the permit would pick me up at the airport.

Since the "negotiations" in Beijing would only take a couple of afternoons, and I knew the CMA would be a good host and provide an interpreter and tour guides as needed, it seemed like a great opportunity to make a vacation of it with Ann. We had bought a house together earlier in the year, and this would be our first international trip together. Ann and I started our vacation in Hong Kong, where we spent a few days before flying to Beijing. On our first day in Hong Kong, she saved my life. I had forgotten they drive on the left side and had started crossing a busy street, looking the wrong way. Just as a double-decker bus sped by, Ann grabbed me by the back of my jacket and pulled me up onto the sidewalk.

When Jim, Ann, and I landed in Beijing in November 1988, CMA officials welcomed us, saying how pleased they were to help us plan our expeditions to Menlungtse and K2. The permitting strategy Nick and Jim had
helped me to develop worked beautifully. The CMA had assigned us an
interpreter who led us on tours of the Forbidden City and the Great Wall.
Ann loved to travel as much as I did, and it was a new experience for me to
slow down and enjoy the sights rather than rush through these cities with
a group of climbers on our way to the mountains.

Before I headed to Beijing for the negotiations, Greg, Phil, and I had
to settle on who would make up our climbing team. Greg had invited
Greg Mortimer (hereafter referred to as Mortimer) of Sydney, Australia,
and although I had never met him, I knew Mortimer by reputation from
his ascent of a new route on the north side of Mount Everest in 1984
with a small team and no supplemental oxygen. Mortimer invited three
other Australians to join the group in support roles, which I thought
meant they would help with things like fundraising, food planning, medical help, and load carrying (Greg, Phil, and I didn't consider them to be
part of our four-person climbing team). These members included Margaret
Werner, Mortimer's girlfriend; Peter Kuestler, the expedition doctor; and
Mortimer's friend Lyle Closs, who was going to help with fundraising.
Peter was a last-minute addition; the original plan was to bring Carolyn
Gunn, the veterinarian who had been with us on K2 in 1987. She had been
a great medical person to have on the team, and I was disappointed that
she couldn't come with us. Having good medical expertise was especially
important on K2's north side because the river would cut us off from any
help if someone got hurt.

As a small team of four climbers, we didn't have the desire or the capacity to climb expedition style all the way to the Camp IV, as in the 1986
attempt. We agreed to place fixed rope up the steep, icy slopes to Camp II
at 22,000 feet. Then above Camp II, we planned to climb alpine style. We
felt the climb was manageable with this approach and was the only way for
us to be safe on such a long, difficult route. (It can be argued that as of 2016
no one has climbed K2 in pure alpine style.)

Before the negotiations with CMA, I had planned an itinerary that had
us approach K2's north side through Pakistan via the Karakoram Highway (KKH), which crosses the Karakoram Mountains and connects China's

Xinjiang Uyghur Autonomous Region with northern Pakistan. In 1986 it had been very costly for us to pay CMA's prices to travel across China from Beijing. Entering from Pakistan would save us considerable money and time. I spent many hours calculating logistics for this trip based on what I had learned in 1986, and having a few locals to help us carry loads up the North K2 Glacier and cook for us at our ABC was a critical part of the plan. This type of help was not available in Xinjiang. Traveling by road from Pakistan would allow us to bring Rasool and Fida Hussein, who had also cooked for us on K2 in 1987, plus two more high-altitude porters we could hire from the mountain villages along the way. I especially wanted to bring lively and entertaining Rasool because he could manage the other Pakistanis—and he was a good cook.

The team was scheduled to fly to Islamabad in late May, which would put us at the Shaksgam River in the first week in June, when water levels in the river were still low. One week before our scheduled departure, however, I received a telegram from the CMA: "THE BORDER IS CLOSED HOW WILL YOU ENTER CHINA." Changing our itinerary at the last minute was disturbing. After some calls, I learned that there had been recent incidents of ethnic violence between indigenous Uyghurs and Han Chinese in Xinjiang, so they had closed the KKH border crossing into China. The Chinese wanted to prevent any unwanted Islamic influence spilling over from Pakistan. They didn't want any foreigners around to report on any action they might take against the Uyghurs.

I called Phil and Greg. "Our only option now," I told them, "is to fly to Beijing and travel across China, like we did in 1986." This would cost us an additional $10,000 that we didn't have. Phil was especially concerned that the extra time it would take to raise more money would delay the departure. "We might not get to the Shaksgam before it floods," he said. We had financed the expedition mostly from personal funds contributed by everyone going on the trip, but we couldn't afford to pay for this expedition entirely out of our own pockets. Over the previous year we had raised money from individual donors and corporate sponsors. To raise the additional money, each of us put in what we could scrape together and then we went back to our supporters. It took almost three weeks to raise the additional money and to rearrange our logistics and travel plans to fly ourselves, our Pakistani team members, and all our equipment to Beijing instead of Islamabad. We finally got under way and arrived in Beijing just after midnight on June 12. This extra time fundraising, combined with a longer itinerary to travel across China, would get us to the Shaksgam River almost a month later than we had planned.

Another problem we faced with having to fly to Beijing instead of Islamabad was transporting our high-altitude fuel. The stoves we used on the mountain burned a special mix of pressurized propane and butane that came in small lightweight metal canisters. These canisters are a hazardous material, prohibited from being transported on passenger airplanes. We had arranged to have a supply of them shipped to Pakistan far in advance, and we would take them by road into China. With the border crossing closed, however, we had to arrange for a new fuel supply to be delivered to western China. Instead of having months to ship the fuel, we had only a couple of weeks. I eventually found an air cargo carrier out of Los Angeles that was permitted to ship our hazardous canisters to Shanghai. From there the fuel would go by train to Xi'an in central China and by road to wherever they could catch up with us. Besides being a considerable additional expense, we arrived in China not knowing if our critical fuel supply would reach us in time.

At the airport in Seattle before getting on the plane, I called Lance Owens, the leader of our K2 expedition in 1986. By now I had come to accept that border disputes, ethnic and political violence, and religious extremism were all significant obstacles when trying to climb mountains in the Karakoram. "This mountain won't give in easily," I told Lance. "After everything I have been through to try and climb it, we could get stopped by the river and never even see the mountain." Lance was encouraging. "You know how to climb this mountain," he said, "and I'm sure you will get up it this time. Reaching the summit would be a great tribute to David and Catherine." It was hard to believe that it had been four years since I was with them on K2's north ridge before they were killed on Mount Logan in 1987. One of Lance's many vocations was his recent ordination as a Gnostic priest, and he had sent me two palm crosses to take to the summit in their memory.

Our arrival in Beijing coincided with the first anniversary of the Tiananmen Square Massacre. It was unnerving to encounter such a large military presence throughout the city, poised to prevent any demonstrations. China was a closed society, and what had happened in Tiananmen Square a year ago—and what had happened in Xinjiang recently—proved there were limits to the political and religious freedoms that the Chinese Communist Party would allow.

Knowing we would not be able to get the local help we needed in China, we had brought our small team from Pakistan to assist us. In addition to Rasool and Fida, high-altitude porters Anwar and Sarwar would help us carry loads on the glacier and possibly on the mountain. Flown from Islamabad to China the day before we arrived, they were huddled in their Beijing hotel room. Coming from small mountain villages, none of them had ever been on an airplane or in a big foreign city like Beijing. Rasool and Fida were relieved to see our familiar faces, which made Anwar and Sarwar feel less anxious. Water levels were rising in the Shaksgam River, so we were in a hurry to get away. Together with our Pakistani friends, we boarded a domestic flight the next day to Urumchi, the capital of Xinjiang.

In Urumchi we met our liaison officer, Mr. Zhou Xing Lu. Like the LOs we had worked with in Pakistan, he was supposed to assist with our logistics, but we knew his main responsibility was to make sure we obeyed the rules. Next we flew to Kashgar, where we met our interpreter, Ma Xun Kui. Other than in a few small places like Hong Kong, which was still a British colony, English speakers were not that prevalent in China at the time. Unlike in India and Pakistan, where the entire subcontinent was a former British colony so English is common and the LOs were fluent, Mr. Zhou only spoke Chinese and a local Xinjiang language. So the CMA sent Ma, a recent university graduate who had studied English. He, like many young people in China, was frustrated by restrictions imposed by the central government. We could communicate and sympathize with Ma, with whom we had a more open relationship than we did with Mr. Zhou.

In Kashgar we also met up with our Australian expedition members for the first time. It was good to meet Mortimer in person after conducting a relationship for a year via fax. Margaret helped greatly with local food purchasing, and Lyle seemed level-headed. But the team doctor didn't inspire the same confidence. Peter had all the affectations of a California hippie from the late 1960s, complete with embroidery and peace signs—which seemed odd to me because he would have been an infant in that decade. I asked him about the medical kit, hoping he had planned for some of the emergencies we might encounter. "I've been able to find a great selection of acupuncture needles and Chinese herbs here locally," he said enthusiastically. "It will be great to have this stuff since I like to practice Chinese medicine." Phil, Greg, and I exchanged incredulous looks. We needed to be medically self-sufficient on this expedition. The kinds of serious medical problems we might face on K2 couldn't be treated with acupuncture needles or alternative medicine practiced by a flower child doctor. Phil proposed a secret pact to Greg and me: "If any one of us gets seriously hurt, we need to perform climber-assisted-suicide so Peter can't get his hands on us."

Once most of our local food and equipment was purchased, we were driven to the town of Yecheng and spent the night. The next day we followed a rough road over the Kunlun mountains, which stood between us and the Karakoram Range farther south. After crossing a 16,000-foot pass, we ran into several landslides and washouts blocking the road. A few large Chinese trucks were lined up on the road and their drivers didn't know what to do. Mortimer leapt into action. "Let's get everyone organized into work parties," he said, grabbing a shovel. "We can use picks and shovels to repair the road well enough so the vehicles can get moving again." Organizing everyone was chaotic, but we were able to get through, and we reached the military outpost at Mazar late in the day on June 17.

Mazar was in a tight valley at 12,000 feet, surrounded by steep brown rocky hillsides. Some of our team developed headaches because of the sudden altitude gain. Our accommodations were rustic army barracks, and after dinner I went out to use the latrine—a platform perched on the hillside with several holes in the floor over which to squat (human waste fell onto the slope below). After I relieved myself, I heard loud snorting and slurping sounds. Looking down through the hole, I saw pigs eating the fresh feces. I wished I had known this before eating the pork that the Chinese army cook had included in the stir-fry he just served us for dinner. We drove from Mazar to the road head at Mazhar Dara on June 18, and that afternoon we weighed out all our loads for the camels so they would be ready to go early the next morning. At our camp that evening, it felt like a miracle when a jeep rolled up and delivered several boxes of our high-altitude fuel canisters.

On every expedition, it's a relief and a pleasure to finally start walking. All the stress of getting ourselves to this point seemed to dissipate with the simple act of putting one foot in front of the other and enjoying the amazing surroundings. I was even able to ignore my concerns about the river. For the first couple of days on our approach trek, Sarwar had been complaining about a toothache; the next morning he was in terrible pain with an abscessed tooth. He begged us to pull it, so Peter laid him out on the gravel near the river, took out the extractor from our first-aid kit, and pulled Sarwar's tooth. Peter went up a notch in our estimation after getting the team through its first medical problem. After a third night along the Suruquat River, we climbed up a wide grassy valley the next morning to a broad saddle at the Aghil Pass bordered by small peaks on either side. Far below us, we could see the Shaksgam River, snaking its way through a half-mile-wide gravel floodplain between cliffs on both sides. My anxiety about water levels surged now that the river was in sight.

Descending from the pass, Greg and I slid down a gravel gully at the bottom and walked up to the river's edge. I threw a large stone into the rapid dull gray current and listened for the quick thud that would indicate it was shallow enough to wade. Nothing. By now the summer snowmelt from upstream glaciers was nearing its peak, and down in the gorge the river was deep and full of enormous standing waves. I threw another rock. Nothing again. *This expedition might be over before we even see K2,* I thought. Greg's expression went from furrowed eyebrows and pursed lips to a blank stare that I knew from our previous travels together signaled his initial concern had turned into despair.

After all the work and heartache of two unsuccessful expeditions to K2, I couldn't believe it might end like this. I made a silent wish: *If only we could get to the base and at least be able to give it a try.* Our partners, Phil and Mortimer, joined us. The camel drivers soon arrived, yelling and shouting and pointing at the swollen river. They were a tough bunch, though, and saw something in the water that I didn't recognize. They led us downstream to where the river split into several smaller channels. The lead driver, sitting on top of his camel, plunged into the torrent and pulled four more loaded camels behind him. They made it across the first channel, so each of us grabbed onto the tie-down ropes and hoisted ourselves seven feet into the air onto the top of a fully loaded camel.

I was inexperienced at riding on animals, but this felt especially precarious and frightening. As the driver led our caravan into the river, my camel reeled back in fear, pulled hard on its rope, and let out a loud guttural bray that told me it was more afraid of drowning than the severe pain from the wooden spike being torqued hard in the fleshy part of its nose. As my camel hurtled down the steep riverbank into the water, it lurched violently from side to side. I felt like a wild bull rider as I hung onto the tie-down ropes to prevent being tossed into the torrent. Once we entered the water, I felt the camel's feet pawing at the gravel bottom and pushing us across, but soon the river was too deep. I felt it paddling while its huge lungs acted like a rubber raft, holding us afloat until we reached shallower ground on the opposite side. I was almost launched out of my perch when the camel heaved itself out of the water onto the shore. After several more harrowing channel crossings, we made it to our camp that night along the river. I began to hope again.

Depending on the water depth, we had to either wade or ride the camels across the river multiple times over the next three days. Crossing the river on top of a camel was terrifying, so we only did it when necessary. On our second day in the gorge, we waded most of the channels on our own. Phil, Anwar, Sarwar, and I teamed up by linking arms to form a line parallel with the river. We walked across so only the upstream person was exposed to the full force of the current. If one of us had his feet swept out from under him, the others would lift him back up. The four Pakistanis were experts at crossing the bridgeless streams and rivers near their mountain villages, and they helped us choose the best places to cross. They showed us how to cross each channel diagonally, letting the current push us downstream as we moved across. The glacier-fed river was cold and full of brown silt that made it impossible to see the bottom. Fortunately the riverbed was lined with smooth gravel, so we didn't trip over large boulders.

Water levels were continuously rising, and we were in constant fear of coming across a channel that was too deep to cross. On June 24 we made our final river crossing and turned our backs on the Shaksgam. Over my shoulder I could see the river flowing northwest, away from us toward its confluence with the Yarkand, and I felt a surge of relief.

The team climbed over the rise to where I had gotten my first view of K2 in 1986 and then traversed a bench in the hillside above the river draining the Sarpo Laggo Glacier near where it flowed into the Shaksgam. I thought we would soon be at base camp, but we were not done with the river crossings—the worst was yet to come. The river that drained the North K2 Glacier had been a mere boulder hop in 1986 when we had reached it three weeks earlier in the season. But this time it was a raging flood. It cut a channel through the brown, rocky landscape that was only about sixty feet wide—but it was steeper and the current much swifter than anything we experienced on the Shaksgam. This river not only looked treacherous; it also projected a muffled *whump-whump* sound from large underwater boulders being lifted by the current and crashing their way downstream. It would have been possible to swim out of a fall while crossing the Shaksgam, but going down in this river could be deadly. To cross this river, we would have to ride on the camels.

One of the younger drivers approached with his train of four camels. When he got to the river, the driver inspected the ropes that tethered each of his camels together. He looked carefully at the short pieces of thin cord attached to the wooden spikes driven through each camel's nose. These short pieces of cord were tied to the thicker ropes strung between each camel, designed to break and prevent all the camels from being pulled down if one of them was swept away.

Soon each of us was assigned a perch atop a load strapped to a camel's back. Rasool, Greg, and I rode with the first camel train led by the younger driver. None of the Pakistanis knew how to swim, and I noticed that Rasool had tied himself onto his camel as a precaution. I didn't think this was a good idea, since it was more likely that he could drown being strapped to a downed animal than if he were thrown free. The crossing started well, but midway across my camel tripped on the underwater boulders and almost fell.

As my camel stumbled back onto its feet, I looked up and watched in horror as the camel ahead of me that was carrying Rasool lost its footing altogether and was swept away. Both Greg's and my camels' lead ropes had become severed from the rest of the train and we were set adrift. Greg and I swiveled around and hit our terrified beasts on the rear with our hands, eventually getting them to the opposite bank. The driver, Greg, and I ran a hundred yards downstream to where Rasool and his camel had been washed onto a gravel bar near shore. The camel was lying on its side in the water, unable to stand up with the load still tied to its back. Rasool had untied himself and was standing in water swirling up to his thighs holding the animal's nose in the air so it wouldn't drown. As the driver and Rasool cut the load off the camel, Greg and I threw the bags of food and equipment onto the bank. After being relieved of this weight, the terrified animal leapt up and scurried to shore.

Mortimer, Phil, Peter, Lyle, Margaret, Anwar, and Sarwar were still on the other side of the river, having witnessed this near disaster with the five remaining camel drivers. "The rest of the drivers refuse to come across," Mortimer yelled to us. "They have decided to try again in the morning when the water should be lower." We set up a rope crossing farther downstream for the team members, and those of us who had made it across arrived unceremoniously at our base camp, Sughet Jangal. As we were having dinner that night, Anwar quipped in his nasal voice and limited English: "Ahh, today Rasool's lucky number." The water levels were indeed slightly lower the next morning, and the remaining camels made the dangerous crossing without incident.

It was great to be together at base camp and to have the river crossings behind us. But arriving safely at Sughet Jangal was not the end of our problems with the camel loads. The camels were contracted by the CMA to drop their loads there, seventeen miles from the mountain. As before, we needed to move everything five miles to the snout of the North K2 Glacier, then up the glacier another twelve miles to our advance base camp (ABC) at 16,000 feet. The support team we had used in 1986 to move everything to ABC had been expensive, and it hadn't worked that well, so I had devised a different plan. But for it to work, we needed to act quickly.

After we had failed to reach the summit in 1986, knowing I might be back one day, I had taken time before leaving to find an efficient way to move supplies from Sughet Jangal to ABC. First I needed to find a suitable route for the camels to carry our loads the five miles to the snout of the North K2 Glacier. Loaded camels can walk over gently sloping gravel and sand but not through a boulder field or up steep slopes—and for unloading, they need a flat area with a soft surface where they can kneel down. After several days of crisscrossing the hill behind Sughet Jangal, I had found a circuitous way between the large boulders and rocks where the camels could walk. It would require some trail building to establish a crude path leading to my most important discovery—a small but perfectly flat sandy area that overlooked the snout of the North K2 Glacier—an ideal place to unload the camels. In 1986, I had built a few cairns along the route and made a mental map. Our plan depended on it!

To move our supplies the rest of the way to ABC, the four Pakistani porters would do most of the load carrying. But if we couldn't get the camels to carry our supplies to the sandy area, the four Pakistanis would not be able to move everything. We would have to do a lot of this work ourselves. That extra effort would deplete the energy we needed for the mountain, seriously threatening our summit chances.

Our camel drivers had done a great job so far, but unlike the porters we had hired on previous expeditions, these men weren't that friendly to us. There was a pent-up frustration among them that none of us had understood until we started negotiating with them to carry loads for an extra day up the new trail we would build to the sandy area. So far, no cash had been exchanged between us and the drivers because everything was included in the total expedition budget we paid to the CMA. We had already paid the Chinese $100 per day for each camel, and we discovered that the camel drivers were only getting a small fraction of that amount—it barely covered their costs! At first they were unwilling to spend an extra day carrying loads and wanted to go back immediately before the rivers got any deeper. But after we explained that this extra day of work was separate from our budget with the CMA, and that we would pay them $100 per camel directly, they agreed. But we had to do it the following day, which meant making the trail that afternoon.

It was dark by the time we pushed aside the last rocks with our picks and shovels, completing a five-mile-long switchback trail up through the boulders to the sandy area. The morning of June 26 we led the camels up the path, hoping the drivers felt it was adequate and didn't turn their animals around short of the goal. By late morning I felt a huge relief, as one of my key responsibilities as expedition leader was complete: all our loads were now safely deposited at the sandy area. Over the next two days we moved everything the short distance from there to a windy, dusty camp we established at the snout of the North K2 Glacier. I calculated that if everyone carried two fifty-pound loads the twelve miles from the snout to ABC, all seven of our team could move there for the duration. The two Gregs, Phil, and I could start climbing, with the others acting in support. The four Pakistanis would continue to carry loads to ABC for another two weeks. Then Rasool and Fida could move to ABC and cook for us, while Anwar and Sarwar continued carrying loads to ABC for the rest of the expedition.

The river would soon flood and leave us cut off from the outside world. I needed a break from the frenzy of the past several weeks to be alone with my thoughts. All the organizational work to get us this far was like managing the construction on one of my engineering projects; this stress was

much different from the mental and physical effort it would take to climb
K2. Carrying loads for a week to ABC seemed like the perfect opportunity to make the transition from a mind-set focused on logistics to one
that prepared me for the physical hardship, frustration, uncertainty, fear, and
exhilaration that would dominate our lives on K2.

No one had summited K2 since the day in 1986 when Alex and I had
turned around about a thousand feet from the top in a storm that had
claimed the lives of seven climbers. They had reached the summit from the
Pakistan side of the mountain. In the past four years, fifteen expeditions had
failed. As climber Jim Curran, who had been at the Pakistan K2 base camp
that fateful year, wrote in *K2: The Story of the Savage Mountain*: "One cannot
help wondering whether, for a while at least, mountaineers were wary of
pushing too hard on the Savage Mountain."

With the help of the four Pakistanis, we ferried loads up the North K2
Glacier and, with the exception of Margaret, the Americans and Australians
moved up to advance base camp at 16,000 feet on July 3. Things were going
well for the most part, but Phil, Greg, and I became increasingly concerned
about the three Australians whom Mortimer had brought. Margaret wanted
to move up to ABC to cook for us, but she wasn't strong enough to carry a
full fifty-pound load and initially we were short on supplies there. It was a
minor issue, since she ultimately had no intention of going on the mountain, but we had to convince her to wait until the Pakistanis had delivered
enough food and fuel to feed a seventh person.

It was understood that Margaret would never go higher than ABC, and
Greg, Phil, and I had trusted Mortimer's recommendation to bring his other
friends to help the four of us lower on the mountain. But conversations
with Peter and Lyle revealed they had little mountaineering experience rel-
evant to a mountain like K2, and it showed. Peter wasn't properly equipped.
He hadn't even brought a pair of double boots—a basic requirement on K2
to prevent frostbite. Lyle had to be coached on what to do, but he was easy
to communicate with and willing to work things out. He had contributed
significantly by helping to build the trail for the camels and carrying loads
to ABC. Both Lyle and Peter had good intentions and wanted to help, so
for now Greg, Phil, and I decided to postpone a discussion with Mortimer
about our concerns and wait to see what they could do.

Ten days earlier, when we first arrived at Sughet Jangal, we discovered that a large Japanese expedition was already there. A few of their members were at base camp with us, but most were already on the mountain with plans to climb a new route on the northwest face of K2 to the right of our route on the north ridge. They had already established their ABC about thirty minutes' walk down the glacier from ours. As we were setting up our ABC, the Japanese climbing leader, Mr. Fukushima, walked by on his way down from their Camp I. I had met him in 1980, when we shared a base camp below the South Gasherbrum Glacier. That year, Fukushima had been leading an expedition to Gasherbrum II, and I had been making my first attempt on Gasherbrum IV. Back then, one of his expedition members had become sick from the altitude and developed a life threatening case of HAPE. Our team had helped carry the stricken climber down to Concordia, where he was evacuated in a Pakistani Army helicopter and survived.

It was great to see Mr. Fukushima again after ten years. He hung around and helped us set up our tents. Over a cup of tea, he asked if his team could come onto our route at around 25,200 feet. Above that elevation the Japanese had determined that their intended route was too difficult, so they wanted to traverse onto our route at that point. His climbing permit stated that they were on a completely different route from ours, and the CMA rules stated that if they wanted to come onto the upper part of our route, Mr. Fukushima needed to ask our permission. His team was almost a month ahead of us on the mountain and climbing in traditional expedition style with fixed rope, fixed camps, and several experienced Sherpas carrying loads high on the mountain. Since they were so far ahead of us, we weren't going to get in each other's way. I didn't see any problem with his request and told him as much.

That night at about 2:30 a.m., Lyle and I heard a large avalanche. Looking out the tent door, Lyle described the huge debris cloud that was heading toward us. We were a couple of miles down the glacier from the mountain, so the avalanche only hit our tent with a mild blast of air and a dusting of snow. We wondered how it had affected the expedition farther up. Later that morning, some Japanese climbers descended past our ABC and told us that their Camp I had been wiped out. They had already brought three injured team members down to their ABC. Mortimer, Phil, and Peter were bringing loads up to our ABC that morning, and as they passed by the Japanese ABC camp, Peter stopped to examine the two Sherpas and one Japanese climber who had been injured. Later that evening he told us they would all be okay, which was a relief. Peter spent the next several days helping to evacuate the injured climbers back to their base camp at Sughet Jangal, where they convalesced for the remainder of their expedition. The Japanese team reached the summit on August 9 by traversing from the northwest face to the north ridge. It was the first time anyone had reached the summit since the disasters on K2 in 1986.

We got off to a quick start, and by July 5 we had placed fixed rope to Camp I at around 19,000 feet. But after that a series of storms made fixing rope to Camp II a drawn-out process. On the several carries we made up to and beyond Camp I, Lyle and Peter had trouble keeping up. Peter suffered minor cold injuries to his feet from wearing inadequate footwear. By now Greg, Phil, and I believed Lyle and Peter shouldn't be on the mountain at all. The issue came to a head on July 20 at ABC, when the three of us told Mortimer how we felt. I had to be careful because on a small expedition like ours, the leader had to be the person in charge when dealing with the Chinese, but once we were on the mountain that strategy would have backfired. I could hardly order around a group of independent-minded expert climbers. My role was not to be the boss but to try and facilitate decision making.

Mortimer was loyal to his friends and wanted them to determine for themselves what they were qualified to do on the mountain. But Greg, Phil, and I felt that Lyle and Peter didn't know enough about what they didn't know. We needed to set some boundaries. The three of us were adamantly opposed to either of them going beyond the end of the fixed ropes we would place up to Camp II at 22,000 feet. Given their skill level, it would be an unacceptable risk to their safety and to the expedition's success. This was my third and Phil and Greg's second expedition to K2. We didn't want to see our efforts stymied by problems we could avoid.

In the middle of a heated discussion, Mortimer stormed out of the kitchen tent and went to his sleeping tent, threatening to leave the expedition. I resumed the conversation at his tent, where he was sitting with Margaret. Frustrated by our lack of progress, I soon stormed over to my own tent. Just as I started to crawl inside, I felt someone grab my ankles and drag me back outside. Mortimer was looking down at me. "We can't run away from each other," he said. "We want to climb this mountain, and so we need to work this out."

So the two Gregs, Phil, and I calmed down and went back to the kitchen tent together. We agreed on a compromise: Lyle and Peter could operate up to Camp II on the fixed ropes, as long as they carried their own food and fuel and were effectively self-sufficient. This agreement minimized risk for Lyle and Peter as well as for the expedition, and it kept Mortimer engaged. Certainly Greg, Phil, and I—and probably Mortimer too—had no expectation that Lyle and Peter could do anything on the mountain to help get us to the top.

I remained frustrated that Lyle and Peter insisted upon doing things that might help them achieve a personal altitude goal but did little to help (and had the potential to hurt) the team's chance to reach the summit. But I was also proud that Greg, Phil, Mortimer, and I could work things out despite our disagreement.

Expedition accounts often romanticize the kinship between climbers heading off into the mountains. The notion that they can utterly rely on each other for safety, friendship, and success has been called the "brotherhood of the rope," but this expression can oversimplify the dynamics that play out during the course of a months-long expedition. It suggests that teammates will always get along and be of one mind when difficult situations arise and hard decisions need to be made. The dispute we'd just navigated didn't feel like a celebration of that sort of idealized brotherhood; it felt more like a business transaction.

It wasn't until years later that I realized we had judged ourselves against an impossible standard, and disagreements like this were a normal, and sometimes necessary, part of expedition life. The four of us had been privileged to have such strong, committed, and competent teammates. More important, we had taken care of each other.

Finally, in the early morning on July 24, Greg, Lyle, and I left ABC and reached Camp I at 5:00 a.m. After all the storms, it was exhausting to clear the fixed ropes and dig out the tents that were buried from the new snow. After only four hours of sleep at Camp I, we kicked steps and finished fixing ropes to Camp II. It was hard work carrying heavy packs with the tent, sleeping bags, food, and fuel that we needed to spend the night there. Lyle wasn't able to move quickly enough when kicking steps in the deep snow, so Greg and I took turns going first. Along the way we repaired ropes that had been damaged or severed by rockfall. It would have been hard to carry enough equipment and supplies on our first trip to Camp II to enable all three of us to stay, so Lyle turned back short of the camp.

Greg and I continued to the same spot we had used for Camp II in 1986 under a rock wall that protected it from avalanches. After leveling a platform, we were so exhausted we didn't take the time to set up the tent properly and eventually collapsed into it around 1:00 a.m. Establishing Camp II after struggling with weather and conditions for almost three weeks was a major accomplishment. Getting well acclimatized at this elevation would be critical to our success. Camp II would be our launch pad to the upper mountain.

The next day we rested, and Mortimer, Phil, and Peter came up in our track from the day before. Peter went down, and Mortimer and Phil helped to set up the tent properly and make a better platform that was large enough for another one where they could spend the night. Greg and I got back into the repitched tent and melted snow for hot drinks for everyone. The previous day had been an ordeal, and the sore throat I'd been nursing was worse. I had coughed all night and probably kept Greg awake. We found an oxygen bottle hanging from pitons pounded into the rock wall behind the tent that we had carried up in 1986 in case of a medical emergency. We had used it then to assist George when he got high-altitude pulmonary edema (HAPE). We attached a regulator we brought along and it showed the bottle was still about half full. Hopefully we wouldn't need to use it this time.

On July 26, Greg, Phil, Mortimer, and I went above Camp II to acclimatize and do a bit of reconnaissance toward Camp III. I was pleased to find that the seven-millimeter fixed rope we placed in 1986 was mostly still usable. There was enough slack to tie knots around the places where it had been damaged. After the others went back to Camp II, I went ahead to enjoy some solitude. Now that we were above most of the surrounding peaks, the Karakoram began to reveal itself. Before heading down, I worked on the ropes a bit more—glad that the effort I put into this route years ago was helping us now. After a couple more days working on the ropes up to 24,000 feet, we all descended to ABC for some much-needed rest. Rasool and Fida were now living at ABC, and it felt good to be eating their delicious food and enjoying the luxury of deep sleep that came with the relatively thick air at 16,000 feet.

After two days of rest, I headed back to Camp II with the two Gregs and Phil. August 1 was one of the clearest days I'd ever seen in the Karakoram, and we carried all the food and equipment we would need higher on the mountain. We thought it might take a couple of attempts to reach the summit, so we brought enough food and fuel to spend three or four nights at Camp III and a couple of nights at Camp IV. The next day was a test of our acclimatization and strength, as we carried some of the food and equipment we had brought up to 25,000 feet, the site of Camp III. This section of the route was very physically demanding, and in 1986 it had eliminated about half the team from going much higher. But this time, all four of us were strong enough to take turns breaking trail in the deep snow and pulling out and repairing the old fixed ropes.

We cached our supplies and descended back to Camp II, and by August 5 we had all descended to ABC. By then, Greg, Mortimer, Phil, and I were acclimatized and ready for a summit attempt after a few days' rest. Full of excitement and anticipation, we encouraged each other to boost our confidence. All we needed was four days of good weather. Even as recently as 1990, there were no readily available handheld satellite phones to communicate with the outside world. Our only access to weather forecasts was a shortwave radio broadcast by the Pakistan government that usually had nothing to do with reality. We had to rely on our own measurements and instincts to predict the weather. We observed barometric pressure, wind speed and direction, temperature, cloud cover, and precipitation. Without more sophisticated tools, we couldn't predict if a period of good weather would be long enough for us to climb K2. Picking the right weather window took experience and luck.

As we entered the second week of August, there was no clear indication of a stable weather pattern so we stayed put. But on August 9 the weather seemed good, so we launched our first summit bid by climbing up to Camp II. It started snowing that night and into the next day, and we spent hours discussing whether to go up or go down. I preferred to wait until the morning to see what it was like, but Mortimer finally said, "Let's go down." Late that afternoon we decided to head down and wait for better weather at ABC. But after we descended only a few hundred feet, the clouds parted and the sunshine lured us back up to Camp II.

On the morning of August 11 we continued to torment ourselves with discussions about the weather. I thought it looked good enough to climb to Camp III, but then it started to snow as we packed up to go higher. This precipitated another round of talks about how to proceed. Suddenly it cleared around the summit of K2 and we headed up—although there were clouds everywhere to the southwest, north, and east. The snow was deep getting to Camp III, and Mortimer and I did most of the step kicking. We got in late and had to dig two platforms for the small, lightweight, two-person bivouac tents we had brought. We were too tired to eat or brew up properly before going to sleep. My cough and sore throat had been constant companions for several weeks—I could hardly swallow.

In the morning we climbed up mixed rock and ice toward our 1986 Camp IV at 25,800 feet—the flat, rocky perch on the crest of the north ridge called the Eagle's Nest. I got there around 6:00 p.m. and waited a few minutes for Greg. We were venturing into what climbers refer to as the Death Zone, the elevation above 26,000 feet where one cannot live for more than a few days without supplemental oxygen. The weather was deteriorating rapidly—blowing at sixty miles per hour from the southwest and bringing moisture from the monsoon that was parked farther south over India this time of year. It looked threatening and certainly not like summit weather, so the two of us decided to turn around.

Greg and I met Mortimer and Phil not far below us and we discussed the options. They agreed conditions were not good enough to go up, and we would deteriorate quickly waiting at this elevation. We had reached a new high point on the mountain, and it was a hard decision to turn back, knowing we would have to do all this work over again when the weather improved. The four of us descended to Camp III, where we spent another miserable night.

The next morning, on August 13, we struggled with cold fingers to get into our windsuits, boots, overboots, gloves, harnesses, goggles, and crampons in a storm that had engulfed the mountain. After securing the tents, we descended into the raging wind and snow. On our way down to ABC, at Camp II, we passed Lyle and Peter, who graciously volunteered to dry the sleeping bags we had brought down from Camp III. The four of us arrived at ABC at around 4:00 p.m. to good food, smiles, and better sleep than the past five days—but my cough kept me awake.

The failed attempt had taken a lot out of us, and the cumulative effect of our efforts at altitude over the past weeks had left us with only enough strength for one more go. We couldn't afford any more false starts—the next attempt would have to be all or nothing. During the last attempt, it had been so difficult to break trail to Camp III that we didn't eat and drink properly, leaving us weak and ill-prepared to reach the summit. It would save a lot of energy if Anwar and Sarwar could help break trail toward Camp II on the first day. But they hadn't been above ABC, and we didn't think they were acclimatized well enough to do it. Peter and Lyle were well acclimatized, but too slow to break trail for us, so after coming down from Camp II they would remain at ABC with Margaret, who had spent her time there reading, knitting, and helping Rasool and Fida with cooking.

With little rest after only two stormbound days, the skies dawned clear, and we knew we had to take advantage of this opportunity as it could be our last. On August 17 the two Gregs, Phil, and I made the 6,000-foot climb back to Camp II. Although we were concerned about their lack of acclimatization, Anwar and Sarwar insisted on going ahead of us to break trail in the deep snow. They put in a tremendous effort getting us to just shy of Camp II, where they had to turn around from exhaustion. Sarwar had tears in his eyes as he clasped my hands and said, "Insha'Allah [God willing], you will reach the summit." They disappeared down the ropes, leaving the four of us alone with a frighteningly huge task ahead of us. We'd soon be farther out on a limb than I'd ever been before—hopefully it wouldn't break.

On August 18 we broke trail to Camp III at 25,000 feet, and the next day we reached the Eagle's Nest at 25,800 feet, where we had turned back a week ago. I had learned from my experience four years earlier that we needed to put our high camp, or Camp IV, above the Eagle's Nest if we were going to get to the summit and back in one day. The four of us agreed to put Camp IV at around 26,250 feet, where the Japanese had left a tent when they reached the summit ten days earlier.

Climbing above the Eagle's Nest, we made a steep, exposed, rising traverse onto a hanging glacier wallowing in thigh-deep snow but assisted by fixed rope left by the Japanese. We reached the site of our Camp IV at the old Japanese tent as the light faded and K2 cast a giant shadow over the peaks to the east. Rather than set up and squeeze into the small two-person tent we had brought for the four of us, we removed the snow that had drifted into the larger Japanese tent and got inside. The tent was equipped with a tunnel door that was also the only vent. When we left it open, the wind outside blew in snow. We'd close the door to keep the snow out, but then we wouldn't get enough of the thin air to breathe. Melting ice for much-needed drinks and filling our water bottles for the next day took three or four hours on the small stoves that struggled to burn in the rarified air. We all suffered from dry, cracked throats, coughing, panting for air, and cramped, wet conditions that prevented us from getting adequate sleep for the task ahead.

Early on August 20 we brewed up before dawn. We seemed capable of thinking clearly at this altitude, but only in slow motion. After three hours we emerged from the tent to a beautiful but bitterly cold morning. When we set out from our high camp, we knew that we could make no mistakes even though our brains were operating in a hypoxia-induced fog. We were clearly oxygen deficient. In the back of our minds, we were keenly aware of the history of the first ascent of this route by the Japanese expedition in 1982. The two climbers who first reached the summit were forced by darkness to bivouac on a narrow ledge they carved in the steep slope, just wide enough for them to sit next to each other. In the morning they resumed their descent unroped toward high camp, but one of the climbers, named Yanagisawa, either stumbled or collapsed from exhaustion and fell more than ten thousand feet down the north face.

The Japanese climbers were selected from the best high-altitude alpinists in the country, and knowing that one of them fell off made what we were doing even more intimidating. We desperately wanted to get to the summit and back to our high camp in one day. Hanging on the side of the mountain all night without sleeping bags or a stove would leave us in such bad shape physically that the risk of falling would be orders of magnitude higher. We had to move as quickly as we could at this altitude. That meant going as light as possible and not taking the time to belay ourselves up and down. Although it was contrary to everything we had been taught, this was a situation where it would be safer for us to leave the rope behind and climb independently.

I was afraid, but it wasn't the kind of paralyzing fear that would have prevented me from going. It was the kind of fear that put every sense in my body on red alert, and not for just a moment, but for the twelve or so hours it would take to get to the summit and back safely. It was the kind of fear that got my brain to say things like, "Don't fuck up now, kick a step, make sure it's stable, stand up, shove your ice axe shaft into the snow, don't fuck up." Over and over. Managing this state of heightened anxiety for hours on end was what I'd been working on for years. Having success today, and in the future, depended on it.

From the camp there was a hundred-foot low-angle snow traverse over to a crevasse that separated the hanging glacier from the steep upper couloir we would climb about two thousand feet to the summit ridge. On the traverse the wind had formed a soft snow slab that I punched through, and with each step it made a hollow sound that reverberated through the slope. Four years earlier I'd experienced similar snow conditions with Alex, and we had turned around not far from here, afraid that we might trigger an avalanche that would carry us over the ice cliff at the bottom of the glacier and down the north face.

Maybe I just didn't want to be defeated again so high on the mountain, or maybe the piece of thin, fixed Japanese rope gave me some added encouragement, but I crossed the slope over to the crevasse while the others waited. The rest of the team came across, and I climbed over the lip of the crevasse onto the upper couloir that was steep enough for most of the new snow to slide off, making it firm and safe. A few hundred feet up the couloir, the Japanese fixed line ended, and we each climbed unroped, at our own pace. Being roped together would not provide any protection if someone fell—on this steep slope the rest of the rope team would get pulled off as well. After several hours we neared the top of the couloir where it forked, and we took the left branch to the ridge crest.

Phil was moving slower than the rest of us, and as I looked down into the couloir, I could see he had turned back at about 27,500 feet, less than a thousand feet below the top. Back at Camp IV that night, he told us he was moving too slowly to reach the summit and still descend safely before dark, so he had decided to turn around. Remembering the 1986 tragedies, I felt fortunate to be with someone who was keenly aware that getting to the top was only part of the journey. He needed to save enough strength to get down. About ten years later I discovered Phil had been living with Crohn's disease, but he never complained or said anything about it to us. When I asked him then why he had never told us, he simply replied, "I didn't want to get any special treatment."

The two Gregs and I regrouped at the top of the north face, disappointed to find another snow slope between us and the summit. From our vantage point a thickening cloud layer stretched as far south into Pakistan as I could see. With only two or three hours of daylight left, we drifted apart on the final slopes, each with our own idea about a turnaround time. Not far ahead of the others, I walked alone to where there was no higher ground.

Standing on the summit of K2 was not the euphoric experience I had dreamed it would be. A dull feeling of accomplishment was mostly overshadowed by the relief of not having to go any farther. Hypoxia took the edge off everything, as if a translucent screen had been pulled over my senses. A storm was brewing; dark clouds from the southwest obscured the summits of all Pakistan's big mountains. I rummaged through my pockets and grabbed the two palm remembrance crosses that Lance Owens had given me for Dave Cheesmond and Catherine Freer. Reaching out, I opened my fist, and the wind ripped them from my hand. After four minutes at the top, I started down.

Shortly after leaving the summit, I passed Greg and Mortimer on their way up. We had a brief discussion about the lateness of the day and the approaching storm. Greg mentioned that they might have to bivouac if it got dark—a dangerous proposition at this altitude in good weather. With a storm about to break, I urged him to make it back to camp. Where the gently angled summit ridge spilled over onto the much steeper north face, I had to turn around to face the slope to make my way down. A stumble was unthinkable: it would result in a 12,000-foot plunge to the glacier.

As the light faded, my oxygen-starved brain struggled to maintain my balance as I alternated plunging the toe of each boot into the steep slope below me. I was desperate to stay focused. Here in the Death Zone, the key for me was to connect with the living. I dedicated each step to family and friends I loved—starting with Ann, who was six months pregnant with our child; followed by my son, Lars; my parents; each of my brothers and sisters; and many wonderful friends. After cycling through my list of names several times, the beam of my headlamp illuminated our small tent perched on the slope below.

I was disappointed not to share the summit with Phil but happy to have someone there. He gave me a boiling cup of tea that I gulped down (it was only lukewarm at this altitude). That started such a violent coughing spell I couldn't catch my breath, and I started retching. Phil helped me through it by pressing a bowl under my chin. "Don't you dare barf all over the tent," he said firmly.

It started snowing lightly, and we were relieved to see our two teammates arrive about an hour later. Greg and Mortimer had summited shortly after I had, although Greg's hands had turned numb on the descent. Mortimer had helped him the last hundred feet to our camp. Inside the tent, Greg plunged his fingers into the warm water in the cooking pot and then into his down suit, screaming in pain as his hands thawed. Fortunately he had no frostbite damage. We rested a bit, then Phil woke everyone at daylight to announce we needed some water. He brewed up, and we partook before sleeping for a couple of hours.

We woke again to the full fury of the storm. It hit us with wind, heavy snowfall, and limited visibility. The stove sputtered out as we burned the last of our fuel, so we shared the water left in the pot and packed up to leave. Mortimer led the way down through the blizzard in deep snow to the Eagle's Nest, and I went first down to Camp III. The others stopped to brew up and have a drink. But I was impatient to get down and headed straight for Camp II. I was dangerously dehydrated by the time I arrived there. I dug out the tents and started the stove. With plenty of fuel, I melted a lot of water. The lower altitude, warmer temperatures, and food brought me back from the brink. Greg, Mortimer, and Phil joined me at Camp II a couple of hours later.

It continued snowing all night, and in the morning we started down into such thick clouds that I couldn't tell which way was up. I pulled the ropes out from under the new snow down to Camp I, where we rested and Mortimer took over from there. We spaced ourselves apart when descending the fixed lines and finally dropped below the whiteout. For the first time since leaving the top, I could see all the way down to the glacier at the bottom of the mountain. Over the past several days, completely preoccupied with our ascent and safe descent, we'd been cut off from everyone else, but now I saw a line of tiny figures far below advancing toward the bottom of the mountain. Rasool, Fida, Anwar, Sarwar, Peter, Lyle, Margaret, and our LO, Mr. Zhou, advanced to meet us. As the stress of the previous days dissipated, I started to appreciate the pure joy of completing this climb. An overwhelming surge of emotion spread through me after so many years of effort. I stood there alone, holding onto the rope, sobbing, while a slow quiver shook my whole body.

At the bottom of the face, Anwar and Sarwar greeted us. I grabbed Sarwar and pushed him over into the snow with me. We hugged each other and I yelled at him, "Success on K2!" He smiled and nodded. Mr. Zhou, who was behind Anwar and Sarwar, hugged me, crying. Arm in arm we went over to where Rasool, Fida, Margaret, Lyle, and Peter served tea, juice, and cookies picnic style in the snow. Then we walked back together to ABC, where the Pakistanis had built a welcome banner. As we walked under it, they erupted in a great cheer. Once inside the mess tent, Rasool produced a great feast and exclaimed that this was "the happy day the members climbed K2 and come back safely."

Greg, Mortimer, Phil, and I rested for a couple of days at ABC after summiting. I slept much better, but I still had a terrible sore throat from all my coughing. I could hardly speak. Our camels would soon be ready to carry our equipment and supplies from the sandy area to Sughet Jangal, so we needed to move everything down. Hiking on the glacier, Lyle and Peter came into their own and took on the responsibility for getting everything carried down, so the four of us only had to take care of ourselves.

By August 26 we reached our camp at the snout of the glacier, with Greg, Mortimer, Phil, and I still exhausted from our ordeal. Anwar was worried about our condition and stood over Greg and me, trying to get us to eat some cookies. We didn't have much of an appetite and kept refusing. In a final effort to sell us on how good the treats were Anwar exclaimed, "But sir, they have cream inside!" We erupted in laughter over his silly one-liner but also in appreciation for how much he cared for us. By August 30 the camels carried the final loads from the sandy area into Sughet Jangal. We had a great celebration that night around a huge bonfire fueled by dried camel dung.

During the walk out, I couldn't help but wonder: *Was it all a dream? Had I missed some slightly higher point farther along the ridge?* Knowing I had been there alone, Greg and Mortimer decided to play a joke on me by describing the summit area as slightly beyond and above my tracks they had found in the snow. I knew they were kidding, but as we trekked back over the Aghil Pass, I needed a final glimpse to dispel my doubts, so I climbed the slope east of the pass. Initially the intervening ridges blocked K2 from view, and as I moved higher the north sides of the Gasherbrum group appeared first. Gradually the same pyramid that once moved Shipton to awe came into view. Through my telephoto lens, I could clearly see where I had reached the top of the north face as it folded back into the summit ridge with its several false summits—and beyond those points, to where I'd walked to the highest one. From a distance I could confirm that I had climbed K2.

CHAPTER 4

LIFE AND DEATH

GASHERBRUM IV SOUTHWEST RIDGE, 1992

A bout two months after I returned from K2, on November 15, 1990, Ann gave birth to a healthy baby boy. She was thrilled to be a new mom, and we were delighted to welcome a second son to the family. Ann won a last-name coin toss, so we introduced him to the world as John Edward (Jed) Dalton. Lars was nine years old, and he said being an older brother was a big responsibility and took his new job seriously. Ann and I had been through a lot as we built a loving family together, and experiencing that level of commitment enabled me to feel comfortable getting married again. On March 14, 1992, we invited a small group of family and friends to our home to celebrate our wedding. It was wonderful to have the ultimate partnership, one I'd already leaned on countless times.

Six weeks after Ann and I were married, I returned to Pakistan for what would be my third attempt on Gasherbrum IV. The team included Alex

Lowe, Charlie Fowler, Tom Dickey, and me. Alex and I had been together on K2 in 1986, plus several other expeditions including establishing a new route on Kwangde Nup (6,035 meters, or 19,800 feet) in Nepal in 1989. We had spent two years planning this trip to Gasherbrum IV following a pledge to go on another expedition together after he had missed out on our K2 success in 1990. Charlie was a friend of Alex's, with a long résumé of hard alpine routes all over the world. George Lowe was part of the original team but wasn't able to go because of family commitments, and he suggested that his friend Tom go with us. Tom had been to Nepal several times guiding treks and had soloed several smaller peaks in the Khumbu and Langtang valleys.

Our team made what for me was the familiar drive across northern Pakistan from Islamabad to Skardu. This time it seemed more peaceful along the edges of the tribal areas (the Soviet-Afghan war had ended in February 1989). Similar to how they had used the mujahideen to implement their foreign policy objectives in Afghanistan, Pakistan's Inter-Services Intelligence (ISI) agency used some of them after the end of the Soviet war to promote their ongoing dispute with India over Kashmir. With ISI support, groups of unemployed mujahideen infiltrated from Pakistan across the Line of Control to spread radical Islamist ideology and participate in an insurgency in the Indian-administered Kashmir valley. A dispute over local autonomy and a rigged election caused members of the restive Muslim-majority population in the valley to revive their independence movement against the Indian government. The Indian Army's ruthless suppression of this insurgency fomented an escalating cycle of violence. Pakistan supported this insurgency in an attempt to gain international support for their challenge to the legitimacy of Indian rule in Kashmir. The movement of these non-state actors to fight another jihad in Kashmir was not evident to us as we drove up the Karakoram Highway (KKH), but it contributed to a growing radicalization of the region.

While planning our expedition, I had written to Rasool, who agreed on a date to meet us in Skardu and accompany us as our cook. On both our K2 trips, Rasool had proven he understood that our Western stomachs couldn't tolerate the usual Pakistani diet. I had seen poor hygiene and a rapid introduction of heavy curries and other unfamiliar dishes by the kitchen staff on some expeditions result in getting what we called "butt sick." With Rasool we had stayed healthier. We could also rely on him for humorous distractions from the dangerous and physically demanding work of mountain climbing and to boost morale during long periods of bad weather. He had developed pretty good on-the-job English skills, which expedited our team's communications. Rasool and I had become friends, and I was looking forward to seeing him again in Skardu.

When we reached Skardu on May 7, I was surprised that Rasool was not there to meet us. Worried that something was wrong, I hired a jeep to take me to Rasool's village of Hushe. The rest of the team purchased our local food and supplies in Skardu and packed everything into fifty-pound porter loads. The next day I reached Hushe, a beautiful small village that sits at over 10,000 feet surrounded by granite peaks rising 5,000 feet above the valley floor. A short distance away the sun reflected off the snowy flanks of 25,659-foot Masherbrum (7,821 meters), which stood 10,000 feet higher than the mountains around the village. Surrounded by a formidable, dry rocky landscape, Hushe stood out as a lush green oasis. The terraced green fields around Hushe had been recently planted with wheat and peas. The dwellings for the village's hundred or so families were uniformly made of rock and mud walls with timbers supporting roofs of branches, leaves, and dried mud. They were all connected to each other. Dirt and stone walkways wound throughout the village, which made it difficult for an outsider to find a particular house.

Rasool was on the road in the center of the village waiting for me when I arrived. As I got down from the jeep, he threw his arms around me and started to weep. "Steve sahib, my son he dead now just one, two weeks," he said, sobbing. Rasool's wife, Bedruma, had given birth to a baby boy the previous fall, but the child had become sick and died. He had been only eight months old. Heartbroken, Rasool hadn't come to Skardu because he wanted to stay with his family. I thought maybe I'd made things worse by coming. Part of him wanted to stay with his family, and part of him felt that he was obliged to go with me to Gasherbrum IV. "Rasool," I said, "I think it would be a good idea for you to stay here and take care of your family." I wanted to make sure that his decision wasn't based on money, so I offered to pay him his cook's wages whether he came with us or not. But he would have none of it. No matter how much I pleaded with him to stay, Rasool insisted that he come with us after all.

Having sons is a big deal in Pakistan. According to their version of Islamic law, when the father dies, the mother gets a fixed amount of the estate (usually an eighth) and the rest is divided among the children, with the sons getting double what each daughter receives. In return for receiving most or all of the estate, the brothers agree to provide their sisters and mother with financial help whenever they need it for the rest of their lives. Fathers want to have sons that can carry out this responsibility. Fulfilling this desire for Rasool was not so easy, however. Rasool and Bedruma had two healthy girls but had lost a baby girl. Since the last daughter was born, Bedruma had given birth to two boys—both of whom had died before reaching their first birthdays. Rasool and Bedruma's tragedy was all too common in villages like theirs.

These rural areas in Pakistan were grossly underserved by the government. A series of military dictators and weak civilian administrations, endlessly preoccupied with their archrival India, have fabricated the need for a huge army that consumes most of the country's resources. The basic needs of poor villagers like Rasool will not be addressed until there is the political will to create stability in the region and to prioritize the needs of the majority of the population over militarism.

Rasool and I had to leave for Skardu the next morning, so I spent the night in their home. The front door opened into the main room that also served as the kitchen. It had a packed-earth floor with no furniture. A small wood-burning cookstove stood in the center, with a stovepipe that extended up only a few inches, allowing the smoke to spread throughout the room before exiting through a hole in the ceiling. Over time, the smoke had blackened all the cupboards and surfaces that lined the walls. Several sleeping rooms and storage areas that extended off the main room had ceilings so low that I had to duck my head.

I slept on a rug in an otherwise empty room in the back of the house. During the night my stomach was upset from some bad food I had eaten on the long drive to Hushe. In the morning, when they heard I had been sick, all of Rasool's extended family (which was most of the village) arrived and started fussing over me and plying me with tea and other home remedies. It amazed me that here, where they had no material goods to speak of, the people wanted to give me everything. At home, we have everything, but we keep most of it for ourselves.

Rasool and I arrived in Skardu, and I introduced him to the other expedition members before driving to the roadhead that morning. On the trek to base camp, I listened to Rasool's constant chatter with the other Balti porters and staff. Even though I couldn't understand what he was saying, Rasool seemed genuinely interested in everyone's story. For several hours one day, he actively engaged in a serious conversation with one of the porters as they walked along. Afterward I asked Rasool, "What were you two talking about all afternoon?" Rasool explained: "His yak died."

After ten days covering familiar ground, we reached Gasherbrum base camp in late May. It had been a very cold, wet spring and the mountains towering around us were fully loaded with fresh snow, creating a high avalanche hazard. The elevation of our base camp was at around 16,000 feet, and the summits of the Karakoram giants around us were over 26,000 feet. Snow conditions near base camp might seem safe, but wind and colder temperatures up high could be forming slabs that release spontaneously once they are overloaded. Before we started climbing beneath them, we needed to know how dangerous the slopes were 10,000 feet above us. We looked at them through our spotting scope. If we saw crown lines—abrupt edges like a scar in the snow where a slab had broken off, indicating recent avalanche activity—we had to avoid those slopes. We found a few of them, but they were not everywhere, which told us that we could climb. But we must pick our route carefully, and keep testing the snow to make sure it was safe.

When we were planning our trip in early 1992, we didn't know that the unusually heavy winter and spring snow season would make it better to come later that year, when warmer temperatures stabilized the snow. We had come in the early part of the season, thinking that weather and conditions would be good in June, hoping to avoid the low-pressure systems to the north that typically pull monsoonal moisture up into the mountains from the south in July and August.

After we reached base camp, I became concerned about Rasool. He was his usual cheery self on the trek when there was a lot of activity, but at base camp he would become depressed thinking about his family. Despite being focused on our climb, I also thought about how to help Rasool.

I was concerned about Alex too. Typically at the start of an expedition he was full of enthusiasm and drive, but this time he seemed distracted. Over the past several years Alex had been frustrated in his efforts to find a career that enabled him to support his growing family while allowing him to climb as much as he wanted. He had tried going back to school, then spent time working for an oil services company. He just couldn't sit at a desk so he quit. We called him "the shark," because he was like an animal that had to keep moving to breathe. Alex hadn't found balance between all the competing interests in his life, and it weighed heavily on him. I loved being on trips with him because he was usually full on, but unfortunately his other mode was off. He had been uncharacteristically short with Tom, our least experienced member, on the hike in. All of us needed to play the long game and patiently wait for the moment to go climbing when weather, conditions, and health all lined up. That could be a challenge for Alex.

The northwest ridge had been climbed by Greg Child and friends in 1986, and our team was going to make another attempt on the southwest ridge, which I had attempted in 1980. Like before, we approached Gasherbrum IV from base camp, by walking and skiing about six miles up the South Gasherbrum Glacier. Alex, Charlie, Tom, and I had to find a safe way through the same two large icefalls, one after the other, that extended across the glacier between the mountains on both sides. This time the second icefall was particularly steep and broken up. It seemed easier to go around it by climbing up a snow slope that extended down from Gasherbrum I on the right. This would get us to an elevation higher than the dangerous icefall, and we could then traverse back left onto the glacier above the jumbled mess.

I started climbing up this slope, but after a couple hundred feet I realized that the snow was unstable and avalanche prone. I came down and we spent the rest of the day carefully finding a safe but circuitous route through the icefall. Once we reached the flat glacier on top of the icefall, we cached the supplies we had carried up and went back to base camp. An international expedition on Gasherbrum I was using the same approach we were up the glacier, and part of their group had been following us all day. To acclimatize, they camped on the glacier above the icefall that night.

The next morning, Alex and I carried a load of food and equipment up to the cache. Instead of descending back through the icefall, the international group was coming down the same snow slope I had retreated from the previous day. Alex said, "I don't like the looks of this." We watched nervously as two of their climbers plunge-stepped down the snow, placing a fixed rope as they went. They were not attached to this rope; they were just walking down the slope using it as a hand-line. When they were halfway down, what looked like a one-foot-thick slab of snow around them started moving. It seemed so innocuous, not a huge avalanche, but it swept them down into a depression in the glacier below. Grabbing our snow shovel, I ran with Alex over to where they had disappeared. One of the climbers, tossed aside by the power of the avalanche, was sitting stunned on the snow. He seemed responsive and not obviously hurt. The other climber was missing, probably buried somewhere. The chance of finding, uncovering, and resuscitating him drastically diminished over time. We quickly left the one climber so we could search for his companion and hopefully dig him out before he suffocated.

I noticed a bit of red fabric sticking out of the snow and rushed over to it. Alex and I were not acclimatized yet and running at nearly 20,000 feet left me completely out of breath. We took turns digging furiously until we found the other climber, completely buried but standing upright. Within about five or ten minutes of the avalanche, we exposed the climber's head but he had no pulse. We couldn't revive him. His eyes were open, staring at me with a haunting faraway look. I reached down and gently pushed his eyelids closed.

Alex and I helped the surviving climber to a safer spot on the glacier and finished excavating his partner. We moved the body out near him. Soon the expedition leader, several other team members, and Charlie and Tom arrived. The only thing our team could do was to sit with them as they tried to comprehend that their friend, so vibrant and alive just minutes before, was now lying dead in front of them on the snow.

After several hours we retreated to base camp, where news of the accident had already been transmitted by radio. Rasool gave each of us a long hug, saying over and over, "I'm so sorry, I'm so sorry." He knew the only thing he could do for us was to just be supportive. Everyone needed to process this sudden death in their own way. Rasool also knew that in times like this it was important to bring everyone from both climbing groups together, so he worked with the international expedition kitchen staff to prepare a dinner that was served to all of us in their large mess tent. It was a somber occasion, but we had a chance to get to know each other and celebrate the life of their friend.

The international expedition discussed arrangements by radio with the family of the deceased, and everyone agreed that bringing the body down to base camp and flying it from there would be too dangerous and difficult. So the next day our entire team went with the other group back up the glacier. We helped wrap their friend's body in a sleeping bag, then listened to some words the international expedition members said about him and his family. Similar to a burial at sea, all the climbers pulled on a rope attached to his body and moved it over to the lip of a nearby crevasse. When prompted by their expedition leader, everyone let go and the body fell into the glacier's icy depths.

Dealing with this tragic event profoundly affected us. The events felt unnervingly close to home. The day before it avalanched, I had led the way up that same snow slope. If I hadn't listened to the small uneasy voice inside, several of us could have suffered a similar fate. Before the accident, Alex hadn't displayed his usual enthusiasm about the expedition; after the accident, his heart wasn't in it at all. He was such a strong contributor and had such a positive effect on others when he was excited about climbing, that the absence of it severely impacted team morale. I tried to rally everyone, but after several more attempts on the southwest ridge of Gasherbrum IV in unstable snow, we all realized it wasn't safe. As a group we were not mentally prepared to wait around for another month to see if snow conditions improved. We were not going to climb the mountain this time. By mid-July we decided to leave.

On the mountain I had been thinking about life and death, and our best efforts to promote the former while risking the latter. A few days before our porters arrived to transport our gear, I sat down with Rasool for a serious talk. "Would you move your family to Skardu if Bedruma gets pregnant again?" I asked him. "She could see a doctor during her pregnancy, and when she is having the baby. If the baby gets sick, then you can take it to the hospital." I'd read that a child's risk of dying is greatest in the first month of life. It could make a big difference being in Skardu, a large town with a well-staffed hospital and health clinic, instead of tiny Hushe, where there was no medical care or emergency services. I told Rasool that I had discussed the idea with my climbing friends, and we had all agreed to pitch in and cover the costs. "You can live in Skardu for a year so the baby gets strong before you move back to Hushe," I said.

Rasool, bowing slightly, replied, "So very much thank you sir, but my house and my fields will be wanting someone." I had anticipated his reaction and had my answers ready. "You have been very sad about your son, and I don't want you to be sad again," I said. I suggested that Rasool's brother could watch his house and farm for one year, and that he could pay someone to help in his fields. I asked him to think about it. The next morning at breakfast Rasool greeted me with an enormous smile. "Steve, sahib," he said, "this is a good idea."

Not long after I returned to the United States, Rasool had someone write to me saying that Bedruma was pregnant. The cost of living in Skardu is relatively small, and it didn't take a big effort to collect the $1,500 from Rasool's climbing friends to support the family for over a year. I wired the money, and they moved to Skardu. I heard later from a friend that Bedruma had delivered a healthy baby boy they named Fida Ali.

CHAPTER 5

EVEREST

EVEREST KANGSHUNG FACE, 1994
NORTH RIDGE, 1994

ll the expeditions I had been on to the Great Ranges, whether climbing alpine style or expedition style, we did most of the work on the
mountain ourselves. I had either climbed with all my partners before
or they were friends of people I had climbed with. Most of the funding for
these trips was out of pocket; we couldn't afford to hire high-altitude porters to carry loads. And besides, I didn't want to feel responsible for employees doing such dangerous work. So I had mixed feelings when Alex Lowe
called me in December 1993, inviting me on a large expedition the following year to the Kangshung (East) Face of Mount Everest (8,872 meters,
or 29,108 feet). Alex had been hired to guide socialite-author Sandy Hill,
a former fashion editor who had raised corporate sponsorship to fund an
attempt on this difficult route.

The expedition's main sponsors included Vaseline Research (a source of much ribbing) and the NBC *Today Show*. David Breashears, a well-known American climber and filmmaker, was the expedition leader; he was to send film clips to NBC via runner, jeep, and airplane. These clips would support live interviews with Sandy for the popular morning television program using a newfangled satellite telephone. From Alex's description, Sandy didn't have the strength to climb Everest without oxygen nor the technical expertise to lead any of the pitches on this difficult route. The expedition would therefore fix ropes and employ high-altitude Sherpas to carry the oxygen bottles, equipment, and supplies needed for her ascent. I would get a free trip if I helped fix ropes and would be given a chance to try to reach the summit. I was free to climb without using supplemental oxygen if I choose.

Because Alex was going, I was interested. He had a new position as a professional athlete for a major outdoor retailer, and his private guiding was going well. He seemed full of enthusiasm about this trip. In addition to his tremendous skill and strength, when Alex was excited like this, he brought a joy to the mountains that made him one of my favorite climbing partners. Everest's storied appeal was a huge draw, of course; this would be a rare opportunity to go to the side of Everest climbed by the team I'd been unable to join over a dozen years earlier.

Concerns loomed as well. For starters, I hadn't climbed with anyone on the team besides Alex. The size and style of the expedition were driven by sponsorships tied to getting Sandy to the top. I also felt that Everest had become overhyped in recent years, given its stature as the world's highest mountain. Despite these concerns, the opportunity to climb the Kangshung Face without supplemental oxygen seemed like one of the most exciting ways to do it. The expedition was fully funded, and I knew the Chinese would make it very expensive—something that I would never be able to afford myself. I decided to accept this invitation to Everest.

Mount Everest is in the Himalayas, eight hundred miles southeast of the Karakoram Range on the Nepal-China/Tibet border. Other than my trip to Nepal with Alex in 1989, I had little experience in this mountain range. The remote east side of Everest had only been climbed three times. An American expedition that included George Lowe and Dave Cheesmond had made the first ascent of the Kangshung Face in 1983 via a route that went directly to the summit.

Our expedition would follow a different line on the east face first climbed in 1988 by a small American-British expedition without the use of high-altitude porters or oxygen. That route was repeated by a Chilean team in a similar style several years later. The heavy-handed style of our expedition would be in stark contrast to the first and second ascents. The lower part of our proposed route was up steep ribs of rock, snow, and ice. Theoretically, climbing on these features that protruded from the wall would protect us from avalanches that fell down either side. Above, the route followed lower-angled snow slopes to the South Col (the saddle between Everest and Lhotse) from the China/Tibet side. From there, our route finished by joining the popular southeast ridge route on Everest that ascends from the south through Nepal.

We arrived in Kathmandu on March 18, 1994, and I immediately realized this expedition would be dramatically different from my previous trips. The amount of money, the huge mounds of gear, having Sandy along as a guided celebrity, and David, who seemed overworked and stressed out by sponsor obligations—all gave me an uneasy feeling. At the airport we met with Wong Chu and several Sherpas who were going with us, and Chongba, our cook. Barry Blanchard, an experienced climber from Alberta, well-known for numerous first ascents of ice climbs and alpine routes in the Canadian Rockies, met us at our hotel.

The next morning, I was asked to be part of a videoshoot with Sandy purchasing food and supplies in the open-air market. After that we tried out the satellite telephone. It looked like a briefcase that split in two, with the top half being the antenna and the bottom half the receiver with a handset. Loaned to us by NBC, this $35,000 piece of equipment was worth more than the total budget of most of my previous expeditions. Before leaving Kathmandu a few days later, I called Ann. She said I had been on the *Today Show* with Sandy bartering in the vegetable market, telling a vendor, "One hundred rupees [ten cents] is too much." I told Ann, "I better be careful what I say now. The whole world must think I'm a cheapskate."

On March 23 we rode in a small bus from Kathmandu to the Nepalese border town of Kodari, where we had some difficulties with the Chinese customs official. Eventually they allowed us to go ahead, after leaving a 15,000-rupee "deposit." Once inside Tibet, we traveled in the back of a truck to Xhangmu, where we spent the night. In the morning we drove

to Nylam and had a dusty ride to Shekar. Two days later, we rode on top
of our loads in the bed of a truck, up over the Pang La. From the pass I
enjoyed a spectacular first view of the mountain I had come to climb. In
the distance only a few peaks protruded above a sea of clouds, and Mount
Everest stood above all of them. The north ridge was facing us, the route
taken by several British attempts in the 1920s and 1930s. The Kangshung
Face was hidden behind it.

On the other side of the pass it was spitting snow as we reached the
village of Kharta. Setting up camp, I was amazed at the amount of luxury
involved in this expedition. Although it is customary on most Himalayan
expeditions, I was not used to having two enormous tents—one for cooking and one for eating. The dining tent was complete with table and chairs,
serving bowls, place settings, and Thermos jugs of hot water and tea available any time of day. The staff in the cook tent had five big stoves all going
at once, turning out meals for the entire team.

David had arranged with the CMA for one hundred porters, each one to
carry a fifty-pound load. Alex, Barry, and I were responsible for dividing up
the pile of supplies and equipment into porter loads, and I estimated we had
150 to 160 loads. The Tibetan sirdar sent for more porters, and on March 27
by about 5:00 p.m. the last load left the village on the back of a man or a
yak. We only walked about two miles before stopping for the evening, but it
felt good to start moving. Alex and I were among the few of our climbing
peers who had children, and we had a great discussion that evening about
balancing two of the things we cared about most: family and climbing.

On the morning of March 29 we started the trek across the Langma La,
a 17,450-foot-high pass, following our string of porters and yaks slowly
moving up the hillside. The beautiful weather was an encouraging sign. At
the pass I experienced the familiar mix of fear and excitement when seeing our objective clearly for the first time. David, Alex, Barry, Sandy, and I
picked out the features of our route on the east face that were visible from
our vantage point. After dinner at our camp below the pass, Chongba and
the kitchen staff brought out a cake for Barry's birthday. The early spring
air was cold and clear, and the remaining four days walking to base camp
took us along treeless heather benches and meadows still brown after the
recent winter snow had melted. We passed high mountains to the south
that towered over us, including Makalu (8,485 meters, or 27,838 feet) and

Chomolonzo (7,804 meters, or 25,604 feet). In front of us, Lhotse (8,516 meters, or 27,940 feet) and Everest dominated the head of the valley.

Before reaching base camp, Alex and I discovered that Tensing, one of our high-altitude Sherpas, was also a monk we had met at the Buddhist monastery above the village of Thame in Nepal. We had been there to climb a new route on Kwangde Nup five years earlier. Tensing's monk name at that time was Nawang Chuchuk; he had invited us for tea in his room at the monastery, where he gave us prayer flags to take to the summit. Tensing revealed to Alex and me that he had recognized us immediately in Kathmandu but, being soft-spoken and modest, he had waited until now to remind us of our previous encounter. It felt like some kind of spiritual intervention that brought us together again—but this time we'd be climbing partners.

I spent some time hiking with Sandy to get to know her a bit. She wanted to experience a climbing life like the rest of us, but she had difficulty reconciling this with her fast-paced New York media lifestyle. To me, the mountains were the antithesis of Madison Avenue. I wondered what she would be like once we started climbing. We reached base camp at nearly 17,000 feet on April 3. We paid and released the porters, and we set about creating tent platforms on the rock-covered glacier.

Alex, Barry, and I got up on April 7 at 3:30 a.m. for our first day of climbing. Accompanied by Sherpas Pinzo, Tensing, and Kaji, we had a productive day and returned to base camp after fixing about twenty-two hundred feet of rope up to the top of a feature called the Scottish Gully. After dinner, David spent most of the night editing one of his NBC dispatches; he worked very hard for his sponsors. Sandy was up all night writing an article for *People* magazine. A few days later we celebrated her birthday with a little party. She wanted us all to dance, but the batteries in the tape player and speakers were too cold to function.

A week later we finished fixing rope to Camp I at 20,000 feet, which got us above the steepest ice and rock climbing. Weather and snow conditions kept us from occupying the camp until April 18, when Barry and I spent the night there with Tensing, Pinzo, and Kaji. Above camp the five of us spent three days to place more fixed rope and where necessary to excavate steep unconsolidated snow down to firmer ice. We descended to base camp, where a bad cold made its way through the team. Stormy weather, deep snow, and the wind blast from an avalanche destroyed base camp, causing more than two weeks' delay. Then on May 3, Kaji and I plowed through deep new snow to reach the site of Camp II at 24,500 feet. We descended to Camp I for a couple days of rest, while Pinzo and Tensing carried loads to Camp II. I was doing well, except breathing hard with my mouth open had caused sun blisters on my lips and snowglare sunburned my tongue. The ever-present sore throat and cough nagged me.

David, Barry, Alex, and Sandy joined the three Sherpas and me at Camp I two days later. Apparently the plan was for everyone to carry loads to Camp II and then to Camp III at 26,000 feet on the South Col in preparation for Sandy's ascent. I doubted if she could make it all the way from Camp I to Camp II. She was determined, but it was more than 4,000 feet of climbing in deep snow. The logistics for this expedition and the number of camps was based on the two previous ascents. But given that the goal seemed to be getting Sandy to the top, it would have been better to add another camp between Camps I and II. The next day, all of us (save Sandy) hiked to Camp II. We carried nearly all of the tents, food, stoves, fuel, and oxygen that would later be moved up to Camp III. My plan was to spend the night and the next day at Camp II to acclimatize. The others returned to Camp I. After my time at Camp II, I'd descend to base camp for a rest and try for an ascent without bottled oxygen when it was time for our first summit attempt.

On the morning of May 7, just as the sun was rising, I poked my head out the tent door after a bad night of coughing and hacking. The brilliant views of Makalu, Chomolonzo, the South Col of Everest, and a host of smaller peaks to the northeast made all the work so far worthwhile. During my 7:00 a.m. radio call to David and the others at Camp I, I discovered plans had changed dramatically. On yesterday's descent the other climbers thought the snow conditions were unstable and avalanche prone; Alex in particular thought the snow was too dangerous for Sandy. They were not going to come up tomorrow for the carry to the South Col. For more than a month I had been laboring in deep snow conditions, but I didn't think they were that dangerous. A strong team of competent climbers would continue. I figured that when the others made the carry to Camp II, they decided Sandy wasn't physically able to make it to the summit and back safely with the resources available. Getting her to the top was the expedition's commercial goal for David and was Alex's responsibility as a guide. Once they finally realized this wasn't a good route for her, they pulled the plug.

I was furious. I felt so naïve not to see this coming. David said he would still support Barry and me in an alpine-style ascent, but he withheld any Sherpa support. With all the deep snow, that would make it too much work for a party of two. Without anyone else on the mountain to help us, we would be completely on our own if anything went wrong. As I packed up my personal gear to descend, I looked up at the South Col—it seemed so close. I was so frustrated knowing that from there it would be a relatively easy climb on the normal route to the summit.

Back at Camp I, we had a conference. Sandy volunteered that the expedition should support the strongest team on the route, and she released Alex from any of his guiding obligations to her. I still wanted to climb the mountain, but it needed to be a sincere and credible effort for me to go back up. I'd done as much as I could. Alex and I descended the glacier to base camp the next morning. Concerned about the appearance of abandoning a paying client for his own summit ambitions, he was reluctant to go back up without Sandy. Alex was the main reason I had come on the trip in the first place, so that clinched the decision for me to not go back up as well.

At base camp the staff told us more about an incident that had occurred a few days earlier when the entire climbing team had been at Camp I. Our Sherpas informed us via radio that some Tibetans from the nearest village of Kharta had snuck into base camp at night and stolen some equipment and supplies. One of our Sherpa staff, Nawang, was a former Gurkha in the Indian Army (similar to an American Special Ops soldier); these soldiers have a reputation for fearlessness and military expertise dating back to the early days of the British Raj.

Nawang, upon discovering the theft, had pursued the Tibetans, outflanked them, and proudly marched them back to base camp at the point of his long, curved kukri knife. Our base camp staff tied them up, put them in the storage tent, and called us on the radio. David asked them what they planned to do with the thieves. "Rub hot chiles on their penises and let them go," they replied. Knowing we had to walk out through Kharta, David told them the hot chile treatment would probably incite them to murder us when we got there on the hike out. Thus he quickly nixed the suggested punishment and instructed the Sherpas to let them go with a stern warning. Now that we were all back at base camp together, Nawang proudly retold his side of the story to much laughter.

A reasonably strong and persistent person, Sandy seemed capable of climbing Everest by an easier route using supplemental oxygen. She had convinced Alex to hike out with her, take a jeep to the Rongbuk Glacier on Everest's north side, and attempt the north ridge route. By modern standards, that route is a technically easy and safe climb. They invited me to go with them. It was nice to be asked, but my first response was to wonder about my obligations to the rest of the expedition and how David and Barry might perceive this. On the morning of May 9 we held a group meeting during which we officially abandoned the Kangshung Face and the film project because the route was too "dangerous." Alex and Sandy brought up their plan to go to Everest's north side with me. David and Barry graciously agreed that we should go right away. They would stay and evacuate all our equipment and supplies from the mountain and then leave with the porters. I was pleased to get another chance to climb the mountain, curious whether I could reach the top without supplemental oxygen.

On May 13, Alex, Sandy, and I drove to the Rongbuk base camp at 16,500 feet and got our first glimpse of Everest's north face. Our permit was not valid to climb on this side of the mountain, so my main concern was obtaining permission from the Chinese to be there. I wasn't sure how the permitting process would play out with the three of us. The guide-client relationship between Alex and Sandy drove the need for both of them to use supplemental oxygen, which required different logistics. My needs were vastly less complicated, since I was going to climb independently without oxygen. Fully acclimatized after spending six weeks on the Kangshung Face, I was ready to make a summit attempt.

Several expeditions were attempting the mountain from the north, including one from Seattle-based International Mountain Guides (IMG) led by my friend Eric Simonson. Eric and I had both grown up climbing in the Cascades and had known each other for twenty years. His expedition, like most of the others on this side of the mountain, included both commercial and guided clients plus staff to support them. There are many variations on how these paid trips are run, but in this case Eric's commercial clients paid a fee to have IMG secure the permit, provide all the food and group equipment, oxygen bottles, base camp cook staff, in-country transportation, fixed ropes, and a few Sherpas to help carry group supplies up the mountain.

Commercial clients were supposed to be experienced enough to make the climb on their own. Eric's guided clients, by contrast, were supposed to be strong enough but not necessarily experienced enough to climb on their own. So they were provided all the same services as the commercial clients plus American guides who would cook for them, provide direction and advice, and accompany them on the mountain to make sure they remained safe. Eric's clients were responsible for carrying their personal gear up the mountain, including carrying their own oxygen bottles on summit day. (Other companies running Everest expeditions on the Nepal side of the mountain provided Sherpas to carry personal gear and oxygen bottles for their clients, but for a much higher fee; in the future, IMG would do the same.)

Alex, Sandy, and I found Eric in his tent issuing instructions over the radio to his American guides up on the mountain. He stepped out to greet us, a tall smiling robust figure clad in a large puffy down jacket stained with cooking fire soot, road dust, and food—the residue of outdoor expedition life. Soft-spoken but with a no-nonsense disposition, Eric was willing to help us get permission from the Chinese to climb under his permit. I let Eric know that I was climbing on my own, without supplemental oxygen; he knew I had the experience to be self-sufficient with little impact on his operation. However, he understood the logistics of supporting Sandy with bottled oxygen were much more complex, so he made it clear to her and Alex that he needed to use his equipment on the mountain to take care of his clients first. Eric told Alex and Sandy that they would need to have a separate conversation with him about logistics and costs if they wanted to climb under his permit.

Eric's team was divided into smaller groups that would take turns rotating up through the higher camps on the mountain. If Alex and Sandy were to become part of his expedition, Eric said they would be on the last rotation to make a summit attempt. Alex and Sandy thought their chance of success was slim if they had to wait for everyone else in Eric's group to go first. They weren't able to reach an agreement on how they would fit into Eric's group, so Alex and Sandy decided to obtain their own permit from the Chinese in Lhasa. They drove to the Tibetan capital and returned to base camp with a permit several days later, but it was too late in the season by then to get all their logistics in place before the onset of the monsoon in early June. They eventually decided to leave. Sandy Hill would not be successful this time, but she came back and reached the summit from the Nepal side in 1996.

With all of my original teammates gone, I integrated myself into Eric's team, which was larger than anything I had been involved with before. They had forty members: fifteen clients, nine guides, two filmmakers, and fourteen Sherpas including kitchen staff. To afford the many thousands of dollars it cost to go on the expedition, Eric's clients were mostly professionals, similar to those I worked with as an engineer. I spent one afternoon talking to Paul and Jerry, who both looked like they were in their late fifties. Jerry said he was very sick when he first arrived and almost went home, but he was happy about his lower body weight, increased fitness level, and greater confidence in his physical ability. Paul, from Orlando, owned a small engineering firm doing Department of Defense work. Many of the team members had home lives that were similar to mine, with kids who needed help with homework and rides to music lessons and sports practice. But none of the guided or commercial clients were prepared to climb a peak like Everest completely on their own. I enjoyed hanging out in their large mess tent that was full of good snacks and hot drinks, listening to everyone's stories. The camp had a family-like atmosphere full of people excited about their adventure.

I left base camp on May 18 for advance base camp (ABC) with one of Eric's teams that included two experienced New Zealand climbers, Mike Perry (hereafter referred to as Perry) and Mark Whetu (pronounced "fi-tu"), who had been recruited by Eric to make a film about the expedition. Perry did most of the camera work and Mark, a professional mountain guide, assisted him. The group also included a commercial client, Dan Holle, and Mike Rheinberger, a personal friend of Eric's. A fifty-six-year-old Australian, Mike had already tried to climb Everest six times. Apparently Eric wanted to give him a seventh chance to reach the summit.

The group walked thirteen miles up the East Rongbuk Glacier on a rocky medial moraine that was flat enough for the teams of yaks that had carried loads to ABC over a month ago. We passed by two camps (Camps I and II) that the other climbers had used earlier while acclimatizing. They were used to the altitude now and could walk to ABC in one day. But for me it was all new. The huge, stunning mountains were hidden from view, but the moraine wove its way through a forest of tall ice hoodoo-like formations in the glacier that felt like a scene from a wintery fairy tale. We reached ABC at 21,000 feet that afternoon in a snowstorm. Because it was accessible by yaks capable of carrying heavy loads, ABC was well equipped with large communal cooking and eating tents plus numerous smaller sleeping tents. So far we had been hiking on the low-angle, rubble-strewn glacier to get to

ABC, but above there the actual climbing started. ABC was the logistical and climbing launch point for the mountain.

Three days later, I climbed to Camp IV at 23,000 feet on the North Col with the same group that had accompanied me from base camp, plus two of Eric's guides, Alex Van Steen and Dave Staeheli, and a couple of guided clients. I reached the camp before the others and found a row of about half a dozen tents pitched on the lee side of a fifteen-foot cornice (a snow wall formed by the wind into the shape of a breaking wave). It was a spot nicely sheltered from the wind that was blowing at fifty miles an hour just a few feet above my head. I dug out several tents that had been partially buried by snowdrifts and cleaned out the ones that had been left with trash. Starting up several stoves, I melted snow to provide water and hot drinks for the group when they arrived.

After trekking and climbing with Mike for several days, I was worried about him. Struggling with the altitude, he moved very slowly uphill. I appreciated that he was an open person with a big heart and deep attachments to the Sherpa community, but I was concerned because he kept saying he was going to put everything he had into getting to the top no matter what. The combination of inadequate physical strength for the task plus strong determination was disturbing. I'd only been with him for a short time, though, and the others in the group knew him much better and didn't express any concern, so I didn't say anything.

The next day, I arrived at Camp V at 25,000 feet several hours ahead of the group and found two Canadians in one of the two large IMG tents that were already pitched there. I let them know the rest of my group would arrive soon, so the pair moved into a smaller, less comfortable tent they had brought for themselves. I spent the rest of the afternoon cleaning out and repairing the tents that had suffered minor damage to the door zippers from their exposure to the relentless wind. It was well after the rest of the group had arrived and after dark when Dan, Eric's commercial client, showed up. He was assigned to share one of the tents with me. Cold and tired, I helped him into his bag and plied him with hot drinks. In the morning, we decided to stay put because of high winds, which shook our tents so violently all day it was impossible to get any rest. The Canadians were having a difficult time melting snow in their little tent, so I periodically gave them water.

On May 24 the wind abated enough for a move up to Camp VI. At 27,000 feet, it was higher than the top of all but five mountains in the world. It's very hard to live at that elevation without supplemental oxygen, even for short periods. To minimize the amount of time I would spend at that extreme altitude, I didn't leave Camp V until late morning. I wasn't worried about the time, since it had been easy to make progress ever since the North Col, moving up low-angled snow and along a path that wound through the rocks. I arrived at 2:30 p.m., three hours ahead of the others, several of whom had started using bottled oxygen.

At Camp VI our group planned to use four small tents, so I dug out the one IMG tent that was already there, drifted over with snow. Next I took on the exhausting task of excavating snow and rebuilding a rock platform for the tent I had carried up from ABC. After the others arrived, Dave Staeheli held onto my tent to keep it from blowing away while I set it up and tied it down. Mike and I got inside this tent to melt snow and rehydrate. The others arrived too late and tired to build platforms for their third and fourth tents, so several of them moved into a couple of tents still standing that had been abandoned by previous Italian and Taiwanese expeditions. The two Canadians had arranged with the Taiwanese to use their tent at Camp VI, but when they arrived later they found it already occupied by Eric's group. Instead of moving out and setting up their own tent (as the Canadians had done at Camp V), the IMG climbers helped the Canadians build a platform for the smaller tent they had brought up from Camp V.

The two Mikes, Mark, Alex, Dave, Dan, and the other guided clients felt they hadn't had enough time to rest at Camp VI before making a summit attempt in the morning, so they decided to wait a day. It was increasingly difficult for the guided clients and Mike to move up the mountain at a reasonable pace, and they slowed down the whole group. In the mountains, speed is safety—spending an extra day at this altitude was not a good idea. The threat of ailments like HAPE or HACE increases with the amount of time spent at extreme altitude. Using bottled oxygen can mitigate some of these health risks, but it also enables inexperienced climbers to get higher on the mountain than their skills can match.

Without using bottled oxygen, I knew spending an extra day at Camp VI would leave me too weak to reach the summit. I had to either go up or go down. The group's plan was communicated to Eric during their evening radio call, and he tried to discourage them from spending an extra day at that altitude for the same reasons I did. He didn't convince them either, so I got on the radio and said I'd like to make a summit attempt by myself the next day. Eric understood my situation and gave his full support. Besides wishing me good luck, he asked me to check in with him by radio throughout the day so he could monitor my progress. As the light faded, I made my preparations and traded places with Mike in the tent so I'd be by the door.

Just after midnight on May 25, I brewed a pot of tea and forced down a couple of granola bars. I pulled on my one-piece down suit and double boots and left the tent at 3:00 a.m. under a full moon and clear, relatively calm weather. My thoughts were slightly muddled at this altitude, but years of practice and conditioning kicked in, allowing me to move on autopilot. I took only a few essentials—two liters of water, my headlamp, an extra battery, an extra pair of heavy mitts, goggles, sunglasses, a radio, and six hard candies. Above Camp VI the north ridge blends into the mountainside at a feature called the Yellow Band, where climbing becomes steeper and more difficult. But by modern standards it was still relatively easy, and I felt comfortable moving alone without being roped to someone else.

Finding the start of the route through the Yellow Band in the dark was difficult, but after half an hour, I found some old tattered rope that led me to a series of shallow snow gullies and rocky ramps that wound up through the steep rock. The moonlight revealed the terrain with a shadowy luminescence that allowed me to switch off my headlamp. After a couple of hours, I climbed onto the crest of the northeast ridge around 5:00 a.m. as the first light drew a weak line across the eastern horizon.

Far below, the valleys emerged from the darkness. Looking over the crest proper, I watched the pink dawn light up the entire Kangshung Face. For the past three days I had encountered several artifacts (old oxygen bottles and pitons) that looked like they were from British expeditions that had made the first attempts on Everest after World War I. One of the most prodigious climbers from those expeditions, George Mallory, had disappeared in 1924 with his partner, Sandy Irvine, somewhere along the northeast ridge between where I stood and the summit about a mile farther along the ridge to my right and a thousand feet higher. The words of a member of that expedition, Noel Odell, who had climbed up searching in vain for his friends, crept into my mind: "What right had we to venture thus far into the holy presence of the Supreme Goddess? If it were indeed the sacred ground of Chomolungma, had we violated it, was I now violating it? And yet as I gazed again, another mood appeared to creep over her haunting features. There seemed to be something alluring in that towering presence. I was almost fascinated, that he who approaches close must ever be led on, and oblivious of all obstacles seek to reach that most sacred and highest place of all."

Alone in this intensely beautiful and potentially dangerous place, I talked to myself to support the life and death decisions I was making. I talked my way through the intricate route finding along the ridge by invoking Mallory and Irvine's prior passage with encouragement like, *Yes, those guys must have gone left up this gully and then back right along the crest.* The ridge was very exposed, and I imagined that a fall somewhere nearby had determined Mallory and Irvine's fate. The thought prompted me to be even more careful and, given my hypoxia-induced sluggishness, to keep in mind that it would be easy to make a mistake. But that wasn't my biggest concern. From here to the summit the northeast ridge gained a thousand feet over about a mile, and most of that was in three short, steep steps. With so much horizontal distance to cover, it would be nearly impossible to get down if I got hurt or sick. It's much easier to descend both independently or with assistance when going straight down.

Managing cardio strength is a critical safety technique when climbing at extreme altitude, and I kept track of myself as if I were managing a bank account. The sum of my training, experience, acclimatization, and proper rest was the starting balance, and the physical and psychological work to climb up and back down safely constituted the withdrawals. I needed to ensure that, at any point in my ascent, I still had enough left in the bank to get down. The most difficult part would be having the discipline to turn back if I felt I crossed that line before reaching the top.

Summertime high temperatures on the summit of Everest are 0 to −5°F. With modern boots and clothing, climbers can easily protect themselves from these temperatures. This is especially true when using bottled oxygen because the body can produce more heat with higher oxygen saturation levels in the blood. Climbing without bottled oxygen, my body had to prioritize its limited oxygen supply, and my brain and core were first in line. Knowing my extremities came last, I constantly monitored my hands and feet. My left foot had been cold since leaving the tent, but I could still feel it. After climbing some steeper rock to the top of a feature called the First Step, however, my foot started to go numb. I needed to restore some feeling.

I stopped at a flat place around 28,000 feet and took off my boot. After massaging my foot to get the circulation going, I restored some warmth before proceeding.

A layer of high clouds moving in from the south had an insulating effect, making it relatively warm. There was only a light wind, so with these favorable conditions I kept climbing. I had difficulty finding the route to the next obstacle, a 150-foot-high rocky cliff called the Second Step. Talking to myself about where Mallory and Irvine might have gone wasn't helping at the moment, so I called Eric on the radio to ask for directions. He had climbed this route three years earlier, and his memory of it was good enough to walk me through the climbing that led to the base of the Second Step. I scrambled up some rocky ledges with old fixed ropes to where a fifteen-foot aluminum ladder was lashed against the vertical section of the Second Step. The ladder had been placed there by a Chinese expedition in 1975. Most climbers believe that Mallory and Irvine wouldn't have been able to climb the Second Step given the climbing standards and equipment in use at the time. But I could easily step up the ladder rungs and then jam my gloved hand into a crack to pull up onto flatter terrain.

After a quarter mile of easy climbing, I traversed onto the north face to get around the Third Step at the base of the final summit pyramid and then up a gully back onto the ridge. The stress on my respiratory system was terribly painful, and as I struggled up the last couple hundred feet to the top, I experienced fits of panting, resting on all fours, coughing, and hacking. My sore throat was excruciating. Ten hours after leaving Camp VI, I reached the summit at 1:05 p.m. I had beat my turnaround time by an hour. I had planned about four hours to return to Camp VI, which gave me enough time to get there before it got dark at around 7:00 p.m.

I spent about thirty minutes on top, but unfortunately the cloud layer that had been building all day was now just below the summit. Surrounded by whiteness, I didn't get to enjoy the spectacular view I'd seen in pictures from the roof of the world. The summit was littered with an assortment of flags and old science experiments mounted on poles stuck into the snow. The prevailing southwest winds replenished the summit snowfield and formed a cornice that was gradually being pushed farther out over the Kangshung Face. Occasionally chunks of it broke off and fell twelve thousand feet down the face, taking pieces of the oldest junk with it. To avoid a similar fate, I stayed close to where there was exposed rock.

I radioed Eric and told him I was on the summit. I could hear cheering and clapping from others in the background. My enthusiastic supporters couldn't physically help me get down the mountain safely, but their voices jolted me out of my stupor and connected me to the life I was struggling to get back to. I took a few photos and began my descent. Slowly working my way down, I carefully used various techniques depending on the terrain. On the sloped and fractured rock, I faced out and crabbed along using my feet, palms, and sometimes the seat of my pants. I cramponed-down patches of snow and ice, and where it was steep, I used pieces of old fixed rope as a handline.

I completed the long and exhausting traverse along the northeast ridge three hours after leaving the summit. Looking straight down to Camp VI below the Yellow Band and beyond, I saw the north ridge all the way to the North Col. It was steep downclimbing through the Yellow Band, and at one point my crampon broke through a thin layer of snow and slid on the underlying rock, causing me to fall. Sliding out of control, I was headed for a several hundred foot tumble down onto lower-angled ground near Camp VI. I made a desperate lunge with my ice axe and hooked a piece of old fixed rope, which jerked me back onto my feet. If I hadn't stopped myself, would my fate have been similar to Mallory's? I arrived back at Camp VI just before dark.

I found my tent with Mike still inside, and it looked like he hadn't moved all day. Large snow drifts had accumulated around the tent and partially collapsed it. There was barely enough room inside now for him, so he gave me a cup of lukewarm tea and suggested I move to the abandoned Italian tent that was now empty because Dan Holle, Alex Van Steen, Perry, and the other guided clients didn't feel well and had descended earlier that day. Mike wanted to prepare for his summit bid the next day, so I grabbed my sleeping bag and walked over to where the battered snow-filled Italian tent was still standing. I was annoyed at being kicked out of my tent, but I was really concerned about Mike.

After I cleaned out the tent and pulled off my boots and got into my bag, the altitude, exhaustion, and maybe the solitary nature of my venture overcame me. I started vividly hallucinating. The head of an elderly Asian woman appeared just over my left shoulder, and in a slow, gentle voice she gave me step-by-step instructions on how to start the stove, fill the pot with snow, and brew a cup of tea. After drinking several cups of tea and soup, all I wanted to do was sleep, but I was afraid. I felt the need to stay awake and monitor my breathing while sitting upright, to make sure I coughed up any phlegm or other fluids that might migrate to my lungs and cause me to choke. To stay alert, I brewed countless pots of tea, but I kept dozing off. Each time I fell asleep, the elderly Asian woman would rouse me to consciousness in a soft but clear voice. "Don't sleep, now," said the hallucination. "Please wake up and have some more tea." I made it through the night this way.

The sun was shining on the tent by the time I stirred in the morning. As I tried to clear my head and think about the day, I looked up and noticed the head of a Sikh man floating off to the left in front of me. He had a full beard and wore a light blue turban. With a heavy Indian accent he greeted me in a loud and cheery voice: "Good morning, sir! It is time to start moving." Normally I would have found these hallucinations disturbing, but I'd read numerous accounts about other climbers having similar experiences at extreme altitude, so I figured it wasn't that unusual. Besides, the advice from my imaginary friends was helpful; my Sikh friend guided me through what I needed to do with brief instructions like, "Put some snow in the pot" and "Mix up some cocoa" and "Put water in your bottle" and "Put on your down suit before your boots."

By 8:00 a.m. I was up, fed, watered, packed, and out of the tent. I emerged to a clear day with only a light wind. During the night Dave Staeheli, Mark Whetu, and Mike Rheinberger, the only remaining members of my group, had headed for the summit. I vaguely remembered that before leaving camp, Mike had yelled into the darkness toward me that one of the Canadians was suffering from HAPE so I walked to their tent to see if everyone was okay. The sick climber breathed from an oxygen bottle Mike had given him; he was unable to speak through his oxygen mask.

Fortunately his partner was an MD, and he said that some Sherpas and Canadian team members were coming up from below to help them down. From what I had learned about Dave, Mark, and Mike during the short time I had been with them, it seemed uncharacteristic for them to head for the summit rather than help rescue a sick climber. A horrible feeling of dread worked its way into my hypoxia-addled brain. I realized that Mike was on a mission to reach the summit at any cost, that drive trumping even his own convictions about proper conduct in the mountains. Dave and Mark may have felt obligated to go with him, knowing that a team of Sherpas was on its way up to help the sick climber.

The Canadian doctor didn't feel he could evacuate his partner by himself, and I was in no condition to help much either. I waited with them until we heard by radio that the rescue team was nearby, then I started to descend slowly and carefully. My group of imaginary advisers had disappeared.

I stopped for some food and water at Camp V, then met the rescue team on the way up. As I dropped in elevation, I felt stronger in the thicker air, more secure on my feet. At Camp IV, at the North Col, I spent a couple of hours enjoying many cups of hot tea and soup with the other climbers there. I reached ABC that evening and, after a light meal, went to my tent, feeling well enough to release myself into the kind of deep sleep that only complete exhaustion can bring.

As I descended the mountain, Mike, Dave, and Mark were making their summit attempt. All of Eric's clients had descended earlier. Dave and Mark were guides, and Mike was on the trip by special invitation. They were simply a group of individuals trying to get to the top who didn't have paid guide/client responsibilities to each other. Dave and Mark were strong climbers and by themselves should have made rapid progress using bottled oxygen. But climbing with Mike, the group was so slow it became impossible for them to reach the summit and get back to Camp VI before dark. I had reached ABC by early afternoon, and the climbers there told me Dave had turned back, probably because of their slow pace. Mark had remained with Mike, and the two of them continued to move up despite the late hour. Everyone was alarmed when Mark radioed at 7:15 p.m. to say that they had reached the summit of Everest: it was dark.

I woke at ABC to the morning sun on my tent and shook off my grogginess. The Canadian climber with HAPE had been taken down safely and would be okay. I shifted my attention to the radio, when Mark called in with the good news that he and Mike had survived the night. The bad news was they had descended only a short distance from the summit before darkness and exhaustion forced them into an open bivouac without sleeping bags or a stove to melt snow for water or hot drinks. I could only imagine the suffering involved to survive both the cold and the fact that they would have run out of bottled oxygen hours before. I had been able to climb that high without using supplemental oxygen largely because the physical stress increased gradually as I got higher. As the soft hiss of oxygen from their bottles filling their masks went silent, they would have felt a sudden crushing sensation deep in their lungs at 29,000 feet.

Most of us at ABC were gripped by the seriousness of their situation. After a night out without oxygen, Mike was probably badly frostbitten, exhausted, and unable to descend on his own. It looked like Mark's decision to accompany Mike on his quest was going to turn into needing a rescue attempt. People at base camp could see them through a telescope. They radioed to ABC that the two climbers had reached the top of the Second Step by around 2:00 p.m. It took more than two hours for them to descend the 150 feet of fixed ropes and the ladder. At 4:00 p.m., Mark radioed to base camp: "Mike has altitude sickness. It came on during the night and now it is so bad he can scarcely move." Mark was faced with coaxing and pulling an incapacitated climber along the northeast ridge at extreme altitude. Probably semiconscious, Mike was likely afraid that he might not survive.

Those watching through the telescope reported that Mike was in such bad condition now that he could barely stand. By 6:30 p.m. they had progressed only a few hundred feet beyond the bottom of the Second Step. They were going to have to spend another night out, which could be fatal to them both. At ABC we huddled around the radio listening to Eric at base camp talking to Mark. There was a bottle of oxygen left by two guides near the top of the First Step, and Eric was trying to get Mark to descend to it. He was afraid that Mark would perish trying to help Mike.

"Mark," Eric said, "this is one of the hardest conversations I've had in a long time. My concern at this point is you, Mark. I want you to get down. You've got a life ahead of you. You have a family, and a wife, and a business, and a future. I just don't want you to suffer any more than you have." Mark agreed to go down to the oxygen bottle, but with the intent of using it then bringing it back up to Mike. He reached the oxygen bottle and called on the radio. Eric instructed him to breathe the oxygen for a while. Mark's friend Perry was back at base camp by then, and he spoke to Mark on the radio, trying to convince him to continue his descent and not go back up to help Mike. After Mark had a chance to breathe from the oxygen bottle for a while, Perry asked, "Mark, are you cold or warm?"

Mark responded, "Pretty cold." Perry ordered Mark to go down to Camp VI immediately. His voice cracking over the radio, Mark said, "I just can't imagine leaving a man on the mountain, you know." Perry responded sharply. "Mark," he shot back, "I can't imagine going back to Edie [Mark's wife] and telling her you are not coming back! You are going to go directly to [Camp] VI. You are going to go now."

The radio cracked. I didn't think Mark sounded irrational, nor did his reluctance seem to stem from any kind of impairment. He was simply emotionally distraught over the situation. Mark eventually followed Perry's advice and went down to meet the two guides coming up to help him. This group didn't have the resources to climb farther and help Mike, but the two guides were able to assist Mark in getting down safely. Mike Rheinberger must have perished that night. He was the third fatality on the north side of Mount Everest that season.

The next day, on May 28, I walked fourteen miles by myself down the East Rongbuk Glacier to base camp. The previous days had been an emotional roller coaster, and I was glad to have some time to myself. My happiness over reaching the summit of Everest on my own and without supplemental oxygen had been overshadowed by tragic events. I couldn't understand how climbers could have headed for the summit while leaving a man behind at Camp VI with HAPE. I was also disappointed with myself and the rest of the team for not intervening given the warning signs about Mike's mental state. He seemed like a kind and gentle man, but maybe that was why everyone was willing to go along with his obsession. I was having trouble making sense of it all.

I arrived at base camp late, just in time for dinner. As I walked toward the dining tent, I saw Pasang, our cook, standing alone looking through a telescope searching for Mike's body. Pasang had been with him on about fifteen expeditions, several to Everest but also to other peaks in Nepal. He was devastated. I gave him my condolences. Pasang said, "You had a nice summit, but my boss is still there." Several days later, Mark was assisted back to base camp. During his ordeal trying to save Mike, Mark had suffered severe frostbite to his toes. He was placed in one of the large tents for treatment, and we all tried to lift his spirits. He was devastated having to leave a fellow climber behind and kept second-guessing his decision to come down.

The weather on the morning of June 1 was perfectly clear. Eric's expedition conducted a memorial service for Mike. There is a rocky mound near base camp that offered a spectacular view of the north face of Mount Everest above the Central Rongbuk Glacier. Cairns and flat stones engraved with the names of those who have died on the mountain are scattered around the mound. It is a solemn place, and I found plaques with the names of Mallory and Irvine and several other climbers whose stories I had heard or read. Someone had engraved Mike's name on a large flat slab of stone that we leaned against a new cairn we built. One of the climbers made a tearful eulogy, and Eric read several of Mike's journal entries. One was about doing God's will even though you don't always know what it is; the other entry was about being a romantic.

After their eulogies Pasang lit a juniper fire next to Mike's cairn. He bowed all the way to the ground several times, then quietly recited a prayer he had written. This small, humble man walked back to camp to resume his duties. Witnessing the effect that Mike's death had on many of the Sherpas revealed a great tribute. That kind of devotion must have come from his having helped the Sherpa community over many years. The mourners sat around solemnly, with a backdrop of Mount Everest that was so beautiful it hardly seemed real. I didn't ever want to be the subject of one of these memorials, but I couldn't have asked for a more beautiful place to have one.

Although I was glad to have climbed Everest, my experience on the mountain continued to trouble me. From then on, I avoided the popular routes and base camps on 8,000-meter peaks. I mostly enjoyed climbing with smaller groups of friends I trusted. There are countless remote, unclimbed, or rarely climbed peaks of 6,000 and 7,000 meters. These mountains offered something not easily experienced in the twenty-first century: exploration. Exploration is not a goal or projecting an image; it's the act of seeking the unknown. The joy of exploration is enhanced when the level of effort, the uncertainty of the outcome, and the inherent risks increase with our capability to manage them. Increasing those things without the capability to manage them was foolish. A good adventure achieves a delicate balance between that joy and foolhardiness. By accepting the financial, emotional, and physical risks associated with exploration, humans fulfill the urge to discover. This is hardwired into our psyche through an evolutionary process that is as much a part of our humanity as the desire to procreate. It's how we progress and improve as a species.

That quest for exploration pointed me back to the Karakoram. That magnificent range still contained one of the world's greatest concentration of unclimbed, unexplored high-quality mountaineering objectives. Plus, I had a major unfinished project there.

CHAPTER 6

ONE MORE TRY

GASHERBRUM IV SOUTHWEST RIDGE, 1999

A fter returning from Everest in 1994, I took a hiatus from climbing in the Great Ranges. Lars, just about to turn thirteen, was living with Ann and me halftime. Ann worked part-time at the library, as she had since shortly after Jed's birth. She had found her calling helping the children and families that came into the library. I was managing some large engineering consulting projects. I enjoyed watching Lars grow and develop a social conscience. He was very bright but, like most teenagers, reluctant to share much with us. He focused on his artwork (drawing and photography) but was also becoming interested in music. I traded a tent for a basic electric guitar and small amp for Lars, and he started to play. At his school there were parent-teacher conferences, homework, and field trips, and Ann and I helped with fundraisers and other volunteer projects.

Jed's prophetic first word had been "ball." By age four, he had become a dedicated sports enthusiast—T-ball in the spring, summer sports camps at the community center, soccer in the fall, and basketball in the winter. He liked to be busy, asking every morning, "What are we doing today?" Jed was nine years younger than Lars, and because of their age difference there wasn't any sibling rivalry between them. They got along well, and Jed looked up to his older brother. He learned to appreciate Lars's taste in music. When Jed's preschool teacher asked students about their favorite song, most of them replied with "Twinkle Twinkle Little Star" or the "Happy Birthday Song." Jed preferred the Ramones' "I Wanna Be Sedated." He learned math from the sports section of the newspaper, and as he got older, Jed's soccer, basketball, and baseball team activities became more serious and competitive. He had also started to golf with a friend and his dad.

At fifteen, Lars still played electric guitar and was becoming more serious about it. At seventeen, he was part of a punk band called The Catheters. They had a contract with Sub Pop Records and played shows locally and opened for nationally touring bands. Ann and I, more than double the average age of the audience, attended some of the shows. Lars, reserved and serious at home, surprised us by jumping around the stage and off the amplifier stacks and attracting special attention from the young women in the crowd.

Our busy family life included winter ski trips and summer vacations. My work life was also busy during these years, making it difficult to get away for any serious climbing expeditions. I was responsible for building teams to win projects and then delivering the work satisfactorily, on time, and within budget. In helping build and grow a segment of our water resources business, I had become a strong part of the company and was asked to become one of the owners. I felt great about achieving this level of professional success, but I didn't like the idea of continuing to work at this pace without my usual trips to the Great Ranges.

Many of my previous climbing partners were no longer available for those kinds of trips. My window of opportunity to build relationships with the next generation of alpinists wouldn't remain open if I stayed away from the big mountains for too long. I started planning an expedition for 1999. It had been five years since Mount Everest, seven years since I'd been to the Karakoram. It was time to return to Pakistan to climb and to see Rasool and my other friends there.

I had met Steve House in the early 1990s at an informal ice-climbing event that was held annually the week before Christmas near Cody,

Wyoming. Called "The Gathering," it was open to anyone who wanted to show up, and Steve, sixteen years younger than me, was the star. With dark, straight hair and ears that seemed a bit too big for his head, he carried his slight but muscular body in a shy, self-effacing manner that had earned him the nickname Farm Boy. Steve had been on several expeditions to Alaska, where he had completed at least one new route on Denali.

After that event Steve and I ice climbed together in the Canadian Rockies and decided to go on an expedition to Alaska in the spring of 1997. We successfully completed a new route up a rock pillar on the South Buttress of Denali. While hanging out in the tent waiting for better weather, we had plenty of time to talk about other climbing destinations. I told him stories of my previous trips to the Karakoram and my ongoing unfinished business with Gasherbrum IV. Steve was intrigued, and we left Alaska agreeing to plan an expedition to Gasherbrum IV in 1999.

In addition to Steve, I asked Andy DeKlerk, a South African climber living in Seattle, to join us. A powerful rock climber and skilled alpinist, Andy had helped me rappel off a big granite wall on the Eye Tooth in Alaska after a basketball-sized piece of falling ice hit me in the shoulder and broke my scapula. The fourth member of our team was Charlie Mace, from Golden, Colorado, who had summited K2 in 1991. I contacted Rasool to arrange for him to cook for us. It was hard to believe it had been seven years since I'd been to Pakistan. I hadn't heard anything from him in all that time, and I was looking forward to seeing him again.

The team arrived in Islamabad on June 15, 1999, to a depressing and chaotic political situation that had worsened over the seven years I'd been away. After Pakistan's president, General Muhammad Zia-ul-Haq, had been killed in a suspicious airplane crash in 1988, Benazir Bhutto had been elected as the country's first female prime minister. Hers was the first civilian government since 1977, when General Zia had overthrown her father, Zulfikar Ali Bhutto, and hanged him following a sham trial. Over the previous ten years Benazir Bhutto and her rival, Nawaz Sharif (who represented another political dynasty), alternated being removed and elected as prime minister. The civilian government characterized by this political revolving door wielded little power, however, as the country was still controlled by the military. The nation was mired in a repeating nightmare from which it could not escape. To compound matters, militants coming from Pakistan, with support from the army, had snuck across the Line of Control (LOC) in the spring of 1999. They occupied Indian outposts that overlooked and protected the town of Kargil and the Indian National Highway 1D that the Indian Army had not reoccupied after they were abandoned for the winter. The highway was a major supply route for the Indian Army operations on the Siachen Glacier. The Indian Army launched a full-scale attack to drive out the militants and Pakistani troops.

Our climbing team left Islamabad by road on June 21. As our bus headed up the Karakoram Highway toward Skardu, I watched busloads of bloody, bandaged Pakistani soldiers fresh from the battlefield traveling in the opposite direction. I had never seen such a vivid display of the horrors of war. Witnessing these wounded young men, many of whom looked like they were teenagers, overwhelmed me. It seemed like another miscalculation by Pakistan's Army on how India would respond, only to be defeated in short order by their stronger neighbor. The Pakistan Army would accomplish nothing toward its goal of securing additional parts of Kashmir; they would alienate the international community for violating the LOC; and hundreds of young men would be killed in the process.

When we reached Skardu, Rasool was there. We greeted each other with big bear hugs and lifted each other up. He was as lively as usual and much happier than the last time we met. After several days of provisioning, we took the eight-hour jeep ride in the opposite direction from his village of Hushe to the village of Askole. Once again, we hiked from there to base camp up the Braldu River valley and then the Baltoro Glacier.

We spent the usual extra night camping at Paiyu, the last campsite on the trek before the glacier, so the porters could cook their chapatis. My friend Alex Lowe was on an expedition to climb a new big wall route on Trango Tower. His party's base camp was a few miles up a side valley not far from where we were. Soon after we arrived in Paiyu, Alex showed up for a visit. Somehow he knew we were arriving that day and wanted to drop down to recover from a bad head cold. After talking with him, I figured he needed to get away from his group for a bit and vent about participating in a media-driven expedition.

The year 1999 was nearing the height of the dot-com boom, and internet companies were flush with money to acquire content they could post. Alex's expedition had been sponsored by one of these websites, and improved satellite technology allowed them to post progress updates several times each day. (Alex participated in sponsored expeditions that paid him a salary because he made his living as a professional climber.) Our expedition to Gasherbrum IV was financed mostly out of our own pockets, and Alex seemed envious that we could climb unencumbered by all the media products his expedition had to produce. Alex and I exchanged news about our families, and he visited with Rasool. Early the next day our team left Paiyu, and Alex returned to his base camp.

As we headed up the Baltoro Glacier, the military presence was even greater than before. To avoid having to transport all their food, fuel, and equipment by helicopter, the army had hired contractors to run donkey trains up the glacier to supply their troops. Military operations in a war zone are not known for their environmental stewardship, and the glacier was now littered with broken crates, plastic, trash, and manure. Once we reached base camp, we watched army helicopters supply the Pakistani outpost on Conway Saddle above us. A long, broad col, the Saddle sits between Baltoro Kangri and Sia Kangri—two peaks over 23,000 feet (7,010 meters) at the head of the Abruzzi Glacier across from the Gasherbrums. The outpost sits just above 20,000 feet on the Actual Ground Position Line (AGPL) between Indian and Pakistani troops.

We turned our attention to climbing. We had better snow conditions this time than in 1992. We acclimatized and established an advance base camp (ABC) at the head of the South Gasherbrum Glacier below Gasherbrum IV without any incidents. As in 1992, we were trying to climb the southwest ridge. Our plan was to fix rope up the steep snow and rotten rock to the ridge crest, and then spend several days climbing alpine style with what we could carry on our backs to the summit. Although the snow was better, the weather was unsettled, and it took several weeks to gain the crest of the ridge. There, at around 23,000 feet, Charlie, Andy, Steve, and I scratched out platforms in the rock and ice for our small bivouac tents. From our perch we looked down on Concordia, the juncture of the great glaciers in this part of the Karakoram. The four of us spent a night here as part of our final acclimatization and then headed back to base camp to rest and wait for better weather. Small, inexpensive satellite phones were becoming available, and an American expedition on Gasherbrum II had one at their base camp next to ours. Weather forecasts arrived by phone, and we waited for a five-day outlook for clear, calm weather to make a summit attempt.

At 7,925 meters (26,001 feet), Gasherbrum IV has seen little traffic (as of 1999, there had been only three ascents) because of its technical difficulty and lack of 8,000-meter cachet. In contrast, the elevations of nontechnical Gasherbrum I (8,034 meters, or 26,358 feet) and Gasherbrum II (8,080 meters, or 26,509 feet) make these peaks very popular, and they see numerous ascents every year. All three peaks are accessed via the South Gasherbrum Glacier, so we shared the same base camp with other expeditions. This year it was crowded with more than fifty climbers at the Gasherbrum base camp. We visited with them to pass the time while waiting for better weather. Base camp was like a small town, with satellite communications, cricket matches on the ice, and parties with music and dancing. A neighboring expedition had a party one night and the emcee—a climber acting as a lip-syncing rock star—playfully strutted around and several female Spanish climbers, pretending to be groupies, reached under their shirts and pulled off their bras to throw at him. The Pakistani Army liaison officers for all the expeditions had never seen anything like it!

Rasool was happier than I had seen him on past expeditions. He loved being the ringleader for large group dinners and other social activities at base camp. And he talked incessantly about his son, Fida Ali, who was now in grade school in Hushe; Rasool gave me a lot of credit for this. Several times when I sat in the cook tent having tea with him, Rasool turned to me and said, "Many thank you, Steve sahib, now I have a son." Uncomfortable with the appreciation, I said, "Rasool, all we did was provide you and Bedruma with some ideas and money; you and your wife deserve all the credit for the work it takes to raise your children."

The weather finally improved, and the four of us climbed back to our high point on the southwest ridge. Preoccupied with returning to South Africa that fall (and his pending marriage), Andy decided to go down. Charlie went with him. Steve and I had spent considerable time together by now, and I was impressed with his ability to stay motivated. Most impressive, however, was Steve's capacity to keep a cool head where the climbing was steep, difficult, and with loose rock or few cracks to place gear that would protect him. In the Alaska Range, Steve had soloed a new mixed ice and rock route on Denali and had completed several other difficult first ascents besides the climb we had done together. He demonstrated a strength and skill level that was far beyond mine. We pitched our small tent on the edge of the abyss over Gasherbrum IV's west face, which dropped thousands of feet to the glacier. Our paths were at a crossroads. It was a privilege for me to be in such a dramatic place with this talented athlete, but it would likely be our last time on a climb like this together. Steve would be moving beyond my capabilities and would soon team up with the best climbers in the world.

While brewing up in the tent, Steve and I planned the next several days making an alpine-style summit attempt. I had never been this high on the route. The 3,000 vertical feet of climbing between our camp at 23,000 feet and the summit would be difficult. At this extreme altitude, the enormous, steep, compact limestone rock wall would be much harder than I had anticipated. For this challenge, we had brought a lot of heavy rock-climbing equipment. We carried more than forty pounds each, including all our food and fuel, the tent, the stove, cold weather gear, and ropes and hardware for a several-day climb.

Steve spent the night vomiting from the altitude, and the noise from his retching and the tent being pummeled in the wind kept me from getting any sleep. We staggered out of the tent in the morning to stupendous views of all the Gasherbrums, Sia Kangri, and Chogolisa. Here, on our tiny ledge in this vast setting halfway up one of the most difficult mountains in the world, there was an elephant in the tent: we needed to talk about going down, but we couldn't.

Weak from the bad night, we knew the gear was heavier than we could carry. The climbing would be difficult, and good anchors would be hard to get. Plus, the weather was unstable. The risks of going up were greater than we were willing to take, but neither of us could accept that going down was the other option. The realization was excruciating—over the past nineteen years I had led four expeditions to Gasherbrum IV. I would not try to climb this mountain again. "I can't think of anyone I'd rather be with in this situation," I told Steve. "I feel the same way," he said. Not wanting to leave, we couldn't admit the obvious, so we sat for a long time. These steep places, so high above the rest of the world, held such a strong pull that turning our backs on the mountain before reaching the highest point felt like abandoning something we had prepared for all our lives. Eventually, the time passed when we should have started up, so we clipped into the ropes and headed down. It took us a couple of days to reach base camp. Another storm had enveloped the peak. Despite our enormous disappointment, we felt justified—the weather was a tangible reason for coming down.

Before leaving base camp, Rasool suggested we avoid the usual return trek down the Baltoro Glacier by taking a shorter route over the Ghondoghoro La—a pass that would bring us to the road at his village of Hushe. He loved the idea of trekking out of the mountains into his village at the front of the expedition, to be proudly reunited with his family. "Let's do it," I said. "I've been up and down the Baltoro nine times, and I'd like to see some new territory and also get a chance to meet Fida Ali." Andy, Charlie, and Steve agreed, so we followed Rasool for two long days over a high snowy pass and down pristine valleys untouched by trekkers, climbers, and the army.

Over the pass, Rasool basked in his home turf. He had grown up in these valleys grazing animals and collecting timber and firewood. Rasool knew everyone, even the occasional goat herder we met. That night we reached Shaisto, where we came across a shop amid juniper bushes that served tea, Pepsi, chapatis, rice, and curried lentils. Sitting on plastic chairs at a table under the awning of the hut's corrugated metal roof, we luxuriously sipped our soft drinks.

It took about three hours to hike from Shaisto to Hushe the next morning. Rasool was in his element—waving, talking, and joking along the way. He became more confident and animated the closer he got to home. Like Hannibal crossing the Alps, Rasool led us into the village from the mountains, which was not the way the villagers were accustomed to seeing foreigners arrive. After the austere world of rock and ice, Hushe was a lush oasis. I relished the smell of the grass and the sounds of water flowing through stone channels. Like its surroundings, the earth-toned village sharply contrasted with the bright orange rooftops of apricots drying in the sun and the golden fields of wheat and hay. It was mid-September, and all the men, women, and children were working the harvest in the fields. The people were happy. It was warm, there was plenty of food, and they were reaping the results of their labor. The children ran to meet us as our expedition approached. A group of five or six school-age boys reached us first, waving their arms and talking to Rasool and several of our porters in Balti. But Rasool's gaze was fixed on one boy, whom he proudly called to step forward. This was his son, Fida Ali.

About six years old, Fida Ali wore dark blue pants and matching long-sleeve shirt. He held back at first, but Rasool stood behind him, looking down lovingly and encouraging him not to be shy. After leaning over and whispering something in Fida Ali's ear, Rasool smiled, his eyes full of gratitude. He gestured toward his son with the usual flip of his wrist. Although he spoke in Balti, I could tell he was giving Fida Ali an order of dismissal. The boy stood stiffly to attention and snapped me a quick salute followed by a slap on his thigh. It was too much for me—the danger, disappointment, exhaustion, stress, and suffering on the mountain, arriving at this idyllic place so full of life. And this beautiful young boy. I wept as it all welled up inside me.

The team left Rasool and all our porters behind in Hushe and traveled back to Islamabad on the Karakoram Highway. (KKH) Surrounded by friends in the mountains, we were isolated from the increasing political violence within the country. Part of the KKH goes through tribal areas in Khyber Pakhtunkhwa (KPK, formerly the Northwest Frontier Province), and although we felt reasonably safe, the growth of radical Islam and anti-Western sentiment was prevalent on this part of our journey. We had been warned not to travel at night along the most dangerous stretch of highway between the towns of Besham and Chilas.

To our west, a civil war had raged between warlords for control of Afghanistan after the Soviet departure. But the Taliban had recently defeated most of the Afghan warlords and gained control over the majority of the country. The Taliban was the latest group of Islamic militants supported by the Pakistan security forces to serve as their proxy in Afghanistan to keep India from having influence there.

After reaching Islamabad we stayed in a guest house not far from the Presidential Palace, where its current resident, Nawaz Sharif, was embroiled in a power struggle with the military. In October, not long after I left the country, the army staged a coup, and General Pervez Musharraf took over as chief executive. Whether overtly or covertly, the Pakistan Army has always held the reins of power in their country, promoting a self-serving national preoccupation with external threats. This has provided justification for them over the years to spend nearly a quarter of the country's budget on its military; only about 1 percent of spending goes toward health and a meager 8 percent to education.

These expenditures are startling, given the reality for most Pakistanis. In 1999 it was no better than as recently as 2012, when a third lacked drinking water and another seventy-seven million had unreliable food sources.

Forty-eight percent of the children in Gilgit–Baltistan, where Rasool lives, do not attend school; the number for girls is 6 percent higher. The literacy rate is 57 percent, the lowest in South Asia and not much better than the 52 percent literacy rate that prevailed at the creation of Pakistan in 1947. Half of the population is not even looking for jobs, since they know they won't be able to find them. The country needs at least a 9 percent annual growth rate to employ its young adults (the "under-twenties"), who make up 60 percent of the population. I wondered what it would take for the living standards of Rasool and most poor Pakistanis to improve. A democratically elected government could learn to be effective and gain control over the military. A powerful civilian government could be empowered to negotiate a settlement with India over Kashmir and other bilateral issues. Only then could rampant military spending be redirected toward improving the lives of ordinary people—the necessary ingredient for stability.

I returned to the United States from Pakistan in September. A few weeks later, I received a call at work that Alex Lowe had been killed in an avalanche on Shishipangma (8,027 meters, or 26,335 feet), in Tibet. After I had seen him at Paiyu, just months earlier, Alex and his team had completed their route on Trango Tower and returned to the United States. He had then left on another expedition, to Shishipangma. While Alex and two team members were exploring the lower reaches of their route, an avalanche was triggered thousands of feet above them by unstable snow conditions that they could not have detected from so far away. They had tried to flee to the side as the avalanche approached, but it covered such a wide swath that only one of them escaped. Alex and his other teammate were buried, their bodies not found. (In the spring of 2016, the bodies of Alex and his partner melted out. In June, the families of the two climbers traveled to Tibet and cremated their remains.)

I left my office early to go home and tell Ann. My whole family had spent time with Alex's wife, Jenni, and their three young boys. This was a difficult personal loss. As a climber, I have seen a lot of death, but losing a friend as close to me as Alex hurt so much that it called into question my climbing life. He wasn't the first friend to die in the mountains, and he wouldn't be the last. My initial reaction to a death like this is to tell myself, "Okay, this is it. I'm done with this shit. It's time to stop." But I know from past experience that this perspective doesn't work for me. If I stay away from the mountains, I become sad and depressed. Over time, I've learned that I can't change this fundamental aspect of who I am any more than I can change the color of my eyes.

I realized at a young age that climbing is my life's calling. I've spent many years experiencing the powerful forces of nature in the mountains. I wouldn't trade it for anything. I find greater happiness when I embrace this, which isn't always easy. Climbing is hard and dangerous, and it takes me away from the people I love. After a friend dies, it never gets any easier. It is extremely difficult to get motivated, to return to the mountains, to work hard on a route again. But doing so helps me process and grieve, which is what my lost climbing friends would want me to do. I know this is true because if anything ever happened to me, I would want them to continue to embrace who they are as climbers.

Perhaps my reasoning is better captured by French surrealist writer René Daumal: "You cannot stay on the summit forever; you have to come down again. So why bother in the first place? Just this: What is above knows what is below, but what is below does not know what is above. One climbs, one sees. One descends, one sees no longer, but one has seen. There is an art of conducting oneself in the lower regions by the memory of what one saw higher up. When one can no longer see, one can at least still know."

There are many things in life I can't understand, especially mortality. I think about Alex often and talk about him with friends and family. I try to imagine what his opinions might be about such things as modern climbing or politics. Like other friends I've lost, Alex still inspires me to be strong when I feel weak.

Nayser Brakk
(Photo by Doug Chabot)

CHAPTER 7

AFTER 9/11

KONDUS VALLEY, 2001

CHARAKUSA VALLEY: NAYSER BRAKK, KAPURA, AND

K7 WEST NORTHWEST RIDGE, 2004

fter the Gasherbrum IV expedition in 1999, I received permission to climb in Pakistan's Kondus valley in August 2001. The objective that year was to attempt Link Sar (7,041 meters, or 23,100 feet), which was unclimbed. We were unsuccessful in reaching that or any other summits, but I did a thorough reconnaissance of the valley. Immediately west of the Actual Ground Position Line (AGPL), the valley is usually closed to foreigners because it is sensitive militarily. Our base camp was located alongside the road that Pakistani soldiers traveled on their way toward Sia La, one of the major passes crossing the Siachen Glacier and a hot spot for the ongoing conflict with India. One afternoon, a group of soldiers stopped for tea. As they got up to leave I asked the soldiers what they were going to do next. "Soon we will go off to the front to become martyrs," one of them said. These young men were probably encouraged to feel this way by their fathers and male religious instructors. "Does your mother want you to be a martyr?" I asked. With some hesitation the soldier responded, "Probably not." I told him: "You should listen to your mother."

On that trip, I discovered several other unclimbed peaks with safe, appealing climbing routes that had solid-looking rock and ice. I planned an expedition to several of these objectives for 2002 or 2003, but shortly after returning home, the terror attacks of September 11, 2001 put these climbing plans on hold. Soon after, the United States retaliated against the Taliban, who were sheltering al-Qaeda in Afghanistan. Many of the Taliban and their allies, ironically, were the same forces the United States had called "freedom fighters" when they were battling the Soviets over a decade earlier.

The Bush administration gave the CIA the authority to launch Operation Enduring Freedom, and by the end of 2001 the Afghan Taliban were defeated. Most of the remaining Afghan Taliban, along with their al-Qaeda allies, retreated over the border into Pakistan, where they would regroup to fight another day. Several months later, militants (purportedly under the guidance of the Pakistan Inter-Services Intelligence—the ISI) attacked the Indian Parliament in New Delhi, which precipitated a military standoff and a massing of troops mostly along the Line of Control (LOC) in Kashmir. This brought the two countries to the brink of nuclear war. Before returning to Pakistan, I wanted to wait and see how the war in Afghanistan would affect security and, I hoped, a reduction of tensions between India and Pakistan.

After a few years, I felt it was safe to return to the Karakoram. The spillover into Pakistan from the ongoing war in Afghanistan seemed limited to the tribal areas along the Afghan border (on the other side of the country from where I climbed). The violence had not spread up into Baltistan, nor did it seem like it would. Tensions eased between India and Pakistan; in late 2003 they declared a cease-fire along the LOC and AGPL. But my friends and family expressed concerns for my safety. The 9/11 attacks had affected everyone deeply, and traveling anywhere remotely connected with the part of the world where the extremists originated was considered reckless.

Most of the people in Pakistan are peaceful Sunni Muslims, I explained. In the tribal areas along both sides of the Afghanistan-Pakistan border live the Pashtuns, an ethnic group of mostly conservative Sunni Muslims who make up about 15 percent of the Pakistani population and over 40 percent of the Afghan population. All of the Afghan Taliban are Pashtun Sunnis. Many of the Pakistani Pashtuns living in the Pakistan tribal areas along the Afghan border belong to violent militant groups. Farther east, in Gilgit-Baltistan, where the Karakoram mountains are located, the locals are mostly minority Shia Muslims who have been victims of sectarian violence mostly perpetrated by Pashtun Sunnis. These local Shia Muslims are peaceful and welcome foreigners because they benefit from tourism. They often feel a kinship with non-Muslim tourists like us who also feel threatened by these militant groups. Other climbers and trekkers gradually realized that these Shia Muslim areas are safe and learned to avoid or be careful traveling through areas populated by Pashtuns while on their way to Gilgit-Baltistan. Although the numbers of trekkers and climbers did not reach the pre-9/11 levels, the beauty and challenges of the Karakoram lured many of them back.

Security issues in Pakistan were not the only thing that had kept me away from the Karakoram. My responsibilities at work made it difficult to go on eight- to twelve-week climbing expeditions. I was engaged in some projects that were interesting, demanding, and lucrative. But I was feeling trapped. I needed to recruit someone who could maintain my practice when I was gone and help it to grow. I was willing to transition my position to a new manager if that was what it took to get the kind of person the firm wanted and needed. In 2003 my counterpart at a competing company agreed to join us. It was a good fit, and it set me free again.

My two sons were getting older and more independent. Lars had graduated from high school and was living on his own, so we didn't see him very much. Working part-time at a vintage clothing store provided the opportunity for him to become familiar with fashion and the fashion industry. A Seattle recruiting agent offered him a free trip to Paris to work as a runway model. There, Lars met designers who chose him for paid work that turned into international modeling assignments. He bounced between Paris, New York, Tokyo, and home in Seattle. Jed, almost a teenager, focused on soccer and golf and keeping up with his schoolwork. He was competitive but had an easygoing disposition that enabled him stay calm in demanding situations. He could sink a birdie putt on one hole, double bogey the next, and not change his demeanor. Driving Jed to his activities was a part-time job for Ann and me, but soon he would be able to drive himself. It wouldn't be long before Jed, like Lars, would be out of the house. By spending time away on summer expeditions, I missed out on his remaining time at home. As always, I struggled with balancing family and climbing.

I had recently turned fifty, and most of my climbing peers had retired. The majority of the active Himalayan climbers were young. I had been building relationships with them, but I knew these would be fleeting. In every sport, subsequent generations of athletes build on the accomplishments of their predecessors and do things no one has done before. For now, I had experience to offer, but my younger partners would gain this quickly and then push themselves to advance the sport further. The best I could do was train hard and remain strong so these new partnerships could last for a few more years.

In early 2004, I got a call from Steve House, whom I had attempted to climb Gasherbrum IV with in 1999. He was organizing a team for an expedition to the Charakusa valley in Pakistan that summer. I had been planning an expedition to the Kondus valley, but it had been closed again to foreigners, and it seemed unlikely that I would get a permit. "If your permit doesn't come through for the Kondus, you are welcome to join us," Steve said. "We already have a group of five strong climbers." Later that spring, my Kondus valley permit was denied. I was happy for the opportunity to join the Charakusa valley expedition. Our base camp would be only three days' walk from Rasool's village of Hushe, where many porters, cooks, and guides from my previous trips also lived. Eager to get back to the area, I wanted to see how my friends were doing, given the turmoil in the region.

Steve was thirty-four and since our Gasherbrum IV expedition together, he had become a certified mountain guide and one of America's leading alpinists. His "farm boy" mannerisms had evolved into something more serious. Absorbed by his own expectations that only the most brilliant and imaginative climber could satisfy, Steve had completed nonstop ascents of difficult routes on Denali and Mount Foraker in Alaska, attempted to summit the South Pillar of Nuptse in Nepal, and attempted to summit Masherbrum in Pakistan—all with partners. After leaving Masherbrum in 2003, he trekked with Rasool into the Charakusa valley and soloed a steep mixed rock and ice peak that he named Hajji Brakk (5,985 meters, or 19,636 feet) after Hajji Rasool, who had recently taken the pilgrimage to Mecca and was given this new title. He also made several solo attempts of various new routes on K7 Main (6,935 meters, or 22,752 feet). For this latest expedition, Steve hoped to complete a solo ascent of K7 Main.

The group he had assembled included Marko Prezelj, Doug Chabot, Jeff Hollenbaugh, and Bruce Miller. Each climber had an impressive résumé. I had either climbed with them in the past or knew them by reputation. Marko had attempted a new route on the south face of Nuptse in Nepal with Steve in 2002, the next year they were together again on the Masherbrum attempt, and the previous spring they climbed the north face of North Twin in the Canadian Rockies in winter conditions. From Slovenia, Marko was an experienced climber with several Himalayan first ascents. Thirty-eight years old, he had won a Piolet d'Or (the Oscar of world mountaineering) twelve years earlier for his alpine-style ascent of the southwest ridge of Kangchenjunga South (8,494 meters, or 27,867 feet). Part of the next generation of modern alpinists, Steve and Marko were fully committed to light and fast alpine-style climbing that bordered on a religious-like fervor. What it would be like to climb with this group?

I had met Doug, a forty-year-old avalanche forecaster from Bozeman, several times over the years. His infectious cheerfulness made me glad he was on the trip. Although we had never climbed anything significant together, we had both been close friends with Alex Lowe and served on the board of directors for the Alex Lowe Charitable Foundation (ALCF), a nonprofit established by Alex's family after he died to support community-based humanitarian programs in remote regions around the world. The organization's signature project is running a climbing school in the village of Phortse Nepal for Sherpas who work primarily on Mount Everest. I knew less about Jeff and Bruce, but Steve assured me they were climbers with the skills and disposition that would make them good team members. The youngest of the group, Jeff was thirty and had accompanied Steve on several big routes in Alaska in 2003. Bruce was forty-one, and he and Doug had climbed a difficult route on the North Buttress of Mount Hunter in Alaska together in 2001.

On June 13 the team arrived in Islamabad. At the guesthouse we met our liaison officer, Captain Amin, a Hazara from Quetta in the southern province of Balochistan. A minority Shia ethnic group, the Hazara mostly live in Afghanistan, where they are persecuted by the surrounding Pashtun Sunnis. Together with the other minority Tajiks and Uzbeks, the Hazara suffered terribly under Taliban rule in Afghanistan (these three groups made up nearly half the country's population). They comprised the Northern Alliance that defeated the Afghan Taliban in 2001 with help from the United States and were opposed to them returning to power, citing massacres of these ethnic groups during their regime.

We bought Western camping food at a store in Islamabad that imported groceries for expats. This significantly reduced the amount of food we had to ship from the United States; all we needed to bring were climbing food items like energy bars, high-quality cheese, hard salami (Muslims don't eat pork), meals ready to eat (MREs), and some freeze-dried dinners. After a couple of days of working and waiting in Islamabad, we flew to Skardu on June 16, where Rasool met us at the airport. Per our usual greeting, we threw our arms around each other, lifting each other up and down. It had been a long three years since our last meeting (I had visited with him on my Kondus valley reconnaissance trip in 2001), and we had a lot to catch up on. He wanted to know all about Ann and my sons, and I learned that his son, Fida Ali, was in a boarding school in Skardu. Fida Ali's schooling, along with that of the children of several of our other cooks and guides, was paid for by the Balti Education Fund, a small charity that Steve House had started shortly after our trip to Gasherbrum IV in 1999. I was one of about a half dozen climbers who chipped in to pay for an education that cost the equivalent of about $600 per year for each child.

When I asked Rasool how he and his family were doing, he confessed it had been tough to make a living since 9/11. The terrorist attacks had discouraged Westerners from traveling to the Muslim world, especially to Pakistan. Nazir Sabir, who we had first worked with in 1980, now had his own tour company, Nazir Sabir Expeditions, and he had told me that the number of climbing expeditions going to Pakistan was reduced by more than half, and the number of trekking groups by even more than that. Before 9/11, the wealthier villagers, like Rasool, who benefited most from employment in the tourism industry, had accumulated land, animals, and household goods. They had been able to pay for—or their clients supported—their children's education beyond what was available in the village.

The post-9/11 economic impact in places like Baltistan varied and was more severe in towns and villages close to popular trekking and climbing destinations that were highly dependent on tourism. Those villages were usually at higher elevations with a shorter growing season, causing them to be the least able to make up for lost tourism income with increased agricultural production. With decreased income, villagers were able to just get by, selling land or animals, using any savings they might have, eating less chicken and mutton and more lentils and rice, and deferring purchases of clothes, household items, and anything they didn't absolutely need. Some villagers were forced to cut back on their children's education expenses.

The poorer members of the village who didn't own assets to fall back on had to rely on *zakat*, the Islamic system of tithing. Islam dictates that those who can afford it must donate 2.5 percent of their wealth toward charity each year. In villages like Hushe, the elders get together and identify the needy families. The elders work with the families that can afford *zakat* and determine how it will be distributed to those that need it. According to the locals, this system prevents anyone from starving and eliminates embarrassment to their village if anyone were forced to beg. I never saw anyone begging in Skardu, although it's quite different in larger cities like Islamabad or Rawalpindi.

On June 18 we drove to Hushe and packed the seventy loads that would be carried by our porters to base camp. The next day we walked to Shaisto, and I dropped back to keep Captain Amin company and make sure he didn't get lost. While we hiked, Amin told me more about his family background. The situation for the Hazara in Quetta was better than in Afghanistan, he explained. Amin's community was well integrated into the Sunni-majority province, and his late father had also been an army officer. His two sisters were medical doctors, and his mother had moved to Islamabad. But the Hazara in Quetta were now at greater risk because the Taliban leadership moved there after they were kicked out of Afghanistan. Militancy was on the rise there in Balochistan and throughout the tribal areas. Increasing numbers of Hazara were being targeted by Sunni militant sectarian groups. I liked Amin's easy-going nature; he didn't act superior or expect Rasool to wait on him like many of the liaison officers I had worked with. Maybe his background as a Hazara had caused him to be less prone to treat other minority groups, like the Baltis, as servants.

Three days later, we arrived at base camp in a beautiful alpine meadow with a stream running through it. Camping on real ground covered with grass and wildflowers is much more pleasant than the base camps we often had on rock-covered glaciers. This time we wouldn't have to camp on the cold ice, which requires a lot of work to keep moving our tents when the ice surrounding them slowly melts, leaving them draped over several-foot-high mounds of ice.

After paying off our porters, the six of us (Steve, Marko, Doug, Bruce, Jeff, and I) started our acclimatization routine by hiking up the surrounding hills. I wasn't getting left behind, and my concerns about being ten to twenty years older than everyone else subsided. I enjoyed each moment more than ever before. I wondered how the trip would play out. Our group would share a base camp, but given our lightweight style of climbing, we would work in smaller groups of two or maybe three, pursuing a number of different objectives over the next five weeks. It wasn't clear how the team arrangements would be worked out for the peaks we wanted to climb. In the Charakusa valley we had permits for the unclimbed 6,544-meter Kapura Peak (21,469 feet) and 7,040-meter K6 West (23,097 feet). We also had permission for 6,935-meter K7 Main (22,752 feet), which had already been climbed. In addition, our permits allowed us to climb any peak under 6,500 meters (21,325 feet), and there were plenty in the area. I hoped all six of us would have a chance to get to the top of several peaks.

This was my first expedition where we owned a working handheld satellite telephone. On a couple of previous trips we had satellite phones, but they were very expensive and bulky, or they broke down. For the first time while on an expedition, I called Lars on his birthday, on June 25. It was a joy to connect with him in real time, to find out what he was doing, to wish him a happy day, and to tell him that I loved him. His voice sounded so clear it belied the reality that we were half a world apart.

A lot of new snow had fallen on the higher peaks during our first week at base camp, so we decided to do some lower rock climbs until conditions stabilized on Kapura Peak, our first big objective. On June 28, Doug and I climbed the original route on 5,200-meter Nayser Brakk (17,060 feet), a beautiful granite pyramid. Two days later, Bruce and Jeff woke up with fevers of 101°F, and Doug was suffering from a bad stomach problem he had developed on our climb. Steve and Marko wanted to do a new route on Nayser Brakk up a spectacular rock buttress that faced base camp. Since I was the last man standing, they invited me to join them. Going along was an intimidating prospect: these two guys comprise one of the most accomplished climbing teams in the world. As it turned out, I had a great day.

Initially I had trouble keeping up on a long gully approach to the start of the route. As we soloed a couple of short but steep rock steps, I reminded myself to be comfortable at my own pace and climb carefully. Once we started the buttress, I carried most of the gear while Steve and Marko alternated leading. After four pitches I asked if I could lead. Steve said, "You better speak up if you want anything here." It was an offhand remark about our teammate, suggesting that if I wanted something from Marko I needed to be more direct. After that the three of us swung leads for the rest of the climb. We topped out at the summit after ten pitches of great rock climbing with a spectacular finish climbing up steep but easy chicken head–like nobs of granite.

On the descent Marko wanted to downclimb the ridge unroped, which Doug and I had ascended two days ago. I didn't feel comfortable without the rope; even though it was easy, the ridge fell off at least a thousand feet on both sides. Steve helped me convince Marko to tie into one of our ropes with hundred-foot lengths between us clipped to occasional rock anchors along the way. After downclimbing the ridge, we made a few rappels to the gully we had come up. Marko ran ahead after we put away the ropes. Steve stayed with me on the several short steps of rock we soloed on the way up. As we worked our way down the gully, Steve said, "I've been trying to get Marko to go along with what the group wanted to do to be safe all day." I thanked Steve for waiting for me. "No need to thank me," he replied. "Staying together is the right way to do it." Steve had this ongoing frustration with Marko, but they had a kind of extrasensory perception between them about what to do in difficult situations. Like Steve, Marko had a singular focus when climbing that enabled him to accomplish some amazing feats, but he seemed unaware of how oblivious and unsympathetic he could be in the process.

Hanging around at base camp the next day we commented on the beautiful wildflowers blooming in our meadow. Alpine wildflowers look like lowland flowers, but they are miniaturized, with sturdy, tiny blooms. Their purple, blue, yellow, and red colors lit up the meadow for only a few weeks before they withered. We picked a few of these blossoms and pressed them into our journals. Marko photographed them. Doug dropped a few into the aerogram he was mailing his wife, and Bruce and I decided to do the same. I made a bet with the group that I would be able to convince Marko to also do this. I knew I would lose, but the process of trying to convince him of this sentimental nicety made it worthwhile. Marko fostered a gruff, no-nonsense persona, and prodding him about sending little flowers to his wife was one of many opportunities to tease him about how to be a more sensitive guy.

That evening at dinner, the Americans among us discussed relationships with the opposite sex. Isolated in this beautiful environment, so far from home where we come to rely on each other for our very lives, my climbing partners and I often share confidences that we wouldn't necessarily disclose in day-to-day conversations back home. I paused and turned to Marko. "Please pass the salt," I said, and suddenly he jumped up out of his chair with a fierce expression on his face. "Enough of this tasty talking," he shouted with his Slovenian accent. "If you want the salt, just tell me to pass the fucking salt!" We all erupted in laughter, including Marko, who saw the humor. After that, we named the new route we had climbed the day before on Nayser Brakk, "No Tasty Talking."

Steve, Doug, and I had planned to climb Kapura together, so we headed out on July 2, after there had been enough good weather to stabilize snow conditions. Bruce and Jeff were showing signs that they were well enough to climb again, but we weren't sure what they and Marko might do next. Early that afternoon Steve, Doug, and I set up camp on a moraine overlooking the South Charakusa Glacier. We thought the climb would take two days from there, so we brought enough equipment and supplies for one bivouac on the mountain. Before dinner, we walked out onto this expanse of snow and made our way around several crevasses to do a reconnaissance of our planned route. Above us, on Kapura, a snow- and icefield on the south face connected to a narrow snow ramp climbing leftward to the west ridge atop a huge rock wall. We imagined the west ridge would take us to the summit.

We left the moraine at 5:30 a.m. the next day. Steve led the way up the increasingly steeper snow- and icefield, then Doug took over when we got to the ramp. The climbing was not difficult, but it was very exposed. For these guys "light and fast" meant we didn't rope up on this terrain. I lagged a bit behind, because I wanted to go slowly and carefully—a slip would have been fatal. On past expeditions, with other climbers, I probably would have roped up for this. To be safe, I adjusted to the mental strain of having to be 100 percent sure of every crampon and ice axe placement. It took some time, but soon thirty-six years of muscle memory kicked in and I began moving more quickly and confidently. After reaching a broad snow slope on the ridge, we roped up. I led, placing an occasional ice screw so we had some protection as we moved together. Above a small ice cliff, Steve took over kicking steps in calf-deep snow to a flat spot in the ridge at around 6,000 meters (19,685 feet), where we built a snow platform for our small tent. Doug melted snow for water to make soup, tea, and food.

From what we could see from our bivouac, the route above—a steep rock ridge mixed with sections of snow and ice—looked more difficult. Perhaps we would be able to go around the ridge to the left, onto the north face where it might be easier. It had snowed off and on all day, and since we arrived at our bivouac we'd had limited visibility. For a short period at sunset, however, the skies cleared and we had views of K2, Masherbrum, Chogolisa, and Gasherbrum I (a.k.a. Hidden Peak). After snapping a few photos, we tucked into our little perch for the night. I slept poorly, maybe because of the altitude or because of being anxious about the weather, the route, and getting down safely.

Starting again at 5:30 a.m., Doug and Steve alternated leading up the first couple of difficult, poorly protected pitches of thin snow over bad rock. Then it was my turn. Everyone hoped that this pitch would take us up onto an easier snow ridge that led to a short, steep snow and ice headwall below the summit. I hadn't been climbing as much as my partners, so I was slower on these technical bits where efficiency comes with practice. I climbed up easy snow to where we might be able to escape around to the left. Above me was a steep rock step, where I placed a piton in a crack and then hooked it with my axe. Leaning around the corner, I hoped that dropping left onto the north face would bypass the difficulties above.

Going that way looked like a nightmare of delicate ice flutings, so I was forced to climb directly up lousy rock that I cleared of snow as I went. Hooking with my ice tools on delicate, small rock edges was scary. I was tempted to lower down and let Steve or Doug take the lead, but I wanted to contribute something, so I proceeded to climb into the unknown with my rock protection far below, making a fall unthinkable. Fortunately I came to some firm ice where I got a solid stick with my ice tools and climbed up to where I could get my feet on the ice as well. From there it was easy ice climbing and after another 50 feet I placed two ice screws for an anchor and belayed (pulled up the ropes tied to Doug and Steve) them up to me.

Doug took over and we got onto the ridge proper. We continued to swing leads, and by the time we traversed to the base of the final summit headwall, it was 2:00 p.m. Steve had figured we should turn around at 2:30 p.m. to allow enough time to get back to the tent before dark. He was the quickest, so he led two pitches to where we were up against a final compact vertical snow wall. We agreed to keep going, even though it was now past 3:00 p.m. Steve led again up the wall for thirty feet and found he was on top! Doug and I shouted with excitement, "Good work, Steve!" Soon we were on top as well.

We had no time to waste if we didn't want to be caught by the dark, but with only deep unconsolidated snow all around, we couldn't build an anchor strong enough for rappelling. Steve suggested that we pack down a bollard (a large mound of snow to wrap the rope around), and Doug and I thought that making it about four feet in diameter to spread the load might work. Doug said he would rappel first, but to be safe Steve used his body as a back-up anchor by clipping a sling attached to his harness onto the rope on the side of the bollard opposite Doug. Steve backed down the slope to put some tension on the rope, and Doug started rappelling. The rope sliced through the bollard instantly, and Steve was suddenly pulled forward several inches as Doug's weight came onto Steve's harness.

The two of them agreed that Doug should go ahead and continue the short thirty-foot rappel anchored to Steve, since he was effectively holding Doug's weight anyway. Doug slid down the ropes to the base of the vertical snow wall, where it was solid enough to drive in a couple of big snow stakes, or pickets, for an anchor. I joined him soon after. Doug and I pulled in all the rope with the upper end tied to Steve. I fed the rope through my belay device as Steve downclimbed the vertical and insecure snow to our stance. Of the three of us, Steve was the most qualified to perform this scary task, and we were counting on him not to slip. The pickets we had for our anchor were probably strong enough to hold more than our body weight when rappelling, but they might not hold the much greater force of a long fall. Several more rappels to the ridge traverse followed by a few more rappels brought us back to the tent just before dark.

There, we were surprised but pleased to find Marko, Bruce, and Jeff crammed into a two-person bivouac tent. They gave us some water. Steve, our hero of the day, performed cooking duties inside our tent, while outside I collected ice for melting and arranged gear for our descent in the morning. We finished up a long day at 9:30 p.m. after the first ascent of Kapura on the 4th of July—our American Independence Day!

In the morning the weather was poor, but Marko wanted to go up and Bruce went with him. Jeff decided to go down with Steve, Doug, and me. We got lost in the clouds trying to find the top of the ramp that we needed to traverse to get to the steep snow- and icefield on the south face. We all walked by it except Doug, who was in the rear and noticed some faint tracks in the windblown snow going in the correct direction. We unroped at the top of the ramp because there was no possibility of placing intermediate anchors in the snow to protect us. No one would be able to stop a fall if someone slipped. Once we reached the top of the snow- and icefield, we rappelled down the ice to where the angle was low enough to back down and walk the rest of the way to the glacier.

I felt lucky to have had another great mountain adventure and particularly happy to be there with such an experienced and accommodating team. We reached base camp around 4:00 p.m., where Rasool and Captain Amin embraced us and shook our hands to celebrate our ascent. This was followed by a great meal and a toast, and we all went to bed hoping that Bruce and Marko would have a successful climb and return safely the next day. In fact, Marko returned to base camp sometime that night. He and Bruce had reached the summit by noon, but they hadn't bivouacked another night up high like we did. They came all the way down to the glacier, and Bruce had spent the night at the camp on the moraine. He wandered in to base camp around 9:00 a.m. Their quick ascent was a good example of how "light and fast" can be safer. It rained and snowed heavily the night after we reached base camp, and Bruce and Marko were already down before much snow had a chance to accumulate and create dangerous avalanche conditions.

That day, I called Ann on the sat phone and learned that Lars and Jed were fine. Unfortunately she had dislocated her shoulder again, which had happened several times since she had injured it skiing. She was able to reduce it herself right away but she was concerned she might need to have surgery to repair the damage after I returned home. Jed was playing well in soccer, scoring all his team's goals in their league tournament. Lars had just returned from some modeling work in Paris. He enjoyed the international travel associated with his modeling gigs, but he was getting older and seemed ready to try something new. I wondered what he would do next. I spoke to Jed for a few minutes and told him that a small field mouse had gotten into my duffle bag. I had put the mouse back outside, but not before it had eaten the waistband on a pair of underwear and the laces on my rock climbing shoes. Jed thought that was pretty funny.

We had a couple of weeks of bad weather, and by mid-July Steve was tired of waiting. He made a solo attempt on K7 Main in weather that was stormy enough to keep the rest of us at base camp. We expected him back in two days, and we worried when he hadn't returned by the end of the second day. Steve showed up the next morning, telling us he hadn't quite reached the top because of a rock tower that had blocked the ridge near the summit. Getting around it would require more than the few pieces of rock climbing equipment he had brought with him. He wasted time trying to find a different way and eventually climbed the tower without much gear. By then it was too late in the day to reach the summit, however, so he turned around when he was close, maybe three hundred feet, from the top.

That afternoon, Mohammed Khan, Rasool's brother, hiked up to base camp from Hushe with some Australian trekkers. He had an animated conversation in Balti with Rasool, after which Rasool explained to us that their father had fallen off the roof of the house and hurt his upper leg or maybe his hip. He needed to be taken to Skardu for an X-ray, so Rasool left right away to tend to that. Mohammed Khan stayed at base camp to cook for us and the Australians, who planned to stay in the Charakusa valley for five days. Rasool said he would return before the Australians left. I couldn't help worrying about Rasool's father. It sounded like a serious injury, and the old man could die waiting for proper medical attention. Enduring the rough eight-hour jeep ride on the bad roads from Hushe to Skardu would be hard on him.

Another week of poor weather went by, and we had only one more week of climbing before our porters were scheduled to pick us up on August 1. Once we returned to Skardu, all of us except for Marko planned to travel about ninety miles to the south side of Nanga Parbat, the ninth highest mountain in the world at 8,126 meters (26,660 feet), which we had a permit to climb. We needed to reach Nanga Parbat soon: in about a month the summer would be over and the weather would become bitterly cold high on the mountain.

Everyone was healthy, and Doug and Bruce had decided to try an alpine-style ascent of the original Japanese route on K7 Main. Steve said he was going to make another solo attempt on his new route on K7 Main. That left Jeff, Marko, and me to pick an objective. Jeff and I had been looking at the unclimbed 6,858-meter K7 West (22,500 feet). K7 West is a subsidiary peak in the K7 massif, and our LO allowed us to make an attempt on it because we had a permit for K7 Main, the highest peak in the group. Marko had wanted to do a route on the west side of the same peak, but Jeff and I thought the lower part of his suggested line was dangerously close to a small glacial ice cliff that could drop big chunks of ice down the wall. Jeff and I proposed that the three of us instead climb the northwest ridge, which seemed free from any objective hazards. Marko wasn't enthused about it, but he agreed.

On July 24 the weather finally improved, and there was not a cloud in the sky. Early that morning Doug and Bruce left for their route on K7 Main, and Jeff, Marko, and I left for the northwest ridge of K7 West. Steve House was going to leave for K7 Main later that day. Jeff, Marko, and I spent half the day getting to the base of a 2,500-foot-steep snow and rock face that we needed to climb to reach the ridge crest. Shady and cold in the morning, it faced west but was exposed to the sun in the afternoon. When we arrived at almost noon, the rock face was still in the shade.

Marko wanted to continue climbing up onto the face right away. I strongly opposed going on the route this late in the day. After a couple of weeks of bad weather the face was full of snow that would start to avalanche as soon as the sun came around and warmed it up. Marko was unhappy but acquiesced, and the three of us set up our tent on a small col at the head of the nearby glacier where we could wait out the heat of the day. Marko might have been able to climb fast enough to get above the danger before the sun hit the face, but our team had made the right choice. Within a couple of hours we sat by our tent at the head of the glacier watching avalanches and running water pour down the face.

The next morning we left the col by 5:00 a.m. The face was divided into three major rock bands separated by two snow- and icefields. It looked like we could climb through the first two rock bands on thin ice runnels. We couldn't see the third rock band well enough from below, so we would have

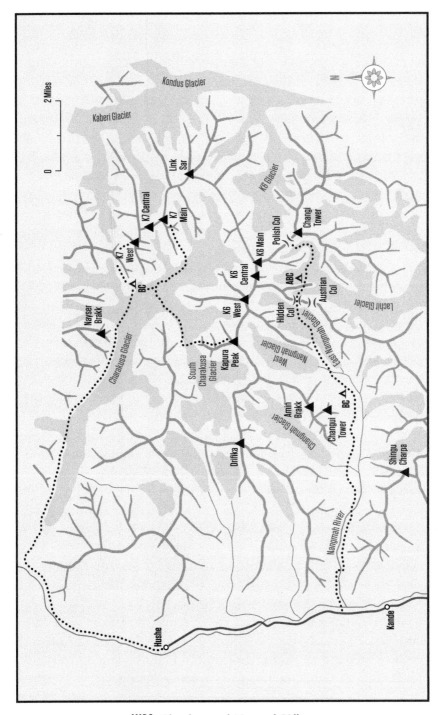

MAP 3: *Charakusa and Nangmah Valleys*

to figure that out when we got there. In the dark we soloed the first runnel, which was pretty solid ice. The next runnel had been running with water the previous afternoon, and it had frozen during the night into vertical, soft, rotten ice. Marko led it safely, and I was impressed with his composure given how insecure it was. Ice screws have no holding power in soft, hollow ice, so there was nothing to keep him from taking a huge fall if his tools didn't stick in the barely frozen water. I wouldn't have been willing to go first and belay up the rest of the team.

With the rope tied between us clipped to intermediate anchors, the three of us climbed together to the second rock band, where I led up an ice gully through the first section. Then Jeff took over and led us through a short rock section that put us onto the second icefield. We climbed together to the bottom of the final rock section that led onto the ridge. This section of rock was a lot steeper, and we again counted on Marko to get us up two very difficult rope lengths of mixed ice and rock. We didn't think anyone else had attempted this route, so we were surprised to find old ropes, bolts, and cable ladders from a previous expedition. It's common to find old gear on mountains or routes that, according to available information, are unclimbed; we figured they were relics from a previous failed attempt. (Later research showed these artifacts were probably from a Japanese attempt on the peak in 1977.) Marko led on the last pitch to the ridge, which consisted of a steep rock slab covered by new snow that had to be cleared so we could climb on the more solid granite underneath.

When climbing at home, it's usual protocol to share the leading responsibilities with your partners. That way, everyone has a chance to work on the technical skills and mental fortitude it takes to put the rope up first. It's easier and less intimidating for everyone who follows the leader, because they can climb with a rope from above to protect them. But on expeditions to difficult peaks in remote places, the primary objective is to get the team to the top—equal opportunity leading is less important. For the kind of technical mixed rock and ice climbing we did, Marko was the most skilled, followed by Jeff, so on the difficult sections it was more efficient for them to share the leading. Unless it was easier terrain that I could lead quickly, I contributed by carrying supplies and equipment behind them.

Once we got to the snow ridge where the difficulties eased, I alternated leading with Jeff up through deeper snow to a flat, narrow section of the ridge. There we dug a platform for the tent. As the day ended, Marko reminded Jeff and me that he wasn't excited about this route. I couldn't tell if that meant he wasn't excited about being with us or if he didn't like the climbing. I probably should have tried to find out what was bothering him. His clear lack of enthusiasm was taking the fun out of our effort and an attempt to address his concerns might have improved the team dynamic. Climbers all have their quirks. For all of Markos's insensitivity while he was on the mountain, he was more aware of the people around him when he wasn't climbing. Later, he would remember my birthday and send photographs or a Christmas gift—things that most of my climbing friends never do. The weather on the mountain had been perfect all day, and that evening we had great views of the sun setting on K2, Chogolisa, Gasherbrum I, Gasherbrum II, Gasherbrum IV, Masherbrum, and the other major peaks in the Karakoram. The idyllic setting helped me put aside the team's problems for the moment and enjoy being in such a spectacular place.

In the morning, Jeff led us over the final rock tower on the ridge, which put us on easier snow slopes leading to the summit. I took over and kicked steps for a couple of rope lengths before I belayed up Marko and Jeff. They climbed up to me in what I thought were pretty typical knee-deep Himalayan snow conditions, but Marko continued to complain—and now Jeff joined in—about how bad the choice of route was. Jeff went ahead for about a thousand feet until he encountered waist-deep snow that almost brought us to a halt. We were concerned about the snow, which had become so deep and unconsolidated that there was serious risk we might trigger an avalanche. After fifty or sixty feet of the stuff, Jeff stopped and Marko went up to where he had dug a hole in the snow to try to reach a more solid layer of snow or ice to anchor himself. Marko tried another thirty feet before he said he wasn't interested in going farther. He started toward me so I could give it a try.

In the meantime I had dug a small hole and drove both my ice tools and a picket deep into the snow. I used some slings to equalize them for an anchor that I hoped could hold us if the snow layer above slid off. I took off my pack and put it in the hole on my right. As Marko approached me, he triggered an eighteen-inch-thick avalanche slab that cut fifty to sixty feet across the slope immediately on our right. As the avalanche slid by just twelve inches to my right, it took my pack with it. Jeff held Marko with the rope that stopped him where the avalanche fractured across the slope. Given this patch of obviously unsafe snow, we turned back. We down-climbed to the top of the rock pitch that Jeff had led us up earlier, then rappelled back to the tent by 1:00 p.m.

At this point we had little fuel, but enough for the night and morning. Marko wanted to continue down to the col where we had spent our first night. But that meant we would be rappelling the west side of the ridge during the heat of the day, when rock, snow, and water would be running and falling down the face. Tired of arguing, I said I would go along with whatever he and Jeff decided, which was to go down. By the time we reached the top of the face, the sun had not completely come around and it was not that hot yet, but as we moved down the face, I became more concerned about falling rocks and ice.

Below the second rock band it was hot. We would not be able to rappel the way we had come up because that runnel had turned into a full-fledged stream of running water and falling rock. Jeff and Marko suggested we dash across this zone and traverse to where we could rappel down the wall just above our previous camp. It was risky, but it was our best option. We all got across a few moments before a large rockfall swept by. After a few more rappels, we arrived at our camp just at dark. We had cached extra fuel and food there, but we were surprised to find our one remaining fuel canister had exploded, probably from sitting in the intense heat. We had just enough fuel to make some soup and instant potatoes that night and a cup of tea the next morning.

When we got up, the wall above was frozen again, and Marko and I walked out onto the glacier below the face to look for my pack. Amazingly, it hadn't been buried in the avalanche—we found everything strewn around in the snow. We arrived back at base camp just before lunch and found Steve House there. He reached the summit of K7 Main this time in an incredible forty-hour nonstop push.

The next day, on July 28, Doug and Bruce returned after making the first alpine-style ascent of the Japanese route on K7 Main. Everyone was safely back in base camp. Thrilled that the other two teams had been successful, I wished we could have reached the top of K7 West too. I felt all right about the outcome for myself, especially given our close encounter with the avalanche, but I was concerned that Jeff might be feeling discouraged about the expedition. Due to illness, bad timing, and inexperience in a big mountain environment, Jeff hadn't gotten to the top of anything on this trip. I never found the right time to have a private conversation with him to tell him not to feel disheartened; it had taken me almost ten years of trying before getting to the top of anything in the Great Ranges.

Now that I was older and had reached several major summits, not reaching the top of a peak didn't bother me so much. Having fun with my partners and encouraging each other was as important to me as the climbing. The lack of camaraderie on our K7 West attempt had made me feel empty, though. It made me question my decision to go with Steve, Bruce, Doug, and Jeff to Nanga Parbat. (Marko was not able to go on the next phase of the expedition.) No matter how much I love the climbing, a specific combination of various elements has to fall into place for me to stay motivated to throw myself at big, dangerous, difficult mountains over and over. These include route safety, health, fitness, adequate rest, and nutrition, but—most important—a relationship with my partners based on mutual trust and caring. I was awake most of the night wondering whether our teamwork would improve on Nanga Parbat. Could I contribute anything useful to the team?

I approached Doug and Bruce that morning about my misgivings. Shocked that I even considered leaving, Doug said, "You have to come! One of the main reasons I agreed to go to Nanga Parbat was because you were going!" I was flattered but unsure if Steve felt the same way. When I approached him later, he gave me a similar pep talk. Contrary to the relationship I had with my partners on K7 West, I'd known Doug and Steve for a long time. I was reminded of the strong partnerships we had forged over the years. This was a good group for me to be with, and I looked forward to the next part of the trip.

The team hiked out from base camp and reached Hushe (and Rasool) on August 2. Rasool's father had broken his femur when he fell off the roof, but Rasool had not taken him all the way to Skardu. Instead, an orthopedic doctor in Khaplu took an X-ray and did an examination. The doctor recommended surgery, which Rasool declined, probably because of cost. I doubted if it would have been very expensive, and the climbers in our group could have easily covered it. But without one of us there to offer that option, Rasool had decided to have what the villagers call a "local doctor" set the bone. With no formal training, this "doctor" had some medical skills handed down from one generation to the next.

Steve and I agreed it was not a good idea to take Rasool with us to Nanga Parbat. His father was still recovering, and it was unclear if the local doctor had successfully repaired the leg. Since I had known Rasool and his family for a long time, Steve suggested that I have a talk with them after lunch. Captain Amin, our liaison officer, would come along to translate for those who didn't speak English. We were served a great lunch of French fries, fried chicken, soup, and pudding. Amin and I went to Rasool's home, where his father was recuperating. As soon as we walked in the door, everyone started crying. Rasool's father thought he was going to die. Rasool said his father needed help with things like going to the bathroom, and it was better to have a man—preferably his son—do that. They showed me the X-ray of his leg, which clearly showed a broken and displaced femur. I was amazed he was still alive. Eventually I realized that all of the weeping was about Rasool wanting to stay home with his father instead of coming to cook for us at Nanga Parbat.

I told Rasool that it was important for him to do what was best for his family and that I completely understood his desire to stay home because I have a family too. Then Rasool started crying all over again and said he was ashamed for not going with us. I didn't want him to have to choose between caring for his father and working for us, so I told him I would pay him for the time that he would otherwise be with us on Nanga Parbat. He and his wife, Bedruma, were very thankful. All we needed to do was find another cook. Fida Hussein, who had cooked for us on K2 in 1987 and 1990, was available and could come with us. That made Rasool happy because he knew Fida would do a good job. Rasool insisted on accompanying us for a couple of days on the jeep ride to Nanga Parbat, after which he would return to Hushe.

Our expedition left Hushe and arrived at the tourist hotel in Khaplu just before dark. The hotel had clean rooms, hot showers, fresh sheets and towels—the simple things we take for granted at home but seem so luxurious after doing without them in the mountains for over six weeks. While waiting for dinner, Steve told me that Jeff had decided to go home. In addition to an unsuccessful climbing trip, Jeff faced issues at home that he couldn't ignore for another month. I certainly understood. I had grown to truly appreciate how Ann made an effort to resolve—or at least postpone—any issues between us before I went away on trips. "We will be fine," she said. "Have fun, focus on what you are doing, and we can talk about it after you come home. Always remember how much we love you." I really liked Jeff, and I wished I could say, "Come with us to Nanga Parbat. You will learn a lot, and going home may not make a difference in the long run anyway." But it was knowledge he'd have to gain for himself.

As we left Khaplu the next morning, Rasool and Fida, perched on top of our loads in the back of our jeep, looked homeward with expressions of concern. We had been through a lot together, and they were very loyal to us. When I asked them about our journey, Fida replied, "Where we are going, these are very bad men." It hadn't occurred to me that we were asking them to travel from Baltistan, where they felt comfortable among their fellow Shiite Muslims, to an area that is mixed but populated mainly by Sunni Muslim tribesmen. They were probably afraid. At the time I didn't take Fida's comment too seriously; I thought he and Rasool were just reluctant to go very far from home.

Nanga Parbat is farther to the southeast and closer to the tribal areas adjacent to Afghanistan. The Afghan Taliban and al-Qaeda exiles that had been allowed by Pakistan to settle just over the border created a dangerous security situation in the Federally Administered Tribal Areas (referred to as FATA), parts of Khyber Pakhtunkhwa (KPK, formerly the Northwest Frontier Province), and parts of Balochistan. Impoverished and underserved by the Pakistan government, these areas were governed by an antiquated system of tribal law. The economic and social problems in the tribal areas created an opening for the newly arrived Afghan Taliban and al-Qaeda militants to recruit disenfranchised local tribesmen while they brutally attacked the existing system of tribal rulers. The fundamentalist system of Islamic law preached to these tribesmen by these outsiders was an appealing alternative to the status quo. These converted tribesmen created another source of foot soldiers, known as the Pakistan Taliban, who were willing to support the global Islamic Jihad alongside their new neighbors and fight their own government to implement Sharia Law.

All three militant groups—the Afghan Taliban, al-Qaeda, and the Pakistan Taliban—had a similar ideology with overlapping agendas, and by 2004 they controlled most of the Pakistan province of FATA, parts of KPK, and Balochistan. After 9/11 the ISI and Pakistan Army had been rounding up al-Qaeda members in these provinces to show the United States they were helping fight the War on Terror and thereby maintain the recent surge of American funding for this supposed purpose. This caused tensions with the Pakistan Taliban, who began to attack the Pakistan military—composed mostly of Punjabis—whom they viewed as an invaders. Although they were fighting al-Qaeda and now the Pakistan Taliban, the Pakistan government security forces continued to support the Afghan Taliban. They viewed the Afghan Taliban battling the United States– and NATO-backed government in Afghanistan as an important proxy force that enabled them to influence the political process there and provide "strategic depth" on their western border by helping to keep India out.

This policy of supporting what the Pakistan security forces considered "good Taliban" while fighting the groups they viewed as "bad Taliban" defied logic, given the close ties among all of these militant groups. Pakistan's support of the Afghan Taliban seemed at cross-purposes to their proclaimed support for the War on Terror and their efforts to quell the violent activities of the Pakistan Taliban, who were trying to start a civil war. General Musharraf discovered that playing this double game was dangerous; in 2003 tribal militants made two attempts to assassinate him. As our team drove west, we didn't realize that the process of local tribesmen becoming influenced by the militant form of Islam that had taken hold in FATA and parts of KPK was slowly working its way eastward toward Nanga Parbat.

Crossing a river on the
Deosai Plain headed to
Nanga Parbat

CHAPTER 8

THE KILLER MOUNTAIN

NANGA PARBAT MAZENO RIDGE, 2004

ugust 3 was Steve House's birthday. After the six of us—Steve, Doug Chabot, Bruce Miller, Marko Prezelj, Jeff Hollenbaugh, and I—arrived at the Indus Hotel in Skardu, Doug led us on a hunt around town until we found a cheap, eight-inch-tall, gold-painted plastic trophy. With his most careful lettering, Doug used a Sharpie to print on the base, "Congratulations on Your Solo Ascent of K7!" All of us signed the cup and presented it to Steve at his birthday dinner at the Masherbrum Hotel. Steve's farm boy mannerisms that had been so dominant when I first met him came to the fore as he accepted his celebratory gift. Sheepishly bowing his head, he muttered a thank you.

Leaving our beautiful mountain existence in the Charakusa valley ramped up Marko and Jeff's desire to get home. The weather had been cloudy since we had arrived in Skardu, and flights to Islamabad had been cancelled for days. Marko and Jeff hired a vehicle the next day and left by road. Over the subsequent years I've lost track of Jeff, but I cross paths or hear about Marko regularly. He continues to climb hard and has become an active mentor for young Slovenian alpinists. I have run into his protégés in places like Patagonia; they tell me he still likes to be a hard man but that he has mellowed considerably. I send messages to Marko via these climbers asking if he is still learning to be a sensitive guy. His joking response to me is usually, "Fuck you!"

Steve, Bruce, Doug, and I were looking forward to Nanga Parbat. We spent three more days in Skardu recovering from the rigors of the Charakusa—eating, resting, and provisioning. After our six weeks in the high mountains, we were healthy, acclimatized, and able to move efficiently over difficult terrain. I felt lucky to be a part of this happy crew. The common objective fueled a spirit among us that had me feeling optimistic that we would accomplish something special.

The ninth highest mountain in the world, Nanga Parbat (8,126 meters, or 26,660 feet) is a solitary sprawling massif standing well to the south of Karakoram giants like K2. It is the first major peak in Pakistan to be hit with storms blowing up from the Indian Ocean, and this precipitation deposits thick blankets of snow that feed its massive glaciers and cause spectacular avalanches. Not technically part of the Karakoram Range since it is south of the Indus River, Nanga Parbat instead sits at the western terminus of the Himalayan Range. From Nanga Parbat the Himalayas extend 1500 miles to the east across northern India, Nepal, Bhutan, and into eastern Tibet. The range terminates at Namche Barawa, the mountain that sits above the great bend of the Tsangpo River that has carved a deep gorge through the range. The first attempt to climb Nanga Parbat was made in 1895 by a British mountaineer Albert Mummery. Then the mountain captured the attention of German climbers, who made five pre–World War II expeditions. None of those expeditions was successful, however, and the attempts resulted in twenty-six deaths, earning Nanga Parbat the nickname "the killer mountain."

The first successful ascent of Nanga Parbat was in 1953 by the Austrian Hermann Buhl as part of a German-Austrian team. They followed the route used by previous attempts from Fairy Meadows up the Rakhiot Flank above the Rakhiot Glacier to the east ridge. In 1962 the second ascent of Nanga Parbat was made from the Diamir valley on the north side of the mountain by Germans Toni Kinshofer, Siegfried Löw, and Anderl Mannhardt. The Kinshofer Route on the Diamir Face above the Diamir Glacier has become the popular route on the mountain.

The huge Rupal Face on the south side of Nanga Parbat is the world's highest mountain face and rises over 15,000 feet (almost 4,600 meters) above the valley. In 1970 the third ascent of the mountain was made by brothers Günther and Reinhold Messner as part of another large, German-led expedition that ascended a steep and difficult line on the left side of this face. Thinking it was too difficult to descend the way they had come up, Günther and Reinhold went down the Diamir side of the mountain, west of the Kinshofer Route. Sadly Günther was killed in an avalanche before they reached the safety of the valley. The fourth overall ascent of the peak (and only other ascent of the original route, because of its length and danger from avalanches), was by two Slovaks in 1971. In 1976 the Austrians Hans Schell, Robert Schauer, Hilmar Sturm, and Siegfried Gimpel made the fifth ascent of the mountain via the southwest ridge from the Rupal valley to the west of the Messner Route, which became known as the Schell Route.

Our plan was to establish a base camp in the Rupal valley. Steve had been planning to climb a new route on the direct southeast face of the Rupal Face to the east of the Messner Route. It was an audacious goal to attempt an alpine-style ascent of the most difficult route on the highest mountain escarpment in the world. In 1990, when Steve was a nineteen-year-old high school exchange student, he had reached 21,000 feet on the Schell Route with a Slovenian expedition that put two climbers on the summit. That early experience fostered his desire to climb in the Great Ranges and Nanga Parbat in particular. After years of preparation he had come back to climb the mountain—but this time on a much bigger and more difficult route.

Doug and I were planning to attempt the unclimbed Mazeno Ridge, the longest ridge on any of the world's fourteen peaks higher than 8,000 meters (26,250 feet). Most of the ridge, which included several unclimbed peaks, soared at around 7,000 meters (23,000 feet). The Mazeno Ridge starts where a trekking route used by skilled hikers crosses the ridge low down at Mazeno Pass and it ends six miles later—and 7,000 feet higher—at the Mazeno Gap. There, the Mazeno Ridge joins the existing Schell Route, which climbs straight up from the Rupal valley to this point. After completing the Mazeno Ridge, it was our plan to climb the upper portion of the Schell Route for another 3,000 feet to the summit of Nanga Parbat and then descend that route back to the valley. Six weeks earlier, I had a good view of our objective from the jet window flying from Islamabad to Skardu. The Mazeno Ridge extends out from Nanga Parbat like a giant tentacle that seemed close enough for me to reach out and touch. Our route was daunting, given that veteran Himalayan climbers like Doug Scott, Wojciech Kurtyka, and Erhard Loretan had completed only about half the ridge on earlier attempts.

Jeff and Bruce had been part of Steve's original Rupal Face team. But after Jeff went home early, Bruce said he needed to see the Rupal Face and assess the danger before committing to it. "I'm concerned about how safe it is to go up on the Rupal Face," he said. "If I don't like it, I might want to try to climb the Mazeno Ridge with Doug and Steve instead." I thought this might come as a shock to Steve, who faced the prospect of not having a partner. But he simply said, "I came on this expedition prepared to climb the Rupal Face alone if need be, and I'm totally comfortable with that." Bruce was a strong climber with deadpan humor and a laid-back attitude. He would strengthen our team on the Mazeno Ridge, so I welcomed the idea of him coming with Doug and me. But if he did, I was concerned about Steve going up on the Rupal Face on his own. He had done well on K7 Main, but this was a much bigger and more dangerous objective.

On August 7 the four of us (plus Rasool, Fida Hussein, and our liaison officer, Captain Amin) loaded into two jeeps in Skardu and headed up and over the Deosai Plain toward the village of Tarshing. The road climbed steeply up to Satpara Lake, where the government was building a dam that would greatly enlarge the lake and provide hydropower, a domestic water supply, and irrigation water for the Skardu valley. Beyond the lake, the road leveled off on a 13,000-foot-high plateau at the entrance to the 1,100-square-mile Deosai National Park, which was established in 1993 to protect the critically endangered Himalayan brown bear, a subspecies of the brown bear like the grizzly bear found in North America. Our jeep wound through the park along broad valleys with clear streams and alpine meadows full of wildflowers. Above the valleys, rounded mountains rose two to three thousand feet above the plain.

Near the end of the day, our drivers pulled off the gravel road near a deep blue lake to camp for the night. We hiked through the wildflowers to the top of a nearby peak and looked off to the southwest beyond rows of blue-gray ridges that faded into one another. There in the distance, towering above everything among a large bank of clouds, patches of dark rock stood out from the snowy whiteness. It was our first view of Nanga Parbat. As the soft glow from the afternoon sun illuminated this apparition, it revealed different facets of the mountain, giving it an ethereal, mysterious quality. It took my breath away, leaving me with a sense of fear and wonder.

Early the next morning, for some exercise, Steve and I hiked to the top of a 16,500-foot peak on the other side of the road above camp. It was cloudy, and along the summit ridge a crisp wind penetrated my sweaty shirt. The sky to the northeast was black with clouds backed up against the Greater Karakoram, where we had spent the past six weeks. These brief glimpses of the high mountains acted like a powerful magnet, pulling me to the heights where a new adventure awaited. The dark clouds were an intimidating reminder of the danger and physical tribulations to come. Without a jacket to keep me warm, I got chilled and didn't stay long on top. We headed down to camp for breakfast.

On the main road headed toward Astor, Rasool and Fida were visibly nervous and made several more comments about this valley being full of "bad men." I found out later that Pashtun Sunni militants fleeing Pakistan Army operations in the tribal areas to the west had settled farther down in this valley below Astor, near the town of Chilas along the Karakoram Highway and up the Diamir valley on the north side of Nanga Parbat. The Pashtuns from the tribal areas had a long history of resisting outsiders like the British and were now resisting Pakistan's attempts to govern their territory. Here all of us, including Rasool and Fida, were considered outsiders.

We left the road leading down to Astor and climbed up a narrow jeep track into the sparsely populated Rupal valley and to the village of Tarshing.

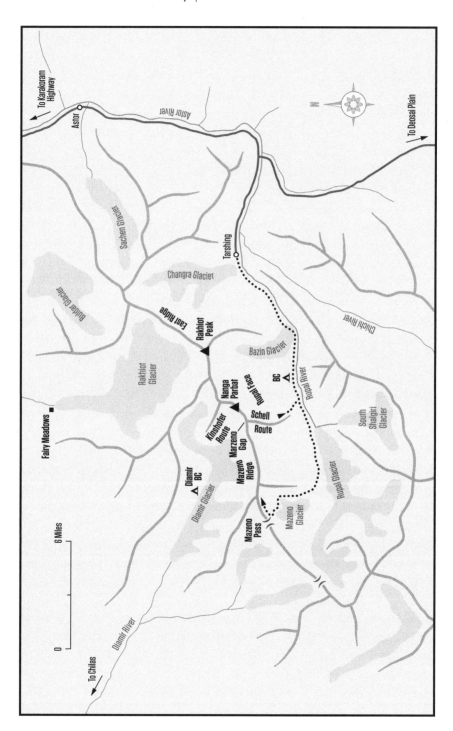

MAP 4: *Nanga Parbat*

As we headed up into the mountains again, Rasool and Fida became more relaxed. The east side of Nanga Parbat towers over Tarshing in the same way that Masherbrum dominates the skyline above their home village of Hushe. We reached the village around noon and said good-bye to our drivers and to Rasool. Not sure when I would be back, or if Rasool would still be around, I found it hard to say good-bye. We gave each other a big hug, and I wished him a safe journey and good luck taking care of his father. Rasool climbed into the back of the jeep, and we waved to each other as it pulled away and finally disappeared around a bend.

The expedition would rely on the local community for fresh food, porters, and animals to carry our equipment and supplies to a safe place for our base camp. It had been fourteen years for Steve, while Bruce, Doug, Captain Amin, Fida Hussein, and I had never been here before. Thus it behooved us to become known and liked by these people as best we could. We hired a local man in Tarshing by the name of Meaboob, referred to us by friends in Skardu as an experienced sirdar. That afternoon he helped us pack our base camp loads that would be strapped on animals or carried by porters in the morning. That evening we stayed in a small guest house and invited the headmaster of the local school for dinner. He gave us some basic information about the Rupal valley, how the people lived, and how our expedition might impact their activities. Before he left, we gave him some notebooks and classroom materials (bought in Skardu with money provided by the Alex Lowe Charitable Foundation).

It was a relatively flat and easy walk to base camp on August 9, with the sprawling ridges of Nanga Parbat towering above us to the north. Trekking through patchy pine, juniper forests, and grassy meadows was a refreshing change from the dry rocky valleys farther north in the Karakoram. Long glaciers descended from the mountain far out into the valley, and we had to walk across a couple of them. We met children in smart blue uniforms walking in the opposite direction to their school in Tarshing about five miles away. Although it was a relatively easy trek for mountain climbers, portions of the trail went across rubble-covered ice, and I was impressed that students as young as five or six walked this way every day. No American's story about a long, cold walk to school could beat the ones these children could have told.

We set up base camp at nearly 12,000 feet in a meadow next to a clear spring. Nearby was a summer dwelling for several families who were herding their livestock in the surrounding meadows. The valley was over-run with donkeys, cows, and sheep. We removed all the dried manure from our campsite so we wouldn't have to live in it. Captain Amin told us the people in this valley viewed Fida Hussein as an outsider and thought we should have hired one of the locals to be our cook. A hygienic cook is critical to staying healthy, so we would never have trusted someone we didn't know. To smooth things over, we hired a local assistant cook and a few porters to periodically bring us fresh vegetables. That evening we cel-ebrated Amin's birthday as Fida and his new helper presented him with a cake topped by a lit candle.

Now that Bruce had a chance to see the mountain, he thought the Rupal Face looked safe enough to climb and he would accompany Steve on that endeavor. For the past week Steve had been preparing himself to attempt the route alone, and he seemed relieved to have a partner. Their route began directly above base camp, so they remained there to discuss plans while Doug and I set off on a day trip to explore the start of our route. We followed the trekking route up the Rupal valley for several miles to the Mazeno base camp at 13,000 feet, and from there went north and gained 2,500 feet in elevation to Mazeno Pass. The trekking route crossed over toward the Diamir valley on the other side, but we left the trail shortly before the pass and scrambled to 16,000 feet. We stopped there to examine the steep ice slopes above us that led to the top of the Mazeno Ridge. Previous attempts on this route earlier in the season had difficulty making progress in the deep snow along the crest of the ridge. Although the lower slopes would be more melted out, we had decided to attempt the Mazeno Ridge later in the season when warmer temperatures had a chance to consolidate the snow farther up. From our vantage point the route looked safe and feasible, and conditions looked as if our theory about firm snow might be true. In preparation for our return, we built a tent platform in the rocks and headed back to base camp. We arrived tired but happy, knowing everything was ready to go.

The forecast indicated some unsettled weather for a couple of days, fol-lowed by a spell of dry, cool air. Doug and I decided to rest the next day and hike up to our tent site the day after. We would launch into the climb when the weather was supposed to improve on what we hoped would be our lucky Friday, August 13. What was especially challenging about this route was not its technical difficulty, but the commitment required. Given its length, it would take multiple days to traverse the ridge at high altitude, and there were no safe options for retreating down either side of the ridge, which was subject to constant avalanche danger. Once we started up the climb, the only way to escape would be to go back the way we came or to complete the entire Mazeno Ridge to the Mazeno Gap, then descend on the Schell Route.

We spent the day sorting what we needed to bring, and despite efforts to cut back, our packs felt heavy. Without a lot of steep climbing, we didn't need much technical gear, but we were bringing more food and fuel than usual. If we got hit by a storm, we would need those supplies to survive while waiting until the weather improved. Fortunately the packs would get lighter as we progressed. We also studied maps and photos to get familiar with the details of our descent options. Our plan was to climb to the summit via the upper portion of the Schell Route after completing the ridge to the Mazeno Gap. From the summit we would retrace our steps back to the Mazeno Gap and then descend on the Schell Route back into the Rupal valley. As Doug and I hiked up the Rupal valley making our reconnaissance of the start of the ridge, we examined the Schell Route below the Mazeno Gap, and it looked like we could come down that way.

Another descent option from the summit would be to descend the other (north) side of the mountain into the Diamir valley via the Kinshofer Route. But since we were in the Rupal valley, we had no way of scrutinizing this route. If the weather was cloudy while descending, we could easily get lost. Also, this late in the season, the snow and ice that froze everything together on the lower part of the Kinshofer Route would likely be melted out, and in those conditions it had a reputation for horrible rockfall. To avoid rockfall, expeditions climbing the Kinshofer Route come earlier in the year, when it is colder and snowier. Going that way, we would reach the bottom exhausted and far from our base camp.

For these reasons we decided not to descend the Kinshofer Route into the Diamir valley unless we ran into unforeseen problems that made it impossible to descend by the Schell Route. Developing our descent strategy felt like a thorough process, but there was a flaw. Since the Schell Route had been climbed only a few times, I hadn't seen much information about conditions. We didn't know whether the rockfall problems we'd read about on the lower part of the Kinshofer Route this time of year would also be the case on the lower Schell Route.

On August 12, Doug and I climbed above what we called the "cow line" at nearly 14,000 feet (the maximum elevation where grass grew and the locals could herd their livestock). We spent the night camped on the platform we had built two days earlier. In the darkness at 2:00 a.m., we climbed unroped up the initial ice slopes. As with every other early morning start over the years, my worldview was limited to the small bubble of light produced by my headlamp. It was intimidating to be confined like that while trying to find a way up the huge dangerous mountain in the dark. As we gained elevation, a helpful kind of fear began to lurk in the back of my head; it made me cautious, but it wasn't crippling. Every step was critical, since hundreds of feet of exposure were accumulating in the darkness below us.

The first hint of light enabled us to see farther than our headlamps and helped us find a way to the left around the shadowy rock towers that blocked the way on the ridge above. This put us on top of one of the many ribs that came off the Mazeno Ridge like flying buttresses. Looking up, we could see that the crest of the Mazeno Ridge was still several thousand feet above us. Noon found us baking in the heat while kicking steps in calf-deep slushy snow. Our goal was to reach the top of the ridge at 21,500 feet and spend the night, but the conditions had slowed us considerably. It would be exhausting and take the rest of the day to get there in the heat, so we stopped 1,500 feet below the ridge at 1:00 p.m. In the morning, with cooler temperatures and a frozen surface, it would take only a couple of hours to reach the crest.

The next morning, on August 14, Doug and I left camp at 3:00 a.m., the steep snow frozen solid under our crampons. We reached the top of the Mazeno Ridge as dawn lit the summits of Lila, Rupal, and the other peaks far below us on the south side of the Rupal valley. Several independent summits along the Mazeno Ridge were named on maps according to their elevation, and we reached the summit of Peak 6880 (22,572 feet) that morning. We continued east along the crest up and down over the tops of Peaks 6825 (22,391 feet), 6970 (22,867 feet), and the first set of rock towers called Peak 6870 (22,637 feet).

At around 22,500 feet, we spent our second night where a large but stable-looking cornice had created an almost-level platform on the crest. Halfway between Mazeno Pass and the Mazeno Gap, we were farther along the ridge than any of the attempts by previous expeditions. All the peaks we climbed along the ridge after this would be first ascents. It was a great day with good progress that made up for having to stop early the day before. Doug and I were optimistic, and the weather and snow conditions were good. A synergy had developed between us that came from our combined years of experience, shared ambition, flexibility, and humor. Things were going very well.

Our third day started with steep mixed climbing on the west side of Peak 7060 (23,162 feet), then down easy slopes on the east side. We went up and skirted around Peak 7091 (23,261 feet) on ice slopes just below the summit and rappelled down over a big crevasse to long easy slopes that led to the top of Peak 7090 (23,259 feet). Another big drop on low-angle slopes took us to a saddle in the ridge, then we kicked steps back up to the top of Peak 7100 (23,290 feet). Now that Doug and I were higher and the temperatures were colder, the snow didn't get soft from the afternoon heat, but it didn't consolidate from melt and freeze either. We were covering long distances kicking steps in ankle- to calf-deep snow that left us exhausted at this altitude.

Between where we were and the Mazeno Gap, the ridge sharpened into a series of rock towers. It made sense to stop early at 2:00 p.m. at a flat camping place before the final obstacle. We had been climbing for three days and hoped some rest would leave us with sufficient strength to go to the summit via the Schell Route on August 17 and 18. But that night I was awakened by the urge to cough up excess mucus, and I coughed and hacked as hard as I could. I found I could keep my lungs clear by sitting upright so I gathered boots, food bags, and clothing to prop myself up in order to get some sleep in a sitting position. My sleep was interrupted by spells of Cheyne-Stokes respiration during which my breathing became deeper and faster followed by apnea that caused me to wake up gasping for air.

Doug had some Diamox that would counter my symptoms. I took a quarter tablet to help keep my respiration rate up, which helped me get a bit of sleep. It was a bad night, though, and by morning I was coughing up bloody mucus balls. I didn't think I had HAPE—high-altitude pulmonary edema—because I didn't feel like fluid was accumulating in my lungs. I was able to cough up the stuff that was interfering with my breathing and then take clear, deep breaths. It seemed more like sinusitis or a respiratory infection that was producing all the mucus—like having a cold when my body was already compromised by extreme altitude.

On Monday, August 16, we woke to high cirrus clouds, which usually precede bad weather within twenty-four to forty-eight hours. The ridge had narrowed to a sharp crest of rocky towers that separated us from the Mazeno Gap. After having such a bad night, I felt pretty weak and asked Doug to do most of the leading to the gap. "Don't worry," he said. "We'll get to the gap today and then have a conversation about whether we have the health and the weather to try and reach the summit, or if we need to descend the Schell Route right away."

We started at 7:00 a.m. along the final series of rock towers, thinking it would take only three hours to reach the Mazeno Gap. But there were more towers to traverse than we had anticipated, and it took us four times that long. Doug did all the leading, and I followed him up, down, and across, rappelling when it was too steep to downclimb between towers. Doug did a great job finding the way, but the work from all the leading and his concern about my health took a toll. As the day wore on and the towers seemed to go on forever, both of us faded into a state of exhaustion. We moved together with our single eight-millimeter, two-hundred-foot rope strung between us. Doug clipped the rope into an occasional cam, nut, or piton placed in the rock, and I retrieved it when I passed. When he ran out of gear, or at convenient locations, he stopped, and I climbed over to join him and return the gear. We repeated this process over and over. It seemed endless.

The last few towers before the Mazeno Gap consisted of very bad rock, and Doug couldn't place any gear for running anchors. We had to trust each other not to fall as we made our way up, over, and around them. We finished the last of the towers, which were all labeled as 7,010 meters (23,200 feet) on the map and rappelled and downclimbed a few hundred feet to reach the Mazeno Gap at 7:30 p.m., just as it was getting dark. After digging a platform and setting up the tent, we spent the next several hours conducting the usual life-sustaining task of melting snow for hot liquids and food. My night was worse than the previous one. With all the coughing and hacking, my throat was raw. By morning, I didn't feel strong enough to spend two more days climbing 3,000 feet up the Schell Route to the summit and back.

Besides my health problems, the weather was beginning to deteriorate, so Doug and I decided to head down the Schell Route from the Gap rather than continue up to the top of Nanga Parbat. Making the decision to go down wasn't that hard because we hadn't given up on reaching the summit. Our plan was to come back up the Schell Route and continue to the summit after resting at base camp until my health and the weather improved. We got up late and left the Gap at 9:30 a.m. thinking the descent would be quick and easy. Our intent was to reach base camp for a late dinner. We had enough food and fuel for several more days, so we cached it at the gap to use when we came back up. To save even more weight on our return, Doug suggested we also leave behind our rope and a snow picket. Steve House had been on this route fourteen years earlier, and he had told Doug that below the Mazeno Gap, he didn't think we would need a rope. The first part involved descending easy snow slopes with no crevasses, he said, and below that the route tapered into a short rock ridge at 20,000 feet where there were old fixed ropes we could follow. I agreed to leave the rope behind.

As we started down the snow slope, our boots broke through an icy crust that scraped our shins as our legs plunged into the bottomless snow underneath. The weather got worse and visibility decreased as the clouds enveloping the mountain blended in with the snow to create white-out conditions. We stopped periodically to wait for brief openings in the fog so we could see the route and continue our descent. When the snow went from breakable crust to deep slush, we glissaded (slid on our butts) to avoid the thigh-deep plunging. Doug fell up to his waist in a crevasse—the first hint that our descent route would be different than expected. With his feet dangling in space, Doug pulled himself out and left behind a dark, bottomless hole. We tied the ends of slings and short pieces of cord to each other for protection. As the snow slope tapered into an icy ridge, we turned toward the slope and backed down several hundred feet standing on the front points of our crampons. When the icy ridge narrowed into a four-foot-wide horizontal rocky ridge, we looked for the fixed ropes Steve had mentioned to Doug.

We walked along the rocky ridge, examining the steep rock walls on either side, but we didn't see any rope. After about fifty feet the horizontal ridge ended, dropping off in all directions into the clouds below. Walking back and forth, we looked for the rope that would lead us to safety, but all we found were several rappel anchors. The horror of our situation dawned on us: We were trapped at the top of this wall without a rope for rappelling and without any fixed rope to use or guide the way. (We later found out that no one had been on this route since 1992. Steve had been there in 1990 with a large Slovenian group that had used fixed ropes, on this part of the route, but sun and weather had apparently destroyed those ropes or maybe another group had removed them.) Standing on the rocky ridge, staring down into the clouds, we resisted despair.

It seemed like we had two options, and neither was good. We could climb, exhausted and without water, up 3,000 feet in thigh-deep snow to retrieve our rope at the Mazeno Gap. It was foolish to try this in our debilitated state; we could easily become exhausted and find ourselves unable to move either up or down. Or we could downclimb the steep, unfamiliar rock without a rope in the fog and face the possibility of falling off the mountain if we encountered a steep wall that was too difficult to descend using our hands and feet. Doug wanted to start downclimbing, but I didn't want to compound our original mistake by rushing into another one. You are never too experienced to make a stupid mistake, and if we made another one now, we might pay for it with our lives.

With the fog swirling around us, we sat on our rocky aerie for nearly three hours trying to come up with a better option to get out of our mess. Suddenly I remembered passing a small loop of old rope protruding from the ice a short distance up the ridge. Maybe we could chop a piece of rope out of the ice that was long enough to get us down. Doug and I climbed up to it and started to hack away at the slope with our ice axes. After three hours we had freed about seventy feet of good half-inch braided nylon rope. We would only be able to make thirty-five-foot rappels with the doubled-up rope, but that would have to do. It was too late to start down, so we were forced to bivouac out in the open. Soon after dark it began to snow, and we spent a miserable night huddled in our sleeping bags with no food or water since we had left all our fuel and supplies at the Mazeno Gap.

The one good thing was that after descending to 19,600 feet, I felt much better breathing the thicker air.

After shaking off the fresh snow that covered us during the night, we pulled on our boots, packed up, and started moving by 6:00 a.m. The visibility was still poor, and I was concerned about getting down with only a seventy-foot rope. Doug led the way, and roped together we downclimbed with me holding the rope from above. That way I could protect him on terrain where it would be easy to fall if he dislodged one of the many loose rocks he had to pull or stand on while finding our way down. We tried to follow old rappel anchors, but in the fog we lost track of any signs of the route. We kept descending and eventually spotted an old anchor in a gully and climbed down to it. The rock wall below the old anchor was too steep to downclimb, so we made five or six thirty-five-foot rappels. We used up a lot of the gear we had for making new new anchors without getting very far.

Doug invoked his uncanny sense of direction and insisted we look around a corner. Sure enough, this was the key to our descent. We dropped into an icy gully and backed down, roped together, alternately placing our two ice screws for protection. Eventually we reached a lower-angled slope with rock that was so loose it wouldn't hold any hardware. So rather than risk pulling the other person off if one of us fell, we scrambled down unroped—but carefully because it was steep enough for a tumble to send either one of us a thousand feet down the mountainside. We continued finding our way down through a series of rocky slopes and ribs, relieved to be losing elevation so quickly.

Just as we thought we were out of our predicament, a rock tower the size of a semitruck collapsed onto the route below us. Doug looked at me in wide-eyed disbelief. In another minute we would have been where the tower had exploded onto the slope. "That was sick," he exclaimed. We decided to abandon our plan to come back up this route. It was just too loose and dangerous this late in the year when there was no snow cover. Enveloped by mist that clung stubbornly to the hillside, we kept going down, never quite sure where we were until suddenly some old tent platforms, the remnants of Camp I on the Schell Route, appeared on the hillside. We stopped there to rest for about half an hour. It was eerie—the small log walls supporting some of the platforms were falling down, like an archaeological site of an ancient civilization. Below the 16,500-foot camp was a faint trail, and by following our noses downward in the fog, we descended out of the clouds and finally could see the grass, flowers, and running water of the valley floor.

Doug and I stumbled into base camp late on the afternoon of August 18. Fida Hussein plied us with plenty of food and liquids. Bruce and Steve were already there, having arrived the day before. They had nearly reached 25,000 feet on the Rupal Face before turning around. Doug and I changed clothes and had more to eat and drink before listening to a quick version of their story. My first impression was that Bruce had forced a decision to go down with only easy terrain left between them and the summit. He thought Steve was sick from the altitude and it would be unsafe for them to continue, but Steve had resisted going down. I was too tired to listen to a more lengthy discussion and went to lie on the thick sleeping pads in my tent. I relished breathing air at this altitude that felt so heavy and moist I could almost chew it. I fell into an exhaustion-induced coma for fourteen hours—a deep sleep that could only come after knowing I was safe. I didn't emerge until late the next morning.

For the most part, the four of us spent the next two days eating, drinking, sleeping, and sharing stories of our experiences on the mountain. Doug's and my story about climbing the Mazeno Ridge and our decision to go down the Schell Route without reaching the summit was uncomplicated. Our personal ambitions had not conflicted with what we both thought was the right thing to do. As Bruce and Steve's story unfolded, however, it was clear that this was not the case for them. There was a tension between them that was revealed not so much by what they said, but by what they didn't say. Now that we were back in the land of the living, Doug and I made light of the things that had happened to us even though some of it had been quite serious at the time. Bruce and Steve were more cautious about how they told their stories, as if they didn't want to say what they really felt in the presence of the other.

Doug and I wondered what really happened to them high up in the thin air on Nanga Parbat. Two days after we reached base camp, Doug declared he was leaving with Bruce. My health had improved considerably, and I wanted to stay and attempt some smaller unclimbed peaks farther up the valley. But no one else was interested, so I decided to go home with Doug and Bruce. I was only interested in staying to climb if I had a partner. Steve announced that he was staying to try the Rupal Face again by himself—but in a way that didn't invite discussion. Bruce and Doug looked incredulous. I worried about Steve taking on such a huge project by himself. That evening, after Steve went to bed, Bruce told Doug and me that he felt guilty about leaving Steve, but he needed to get home. He had spoken to his wife, Michelle, on the satellite phone. "She asked me," Bruce said, "'When can I stop worrying?'"

At breakfast in the mess tent the next morning, Steve gave Doug, Bruce, and me a brief talk to try and ease everyone's concern about him staying alone and to relieve our guilt about leaving. He looked tired and uneasy, as if he had spent much of the night thinking about what he wanted to say and scripting his speech. "I always planned to come here," he said, "even if I had to come alone, since I bought the permit before anyone had agreed to come on this part of the trip." He said he had been surprised there was so much interest in Nanga Parbat. "I thought a lot of people might drop out after the Charakusa portion was over." After a pause, he said, "I've spent the last eight months preparing for this, and I'm ready to go alone. I won't do anything stupid, so don't worry about me." Before we had a chance to respond, Steve told us about his attempt on Nanga Parbat with Bruce. "I appreciate Bruce's ability to recognize my illness and force the issue to make us go down," he said, "but I'm very sad about what happened given all my preparation." He explained that if the roles had been reversed and Bruce was sick, he would not have hesitated to turn back with him. "My reluctance to go down was based on my disappointment with myself," he said, "and not because I'm obsessed with Nanga Parbat beyond being sensitive to the needs of my partner."

After returning to my tent, I thought about Steve's speech, which had the opposite effect on me from what he intended. He did seem obsessed, and now I was even more worried than before. We all had great confidence in Steve's ability, but even the most skilled climbers could get into trouble on such a big and dangerous route. There would be no one to help him if he got hurt or sick. Doug and I had made the first ascent of the Mazeno Ridge to the Mazeno Gap and weren't able to reach the summit, which was disappointing after such enormous effort. But we weren't experiencing nearly as much angst over our failure as Steve was. I couldn't tell if he was blaming himself or Bruce, but it seemed fruitless for him to torment himself about it.

I remembered back in 1990, when Phil Ershler had turned around on K2 just a couple hundred meters from the top while the rest of the team continued to the summit. "You can't question later the decisions you make up there," Phil had said. "What you decided in that moment, in that place, was the right thing to do. It isn't fair to question yourself after coming down when you are safe and comfortable." I liked Phil's attitude, which prioritized safety and friendship over success—although all three elements are important to us. I spent the rest of the morning packing outside my tent. Nearby, a group of the shepherd's children were playing. The sound of their clear, sweet voices as they faded into the magnitude of this vast landscape was soothing. It helped to ground me in a human reality that was easy to forget given our preoccupation with climbing.

Bruce, Doug, and I walked out of base camp the next day, leaving Steve behind with Fida Hussein and Captain Amin. As we stood there with our packs on, Amin started to cry. "I have a hard time with good-byes," he said, "and you people have all been so nice to me." Amin was one of the nicest liaison officers I've ever had.

Typically a cheerful and easygoing person, Bruce was in a somber mood. As we hiked to Tarshing, he shared his version of what had happened up on the mountain with Steve. On their fifth day, above the technical difficulties, they climbed unroped toward the summit. Bruce had gotten ahead and stopped, but after almost an hour of waiting, he doubled back to look for Steve. Bruce found him moving very slowly, intermittently falling asleep and clipped only to his tools on the fifty-degree slope. Concerned about Steve's ability to continue to the summit and get down safely, Bruce decided they should go down. They argued about it, but Bruce insisted, and they came down.

A couple of weeks after I returned to Seattle, I received a call from Steve who was in the UK. He told me he had started back up the Rupal Face five days after our departure, but he didn't go very far. He was still weak from his attempt with Bruce, so he left base camp with Amin and Fida Hussein and went back to Islamabad. From there, he had flown to London to visit a friend. He talked about getting back on a plane to Pakistan right away and trying the Rupal Face again, even though it was very late in the season. We talked for a while, and I suggested several reasons why I thought that was a bad idea. By the end of the call, Steve had decided to come back to the United States and prepare for a future attempt.

Later that year Steve wrote about the expedition: "I had to go down with Bruce because his 'no' was necessarily stronger than my 'yes.' ... Bruce had acted on fear. . . . He poured his fear into me. . . . Our decision was that we descend." Climbers suffering from hypoxia in a high-stress environment have difficulty making even simple decisions, let alone those weighing the merits of a lifetime accomplishment versus the ability to get down alive. In the fog of their circumstance, Steve and Bruce had different perspectives. Thus they each had a different truth.

A year later, on September 6, 2005, Steve reached the summit of Nanga Parbat with Vince Anderson climbing a slightly different line (up the Central Pillar) of the Rupal Face than the route he and Bruce had taken in 2004. An experienced guide from Colorado, Vince had known Steve for decade, but it was the first time they had climbed more than a day route together. The Rupal Face is arguably the tallest and most difficult Himalayan face to ever have been climbed in pure alpine style by just two climbers. The worldwide climbing community heaped accolades on Steve and Vince, and they won the coveted Piolet d'Or in the spring of 2006 for the accomplishment.

Three years later, Steve's book *Beyond the Mountain* was published. He dedicated it to his climbing partners, including Bruce. In the acknowledgments he credited Bruce for saving his life. In an interview Steve said of his relationship with Bruce, "We're better friends now than before Nanga Parbat. We had a hard time and have different memories of what happened up there, which happens a lot at altitude. Eventually I realized he was correct in saying I was on a death march. It took Bruce and his honesty to bring me around to that point of view. It was a shock to me to realize I was going for it with blinkers on."

On March 25, 2010, while rock climbing on an unseasonably warm day in Canmore, Alberta, I received a phone message from Bruce, who was nearby in Banff, Alberta. He and Steve were climbing together for the first time since their attempt on Nanga Parbat in 2004. They were trying to make an ascent of the Greenwood Locke route on the north face of Mount Temple in winter conditions, and Steve had taken an eighty-foot leader fall and was seriously injured. The two of them had been evacuated from the face by a rescue helicopter. Steve was then choppered from the hospital in Banff to the trauma center in Calgary. Bruce drove to my condo to get cleaned up, and together we drove the hour to Calgary. They let us into the ER, where Steve was lying on a gurney hooked up to monitors and IV tubes. Frightened, he wouldn't remember later how he had grabbed onto my hand and wouldn't let go.

Steve was lucky. Bruce initiated a rescue late in the afternoon after the accident, and the helicopter from Parks Canada responded quickly. A skilled warden had plucked them off the wall with a long line. Steve had broken six ribs and his pelvis; he had some minor spinal fractures and a punctured lung as well. But if the helicopter hadn't gotten him off the mountain that afternoon, things could have been much grimmer. By the next morning, a storm moved in and lasted for several days, making a helicopter rescue impossible. Given their position on the mountain, it would have been impossible for Bruce to carry out a self-rescue. Steve wouldn't have survived waiting for better weather.

Steve's recovery took a long time. "After my accident in Canada," he later said, "I discovered that it wasn't more climbing that I wished I had done in my life, but that I hadn't done more for the community of climbers that had given me so much." He created a program called Alpine Mentors, patterned on similar programs in Europe. It's designed to promote advanced/expert alpinism for young adults by encouraging, coaching, and climbing with them. The goal is to help them reach their alpine climbing goals in a lightweight, low-impact style. In early 2013, Steve brought his first group of program participants to Canmore and asked for my help. I spent two weeks with them, climbing frozen waterfalls and some winter alpine routes. I hadn't spent much time with Steve since our Pakistan trip in 2004, and I enjoyed reconnecting with him while passing on to the younger generation many of the skills we had learned over the years. The first group of program participants went on an expedition with Steve to some unclimbed peaks in northern India in the fall of 2014 as part of their graduation from his two-year program. Steve continues this work in Colorado.

The route Doug Chabot and I pioneered up the Mazeno Ridge to the Mazeno Gap was successfully climbed again in 2008, when Germans Luis Stitzinger and Joseph Lunger ascended it starting from the Diamir side. Our objective to reach the summit of Nanga Parbat after having climbed the Mazeno Ridge was completed in July 2012 by UK climbers Sandy Allan and Rick Allen on an expedition that included Cathy O'Dowd (from South Africa) and Nepali climbers Lhakpa Rangdu Sherpa, Lhakpa Zarok Sherpa, and Lhakpa Nuru Sherpa. The team made the third ascent of the Mazeno Ridge to the Mazeno Gap, from where Cathy, Lhakpa Rangdu, Lhakpa Zarok, and Lhakpa Nuru descended via the Schell Route. Sandy and Rick continued, and in an epic seventeen-day climb, became the first to reach the summit of Nanga Parbat via the Mazeno Ridge.

*Doug Chabot climbs on the
second day on Latok II.*

CHAPTER 9

THE WORLD'S HARDEST MOUNTAINS

LATOK II SOUTH RIDGE, 2006
LATOK I NORTH RIDGE, 2007
CHOKTOI SPIRE NORTH RIDGE, 2007

W hen I left Pakistan in 2004, large areas in the provinces along the border with Afghanistan were controlled by militant Pashtun tribesmen. Armed conflict had erupted between the Pakistan Army deployed in these areas to search for al-Qaeda fighters and the tribal militants who viewed this as an attempt at subjugation. To avoid further bloodshed, the Pakistan government had signed a series of shaky peace agreements with the militants. Soon after these agreements were made, the militant Pashtun tribesmen, heavily influenced by the al-Qaeda fighters and Afghan Taliban among them, implemented a system of strict Sharia Law, and they started to export their brand of fundamentalism to other parts of Pakistan. They resisted fighting the Pakistan security forces, but they helped their al-Qaeda and Afghan Taliban partners wage war against the United States, NATO, and the government forces of President Harmid Karzai across the border in Afghanistan.

The irony was that the broader efforts of these groups to impose strict religious governments in the region would soon bring them into conflict with their Pakistan government supporters, proving the original critics correct in saying the agreements were worthless. For me and my climbing friends, the political intrigue and the mystery regarding Pakistan's policies toward its neighbors was part of the country's backdrop. So far the only impact on us was having to deal with a complicated permit process and military oversight of our activities. To this point, none of the violence plaguing parts of the country had affected us as foreign visitors to the region.

In 2005 I felt the security situation in Baltistan was safe enough to bring my wife, Ann, younger son, Jed, and another family trekking there with me. After telling stories to Ann for so many years about Rasool, and the Karakoram mountains, I wanted to share the experience with them. We landed in Islamabad on July 13. Since flights were cancelled because of bad weather, we traveled by road on the Karakoram Highway (KKH) to Skardu, which was well east of the provinces controlled by militants. The violence was escalating in Afghanistan, but that was even farther from where we would be trekking. The locals in Baltistan were very friendly to us, and over the years there had been only one attack on foreigners, even though all the expeditions and trekking groups carried rucksacks full of cash to pay for porters, jeep drivers, hotels, and restaurants.

What I didn't know was that the security situation in the provinces near Afghanistan was deteriorating despite the peace agreements, and religious fundamentalism was migrating eastward toward the KKH as militants fled previous army operations there. (Years later, I learned that Osama bin Laden was about to move into a new compound that his supporters were building in Abbottabad only a short distance from where my family, friends, and I had lunch while driving to Skardu.)

When we arrived in Skardu, Rasool met us at our hotel. I knew that, like other Pakistanis, he felt there was no greater honor than for me to entrust him with the safety and well-being of my family. Ann was touched when he greeted her by holding his hand over his heart. With a slight tilt of his head, he said, "Memsahib, so much thank you for coming to visit us. Your family is same as my family. I would very much like to show you our beautiful mountains." As Rasool shook Jed's hand, he gave me a look of appreciation, reflecting the mutual pride we had in our sons. Our friends were welcomed as my "special guests." After a couple of days provisioning in Skardu, we left for Hushe. One of the highlights of the trip for Ann was when Rasool took us to his house for tea with Bedruma, Fida Ali, Rasool's three daughters, and his father, who was still alive despite the terrible leg injury the previous year.

Because this was their first trip to Pakistan, several in our group got sick from the food or water. The typical stomach and intestinal infection caus, diarrhea and vomiting and lasts for about three or four days. Jed suffered the worst of it while we were still in Skardu but showed a sense of humor when yelling, "gimme the bucket" (the line from the "Mr. Creosote Blows Up" scene in Monty Python's *The Meaning of Life*). Ann came down with it in Hushe, so we delayed our departure.

After a couple of days we hiked toward the Charakusa valley, where I had been the previous year. We only needed a small group of about a dozen Hushe porters, so it was easier to get to know them all by name. Ann enjoyed asking questions about their children and their lives in Hushe. Once we reached the location of our 2004 base camp, we set up camp for three days to rest and make several short day hikes. Ann had a chance to recover there and take in the fantastic surroundings. She was amazed by the size and ruggedness of the mountains. Rasool had brought along his son, Fida Ali, who was now thirteen; Jed was a couple of years older. Fida Ali had been learning English at a boarding school in Skardu, so he and Jed really hit it off. They got to know each other while hiking and playing cards and Hacky Sack. It was an eye-opening experience for Jed to see this part of the world. As we walked back into Hushe at the end of our trek, he said, "The people here are really poor."

We arrived back in Skardu on July 26, and from there Ann and Jed would travel to Islamabad and then back to Seattle. I stayed in Baltistan for another six weeks to climb. As often happens, the flights to Islamabad were grounded for several days due to cloudy weather, and there was a large backlog of passengers waiting to fly. While Ann and Jed waited to catch their plane, I worked with Rasool to reprovision for our climbing trip. The flight from Skardu was cancelled again on the morning of July 28, so our tour operator hired a private car to take Ann and Jed to Islamabad by road. Taking the KKH was the only way they would be able to catch their flight to London a few days later. As we parted, I was concerned about sending my family by themselves through some Pashtun areas on their way to Islamabad. It was a relief to talk to them in Islamabad as they were boarding their flight on the first leg of their trip home. I enjoyed another summer climbing in the Karakoram but without reaching any significant summits.

After the Mazeno Ridge climb on Nanga Parbat, Doug Chabot and I planned an expedition in 2006 to the Latok peaks, a group of dramatic mountains located in the central Karakoram Range in Pakistan. If one measures difficulty by the rarity of successful ascents, the Latok peaks are among the world's hardest to climb. Latok I (7,145 meters, or 23,442 feet), the highest mountain in the group, had been attempted many times, and the summit had been reached only once by a Japanese expedition in 1979. The roster of those who have failed to reach the top of this mountain is a who's who of some of the greatest alpinists in the world.

For the Latok trip Doug and I agreed that a team of three would be ideal. That way, the equipment weight is shared with only the added increment of food and fuel for an additional person. A party of three can divide the loads into one very light pack for the leader, who is responsible for getting the ropes up to the next anchor, and two heavier packs for the followers, who have the security of a rope from above. With a top rope, the two followers have the option to climb the rope with mechanical rope ascenders if the rock and/or ice is too difficult to climb with a heavy pack. A party of three is also safer. If someone gets hurt, the other two climbers can more easily carry out a rescue than one can.

My first choice for a third team member was Mark Richey. I had known him for over twenty years, and we both had significant high mountain experience. We had not been on a long expedition together, but in 2002 we'd gone trekking with our families in the Peruvian Andes, where we took a couple of days to do a new route on 18,944-foot Tsacra Grande (5,774 meters). Besides the Peru trip, Mark and I had enjoyed climbing together in Yosemite, the Canadian Rockies, New England, and ice climbing in Newfoundland. He had wanted to join Steve House's expedition to the Charakusa valley in 2004, but he couldn't get away from his architectural woodworking business at the time. Mark was strong and pragmatic and liked going to big, remote, technical peaks. He had already been on two expeditions to Latok I.

Doug knew Mark by reputation and from the volunteer work all three of us did for the American Alpine Club. He agreed that Mark would make a strong addition to our already solid partnership. When we asked Mark, he was happy to join us. Our next step was to agree on our specific objective. Doug and Mark were most interested in climbing the west face of Latok III (6,949 meters, or 22,798 feet). I wasn't as enthused. The west face is a 6,000-foot granite wall that tops out on the summit, and stories about previous attempts on it were worrisome. In 2000 the west face had been attempted by a Russian expedition that retreated when rockfall broke one climber's hand and another was swept over a thousand feet down the mountain, where he was found alive but with both legs broken. A year later, many of the same Russians returned, but three-quarters of the way up a rope was severed by rockfall and the climber attached to it fell to his death. In general, I wasn't a fan of big mountain rock walls, where water seeping into cracks was subjected to repetitive freeze-thaw cycles that fractured the rock and caused rockfall. This was especially the case if the climate was warm enough to melt the ice that kept the rock frozen together.

I voiced some reservations about our chosen objective, but I didn't object to getting a permit for Latok III because I wanted to go climbing in the Karakoram with Doug and Mark. Once we were there, we would carefully assess the route and proceed only if it seemed safe. Base camp would be alongside the Baintha Lukpar Glacier that flowed into the Biafo Glacier, one of the main glaciers of the Karakoram, and all of the Latok peaks were accessible from there. If Latok III did not seem safe, we would have several options.

We left Seattle on July 17, and after reaching Islamabad, we hired a van to travel to Skardu. There, we had a happy reunion with Rasool, who was his usual cheery self. Now that he was getting older, we decided to hire

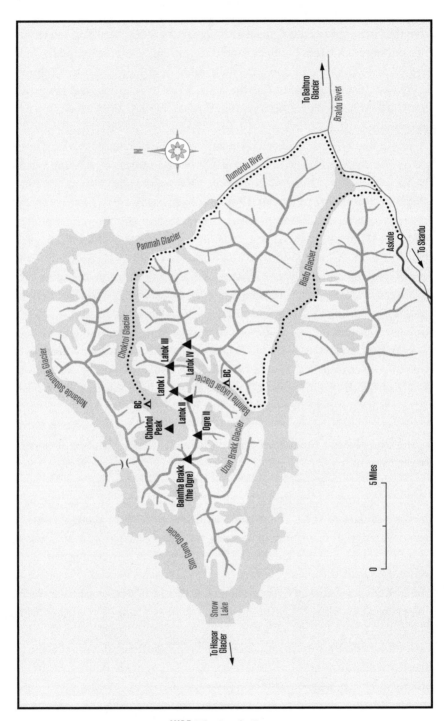

MAP 5: *The Latok Group*

an assistant cook, Ali Khan, to help with such heavy chores as carrying five-gallon water jugs from a nearby stream to the camp kitchen. After the usual provisioning in Skardu, we drove in jeeps to the village of Askole, where we began our trek and reached base camp on July 28. After climbing some easy smaller peaks on day trips from base camp, Mark, Doug, and I set off on August 2 to finish our acclimatization on Latok V, an unclimbed 20,300-foot peak (6,187 meters). Latok V was near the head of the Baintha Lukpar Glacier, beyond the west face of Latok III. Approaching it would allow us to assess conditions on our main objective.

We left base camp the next day and made a camp on the glacier near the col between Latok IV and Latok V. The next morning we reached the col and headed up the east-facing slopes of Latok V. The climbing was easy so we moved roped together, placing gear for running belays along the way. The angle eventually eased off to where we felt the climbing was easy enough that we took off the rope. After a couple of hours, we reached a notch between a small tower and the main peak at nearly 20,000 feet. It had just enough flat space to build two platforms for our small bivouac tents so we could spend a couple of nights there. On August 5 we climbed roped together again and reached the summit in partly cloudy weather that didn't allow the nice views of Latok III that we had hoped for. We rappelled and downclimbed back to camp, where we spent another night acclimatizing.

In the morning, we carefully downclimbed unroped most of the way to the glacier. Before reaching base camp, we stopped to observe conditions on the west face of Latok III that we couldn't see from Latok V. We saw and heard rocks falling down the face. "During the day, especially when the sun comes onto the west face, it's been way above freezing, and all the ice holding the rock together has melted," Mark observed. It was midsummer. "It isn't likely to get much colder for the next couple of weeks," Doug commented, "so we can expect conditions to stay about the same." To my relief, everyone decided the west face was too exposed to rockfall. We abandoned that objective.

Back at base camp, Rasool and Ali had prepared a big meal of pizza and potato-pea curry with chapatis. We slept, read, and rested after that. I called Ann on the satellite phone that night and learned that everything was fine in Seattle. I also spoke to Jed, who had just finished driver's education and was working at one of the municipal golf courses for the summer. He had attended a Red Hot Chili Peppers concert as well as the Real Madrid/DC

United soccer game. Busy with soccer practice, he would start tenth grade in the fall. I enjoyed hearing their voices, but the satellite phone wasn't an ideal form of communication. The air time was expensive: a ten- to fifteen-minute conversation could cost $40 to $50.

This meant Ann and I weren't able to do much more than exchange basic information and reassure each other that, at least for the moment, all was well. (Later, after I returned home from this expedition, Ann told me that satellite phone calls provided some relief from the worry she felt when I was away, but—at the same time—having more information about our climbing sometimes gave her more to worry about. It was different in the "old days" before satellite phones, she explained. When we couldn't communicate in real time, once we'd said our goodbyes at the airport, we just got busy with our lives—me in the mountains and her at home working at the library and being a single parent to Jed. The time for sharing details of our time apart would come after my safe return.)

In addition to calling home, we used our sat phone to get custom weather forecasts from a meteorologist in the United States. We learned we could expect several days of stormy weather and spent that time discussing our options. "We've been walking up and down the glacier for the past two weeks," Doug said, "and we can see that the summits of Latok II, then I, and then III are all lined up from west to east on top of a common base." The glaciers on the upper faces of all these peaks flowed down to form a ring of tall ice cliffs around the massif. The ice cliffs break off, dropping tons of ice thousands of feet to the glacier and pummeling the rock walls underneath. Doug concluded: "It's hard for me to find a climbing route on any of these peaks that isn't exposed to overhead hazard."

We each took turns with the binoculars examining the south sides of these mountains. Mark spotted something. "There's a gully on the south side of Latok II that leads up onto a ridge on the lower part of the mountain," he said. The ridge stuck out far enough that it appeared to be protected from the ice cliffs above, dropping huge avalanches down either side. It looked like the ridge ended at the level of the ice cliffs. "The crux," Mark said, "will be getting through that section." I took the binoculars and found the features Mark had described. "There may be a way to either climb up some steep rock above the ridge," I said, "or traverse left out onto a small lower glacier that leads to an ice face that gets us above the ice cliffs." It was

Doug's turn to scope it out. "If we can find a safe way past the ice cliffs," he concluded, "it puts us on the upper glacier that leads to an ice face and rock wall that eventually puts us onto the summit snowfields."

Once we pieced together what might be a safe route to the top of Latok II, we noticed that it looked possible to traverse down a snow ridge to the notch separating Latok II from Latok I and then to climb up to the summit of Latok I. We examined this ridgeline further and saw we might be able to descend snow slopes from the Latok I summit to the notch between Latok I and Latok III. If we climbed to the Latok III summit, from that notch we could descend the normal route on that mountain. As we realized the potential to link all the major summits of the Latok group into a single climb, our enthusiasm grew. We decided to make the "Latok traverse" our main objective.

No individual section of the Latok traverse seemed that difficult, except maybe the relatively short piece to the summit of Latok III from the notch between it and Latok I that we couldn't see. The intimidating aspects of this climb were its length and position. After reaching the summit of Latok II, traversing over to the Latok I summit and then to the top of Latok III would be a huge commitment. There would be no easy or safe escape route straight down in the event of bad weather, sickness, or injury because of the threat posed by falling ice from the ice cliffs that ringed the lower massif. The Latok traverse was more technically difficult and time-consuming, but it had one thing in common with the route Doug and I had taken on the Mazeno Ridge: The only escape was to either complete the traverse or reverse it.

Before heading out, we spent a day climbing partway up Latok II to verify that we had indeed chosen a safe route. On August 14, during a brief clearing in the weather, we hiked across the glacier to the base of Latok II. After climbing several hundred feet up a narrow but easy gully between two rock walls, we put on the rope and started up a crack system on the left side. We took off the rope after a couple hundred feet and scrambled up low-angled broken granite until we reached a snow ridge that angled up and left. Throughout the day we found bits and pieces of old fixed rope and the remnants of an old camp. "I thought this was a new route," I said to Mark and Doug. "It's a bummer to see that someone has been here before, but maybe they didn't go all the way and their signs will disappear as we get higher."

The snow ridge steepened into a rocky ridge, and we roped up again to climb several hundred feet to a good vantage point. From there we got a detailed look at the route. It involved traversing left from our small ridge onto the small but heavily crevassed lower glacier that I had spotted earlier. A series of ice bridges would take us over these gaping holes to the edge of a hundred-foot-wide trough. The trough was carved by snow avalanches that originated from slopes higher on the mountain and flowed over a small ice cliff looming above it. There was no sign of snow or ice debris scattered on the slopes outside this trough, which seemed to contain everything falling from above. Crossing the trough exposed us to the risk of getting hit by an avalanche. But we could minimize the risk if we ran across this short section, which looked to be the only part of the route exposed to serious overhead hazard. On the other side of the trough an hourglass-shaped ice face ran up through a smooth rock slab onto the upper glacier that curved around above the threatening ice cliff. We decided to accept the hundred-foot dash across the trough, given that the rest of the route looked safe.

Having confirmed this was a feasible route, we headed down. We reached the glacier just as it got dark and found our way to the other side with the beams of our headlamps. In this vast landscape, finding the one spot in the darkness that led up the rocky hillside from the glacier to our base camp seemed impossible. But Rasool always anticipated these kinds of problems, and as we neared the hillside, he and Ali stood above us, waving a lantern. Back at base camp we changed into dry clothes and, just as it started pouring rain, we sat down to a great meal of soup, dal, and chapatis.

Doug, Mark, and I left base camp on August 19 at 5:30 a.m. with six days of food and fuel. We estimated this would be enough to climb the south ridge of Latok II and continue on with the Latok traverse. The sky was clear, but the weather prediction wasn't ideal. It called for some moisture—difficult to know how much—but we launched because no significant storms were forecast over the next week. Our meteorologist said that a major storm would likely arrive in a week, so we needed to hurry. We started up Latok II the same way we had on our earlier reconnaissance, but the forty-pound packs we carried this time made us slower. By 1:00 p.m.

we reached the top of the snow-covered part of the ridge below the vantage point we had reached five days earlier.

This was the first sunny day since recent storms had deposited several
inches of new snow, and the heat triggered wet avalanches that poured over
the ice cliff into the trough through the small lower glacier we needed
to cross. We were only at about 18,000 feet, and to keep to our six- or
seven-day schedule for the traverse, we wanted to camp on the upper glacier above the ice cliff. But the avalanches were coming down frequently,
and there was a much greater chance of getting hit if we tried to cross it
in the afternoon heat. We knew everything would freeze together during
the night, and in the morning this side of the mountain would be in the
shade with almost no chance of avalanches coming down the trough. So
we stopped to spend the night there at what Doug named Ridge Camp.
We made two platforms—one for the six-foot by four-foot two-person
tent that Doug and I slept in and a smaller one for Mark to sleep on inside
a lightweight waterproof nylon bivy sack. To save weight, we had brought
just the one small tent, thinking one of us could sleep outside in the bivy
sack if the weather was calm. But if the weather was stormy, we would need
to squeeze all three of us inside the tent.

We left Ridge Camp at 4:00 a.m., just before dawn, and the mountain was
eerily quiet. Doug led the traverse from Ridge Camp onto the lower glacier.
Mark took over the lead and found a route that wove back and forth across
several deep crevasses on delicate snow bridges. At the trough nothing fell as
we all dashed across together, and then I led as we headed up the hourglass
ice face on the other side. The sun was just starting to hit the rock wall above
the hourglass, and ice clinging to this part of the mountain would soon come
hurtling down, so we climbed as quickly as our lungs would let us. About 800
feet up we reached the top of the hourglass and traversed out of the danger
zone onto the upper glacier, where we found a way across another maze of
crevasses to an ice face on the other side. Doug led over the bergschrund (a
crevasse that separates the ice face from the glacier below it), and we climbed
for six or seven rope lengths up the fifty- to sixty-degree ice face that brought
us to the large rock band separating us from the summit snowfields. The rock
band was split by a series of icy corners and chimneys that we followed until
evening; then we needed to find a place to spend the night.

The terrain was too steep to find a flat or even gently sloping place for the tent. With no other option, Mark and I chose the lowest-angled area in a patch of ice and chopped a tent platform in the slope. It would be easy to get caught up in the work constructing a bivouac and neglect to take breaks to drink and eat. So while Mark and I worked on the tent platform, Doug hung the stove on a small rock face and began the long process of melting ice, filling our water bottles, and handing us hot drinks and soup. It took several hours to create a ledge big enough, but eventually we set up the tent and all three of us got inside. We finished our dinner in cramped but cozy conditions that we dubbed the "Ice Palace." It was a very productive day that made up for having to stop early the day before, and we fell asleep around 11:00 p.m.

On the morning of August 21, we rose at 4:00 a.m. Given our precarious position, it took three hours to finish cooking and packing. Each of us brought different strengths to the team, and Mark was the strongest rock climber among us. I was glad it was his turn to lead as we left the Ice Palace and started up the most technically difficult part of the rock band. Our challenge for the day was to get past this obstacle and camp somewhere on the large upper snowfield. The first two days of the climb the weather had been good, but as we left our bivouac, I noticed clouds blowing in from the south, which was probably the moisture that had been forecast. Given what we knew, I thought we might get some new snow to make life difficult, but not a major storm that could be deadly if we didn't start descending immediately.

The route Mark chose linked a series of snow and ice ramps that wound through several steeper rock sections until we got to the base of a fifty-foot granite wall with no way around it. Too difficult to climb with a pack, Mark left his behind and worked his way up a two-inch-wide snow-filled crack using his hands, ice tools, and crampons until he reached the snow and ice slope above. He used one of the ropes to haul up his pack, then Doug and I took turns climbing up our other rope using rope ascenders. Because the wall was so steep, we used short slings to connect each ascender to our harness and longer ones to each foot. This enabled us to step up in the foot sling each time we slid the ascender up the rope. Climbing this wall brought us to the top of the rock band, where I took over leading and angled left to a series of easy ice runnels that took us through a final lower angled rocky section and onto the summit snowfields.

The stormy weather had reached the mountain, which was now enveloped in clouds, limiting our visibility. We had put in a huge effort over the past three days, and the technical difficulties on Latok II were behind us. But now we were at over 21,000 feet and faced with a lot of work to plow a track up another 2,300 feet of elevation gain through deep snow to the summit. What Doug and I brought to the team was the ability to do most of this mind-numbing work at high altitude. We thought we could reach the top in a day from where we were, and the weather was getting worse, so we looked for a place to camp and plot our next move. We reached the top of a small snow rib around 22,000 feet at a place we called the "Snow Dome," where the angle eased and we dug a platform for the tent and got inside. By that time we were getting blasted by 40-mile-per-hour wind-driven snow. To embark on the Latok traverse beyond the summit of Latok II, we needed better weather. We were buffeted all night in our exposed little aerie and got little sleep.

Conditions hadn't improved by the morning, so we abandoned the traverse and decided it would be an accomplishment just getting to the top of Latok II in such poor weather. We were basically okay—just tired and cramped, but with plenty of food and fuel. Later in the morning, the wind abated and an opening in the clouds allowed us to see all the way down to the glacier for the first time in almost twenty-four hours. This little "sucker hole" in the weather enticed us into making a summit attempt, but we needed to move quickly before it clouded in again.

Getting moving each morning was a time-consuming process. Our comfort—and ultimately our survival—depended on staying dry. To do that we had to perform several tasks in our little tent each morning. Before we could start the stove to melt water, we put away our sleeping bags, otherwise the layer of frost from condensation on the tent walls would drip on everything. With our bags in their waterproof stuff sacks, we scraped the tent walls with our cups to remove most of the frost, to minimize the dripping. Then we rearranged ourselves and all our gear so one of us could reach outside the tent to collect snow and hand it to the person cooking, who needed enough room to put it in the pot and avoid spilling what would soon be a liter of boiling water. After cooking, we moved around again to create enough room to alternate getting dressed. Working together in such a small space was a typical expression of the teamwork that occupied our lives 24/7 while on the mountain. It was easy to get frustrated with each other living in such cramped conditions in stormy weather. I was amazed that Doug didn't get more upset when I bumped him while he was lying in his sleeping bag using a pee bottle, causing him to spill nearly half a liter of urine on himself. These morning rituals usually took at least two hours.

When we finally emerged from the tent, we moved slowly up the slope through deep new snow. We spent hours ascending a series of long series of snow slopes each time, approaching what we thought was the summit ridge only to reach the crest and find another slope climbing into the clouds to another high point. After we crossed several of these false summits, clouds blew in thickly and it started snowing. With only a few feet of visibility, Doug saw a rock outcrop in the fog on the left that he was sure was the summit. Mark thought the summit was farther along the snow ridge on the right. We belayed Doug as he climbed up onto the top of the small pinnacle and then lowered him off an anchor he left on top.

Just as we were going to take turns tagging this "summit," there was a brief hole in the clouds and we could see the real summit was farther along the snow ridge, as Mark had suggested. We left the outcrop (jokingly referred to as Point Chabot), and I led off traversing below the crest, barely able to discern the snow ridge from the clouds, even though it was only a few feet away. To guide me, I ran my gloved hand along the crest of the sharp snow ridge, using it as a handrail. Climbing along the side of the ridge, I felt my way upward. When I could feel the ridge level off and then start down the other side, I knew we must be on top. I pulled in the rope so the others could join me. We had a brief celebration before starting down in the storm, hoping we could find our tent.

We rappelled from Point Chabot and downclimbed to the next false summit, then repeated this process several times from the other false summits. Doug was in front and, like he had done on our descent from the Mazeno Ridge, he used his uncanny sense of direction to find our snow-covered tent. Removing our outerwear, getting into our sleeping bags, and cooking was the reverse of our hours-long morning routine. Once bedded down, we endured another windy, stormy night. That evening Mark told me that he was seeing spots he thought might be retinal hemorrhages that can occur at high altitude. I said they were probably harmless "floaters"—nothing to worry about. Later, after he got home, he had an eye exam and learned that they were from retinal hemorrhages that could cause permanent eye damage. Luckily, it turned out okay for him.

Squeezed together inside the flapping tent, I slept poorly, which allowed my fears to take advantage of my semiconsciousness. I worried about what might happen if we weren't able to go down in the morning because it was too stormy. If we had to wait out a storm, I fretted that we might deteriorate from lack of sleep, and sealed up in this tiny tent, we would eventually get wet, and hypothermia could set in. I tried to purge my negative thoughts by reminding myself that we would be okay, that we could survive on the extra food and fuel we had brought for the traverse. Concerned that it might hurt morale, I didn't share my bad dream–induced anxiety with my partners. They may have had similar thoughts but didn't discuss them for the same reasons.

That morning, I looked outside the tent and was elated to see some clearing, with just enough visibility to start our descent. We brewed up, packed our gear, and downclimbed the snow slope to the top of the rock band. From there we began rappelling, and Mark was back in his element. He led the way, setting anchors using pitons pounded into cracks in the rock for the eight rappels down to the ice face below the Ice Palace. At that point, Doug took over as lead, building V-thread rappel anchors in the ice. To create the anchors he drilled two holes diagonally into the ice about eight inches apart with a long ice screw, so they intersected to create a V-shaped tube. Then he threaded a short piece of rope through this tube and tied the ends together to create a loop of rope anchored into the ice.

Six rappels down the ice took us to the upper glacier above the ice cliff. The cloud cover from the stormy weather kept the temperature cool, so we decided it was safe to keep descending in the afternoon. I took over the lead, and roped together we plowed through the snow around crevasses on the upper glacier to the top of the hourglass. We made four rappels from V-threads down the hourglass to the lower glacier below the ice cliff. Running across the trough, we moved quickly to where we had crossed the snow bridges on the way up. But the fragile snow bridges had melted, so we made a 150-foot free-hanging rappel off the top of a snow and ice wall to get down. For a rappel anchor we used a thirty-inch-long picket (aluminum snow stake) and a nylon stuff sack filled with snow and buried them in separate holes about three feet deep in the glacier. We tied the picket and stuff sack to a twenty-foot piece of small diameter rope that we used to equalize the load on the two anchor points. After this airy rappel, Mark led us up onto the side of the ridge, and we traversed to a final rappel that put us back at Ridge Camp. I decided to sleep outside so we weren't so cramped in the tent. Relieved that most of the danger was behind us, we thought it wouldn't be hard to make it to base camp the following day.

That night it started to snow, but I didn't mind if my sleeping bag got wet since I had a dry one back at base camp. Daylight came, and we packed up to go. After a couple of rappels, some downclimbing, and the final rappel into the gully, we reached the bottom. (We found out later that the gear we had seen on the mountain was left by a 1977 expedition led by an Italian priest, Don Arturo Bergamaschi. This expedition made the first ascent of Latok II via this route in traditional expedition style with eighteen team members fixing ropes and establishing fixed camps. We had just made the fourth overall ascent but the first alpine-style ascent of the mountain.)

About halfway across the Baintha Lukpar Glacier, we saw Rasool and Ali walking toward us. They met us with hugs and congratulations, then broke out the huge picnic they had in their rucksacks. Doug was especially happy to see that they had brought a big thermos of hot water, coffee, and filters—he had wanted a fresh cup of coffee for days. It was a great feeling, sitting there among friends and sharing a simple meal surrounded by some of the world's most spectacular mountain scenery. We packed up when it started sprinkling, and Rasool insisted on carrying my pack. The emotions that follow the completion of a significant climb overwhelmed me: I felt the total relaxation that comes after days of being cautious and vigilant, the relishing of simple comforts, the deep friendship that grows from having shared difficulty and danger, and the joy of experiencing powerful beauty in such an intimate way. These feelings can't be conjured up without having had a sublime experience to prompt them. I keep coming back to these mountains because I want to delight in them again and again.

Mark, Doug, and I wanted to do another trip together, so we decided to return to the Latok group the following year, 2007. This time Mark volunteered to be expedition leader. He worked with our friend Nazir Sabir and his tour company to obtain our permit. Latok I had been climbed only once, by a Japanese expedition in 1979. Their route was east of the ridge we had climbed on Latok II and was so exposed to avalanches that they had had to run away every time it snowed or they would have been swept away. They were threatened by ice cliffs that overhung their route and could break off any time, sending tons of ice cascading down. Several times they escaped being buried by only minutes. The route is considered so dangerous that no one has tried to repeat it.

Mark had previously been to the opposite side of the Latok group, in 1997 and 1998, to climb the north ridge of Latok I from the Choktoi Glacier. That route is more technically difficult but also safer than the Japanese route. It was first tried in 1978 by an American team—George Lowe (a member of our K2 expedition in 1986), Jim Donini, Michael Kennedy (a member of our Gasherbrum IV expedition in 1983), and Jeff Lowe. On that attempt, the team spent twenty-six days on the route climbing what's called capsule style. A hybrid of traditional expedition style and pure alpine style, capsule style meant fixing ropes between two camps at any one time to move supplies from a lower camp to a higher one. Like alpine style, the climbers stay up on the mountain the whole time, but like expedition style they make multiple trips between camps, enabling them to bring along more food and fuel—and therefore have the resources to spend more time working their way up the mountain.

The 1978 American team got to within about six hundred vertical feet of the summit before having to turn around, when Jeff became seriously ill. Since then, around twenty expeditions, mostly climbing in pure alpine style (including Mark's two) had tried and failed to reach the high point of the legendary 1978 attempt. Despite this discouraging history, we decided to make another attempt on the north ridge of Latok I.

Doug, Mark, and I reached Islamabad on June 7 and met with Nazir Sabir, our longtime friend and current president of the Alpine Club of Pakistan, and Nazir's friend Col. Manzoor Hussein. In addition to our expedition to Latok I, we had many things to discuss. I was a member of the American Alpine Club (AAC) executive commmittee, and the AAC had an ongoing project with the ACP to provide financial and material relief to the area in Pakistan-administered Kashmir that had been devastated by a severe earthquake in 2005. The AAC was also organizing a group of American women instructors to participate in an ACP climbing camp later that summer in Hunza. The camp would teach basic mountaineering skills to aspiring young Pakistani women climbers.

In Pakistan's strict Islamic society women were not allowed to go on multiday outings with nonfamily men. The solution that Nazir and I had come up with was to staff the camp with American women instructors, which was acceptable. Because there were hardly any qualified women mountaineering instructors in Pakistan, the American women would help make the camp possible. Security was another concern because fundamentalist militant groups did not believe that women should participate in such sports as climbing. However, the shaky peace agreements between the Pakistan government and the militants seemed to be keeping the violence to a minimum, so it seemed safe for the American and Pakistani women to participate in this ACP program together. We concluded our meal with a long discussion about a wide range of issues in the mountains: conservation, economic development, tourism promotion, and porter training, safety, and welfare.

The next day, the team flew to Skardu and reunited with Rasool and Ali who would accompany us again. We finished our provisioning three days later and drove to Askole to meet up with Asgar, the popular village leader who would be our sirdar. When we hiked out after climbing Latok II the previous year, Asgar had been our sirdar. Having the equivalent of the town mayor manage our porters (instead of asking Rasool to do it) helped ensure that we wouldn't have problems. Asgar invited us for dinner at his house, where we met some of the male members of his family. He had six daughters and four sons and told us he wanted to have five more. I wondered what his wife thought about that. Behind doorway curtains we saw the household's women busy in some back rooms. They prepared a delicious meal that included several chicken dishes, rice, and soup. But the women were not introduced to us, so we didn't have an opportunity to thank them.

Asgar had a terrible toothache, so Mark and Doug went over to the relatively new Italian-built clinic to look for supplies that might help. Like many villages with clinics built by NGOs or the government, there wasn't a medical staff there to run it. It wasn't locked so they went in and borrowed a dental mirror. Using it, they saw that Asgar had a cavity in the side of one of his molars. Doug gave him some Anbesol to apply to the tooth to help relieve the pain. We thought Asgar should go to the dentist in Skardu, but he insisted on coming with us.

On the morning of June 12, we assigned loads to the porters, and before they started off, Rasool delivered a serious speech about environmental protection (no wood-burning and no littering) and told them about all of our climbing exploits. We were American Alpine Club officers, he said, and such important people that they needed to do a good job. Rasool was being such a ham that we had to turn away so the porters couldn't see us laughing. When he was finished, Rasool led them in several cheers for their village, for the climbers, and for Pakistan, after which the porters grabbed their loads and ran up the trail. It is customary for the sirdar to make these kinds of speeches, but while Rasool was talking, Asgar looked at me and shrugged. "Rasool likes to talk," he said, "so I let him do it."

We followed the popular trekking route up the Braldu River that I had taken five times before on my way to K2 and Gasherbrum IV. At midday we left the well-beaten path to follow the Dumordu River at its confluence with the Braldu. In camp that night Asgar complained about his tooth, and he showed us a big ugly canker sore that had developed under his tongue. Someone had told him that a remedy for toothache was to gargle brake fluid, which he had been doing for a couple of days. We told him not to do that—it was probably the cause of the sore in his mouth. The next day he pulled a hard object out of his mouth that wasn't a tooth—an unknown object that had festered out. Nonetheless, he felt better and walked away saying something about how the brake fluid had worked.

On the third day of our trek, Mark woke up with a gastrointestinal ailment that we all get periodically in that part of the world. He threw up before we left camp and was feeling pretty bad, so I hiked with him while the porters and everyone else went ahead. By ourselves we got lost crossing a glacier, but some goat herders far up on the hillside yelled at us and signaled the way to go. Just as we caught up with the others at our lunch spot, Mark lost bowel control and fouled his pants. We were sympathetic with his plight but could still laugh at situations like this that we'd all experienced before.

When we reached camp, Mark crawled into his tent to sleep off his intestinal troubles. Doug, Asgar, and I hiked up a nearby ridge, where we saw two small herds of ibex jumping around in the rocks. We climbed to over 14,000 feet—a good acclimatization outing. That evening, the porters butchered the two live goats that they had been herding along the trail for the past several days. We had bought the goats because government regulations specify we need to give our local staff a meat ration if they are working with us for more than a couple of days. The goat meat was for them, but they gave us some of what they consider to be the choice pieces—like the liver. Unfortunately liver is one of the few things I really don't like, but to be polite I ate several pieces. Fresh meat was not something the porters could afford to eat in their villages on a regular basis, so they were happy to feast on it and the other provisions we brought for them.

Mark was fine after a day of rest, and on June 15 we reached our base camp on the Choktoi Glacier, below the north side of Latok I. We paid off the porters for their hard work. It was a beautiful spot, but camping on ice required us to repitch our tents every couple of weeks as the surface melted down around them. Our first task was to acclimatize, so over the next ten days we climbed several peaks in the area, including the Central and Northern Biacherahi Towers (both around 19,300 feet, or 5,900 meters). We made the first ascent of a 20,229-foot (6,166-meter) triple-summited peak that we named Suma Brakk, meaning "three summits" in Balti. On the summit of Suma Brakk we were visible from base camp several miles away, so we called Rasool and Ali on our line-of-sight walkie-talkies to see if they were looking at us with the spotting scope. Of course they were watching, and they got very excited seeing three tiny specks sitting on top. They yelled encouragement into the radio: "American Expedition! American Alpine Club! Doug Chabot! Mark Richey! Steve Swenson! Pakistan! *Zin-da-bad* [Long Live]!" We waved and yelled back, and everyone had a big laugh while making sure not to fall off our small rocky perch.

By early July we felt well-acclimatized and ready for an attempt on the north ridge of Latok I. The weather forecast indicated clear, calm weather starting around July 4, so we left base camp at 11:30 that same night. We started up an ice couloir that allowed us to quickly gain altitude and bypass a rock buttress that had taken Mark and his team a couple of days to climb on his earlier attempts. We moved together for about six hundred feet as it got progressively steeper and more difficult. To be safe, we stopped and Doug led individual sixty-meter rope lengths, belaying Mark and me up the straightforward but physically demanding ice climbing.

We found ourselves faced with a familiar alpine struggle—moving as fast as our bodies would let us in order to reach the top of the gully before the sun hit and the rockfall started. Doug's duty was to not fall, and Mark and I had the calf-burning job of kicking our way up the steep ice with the front points of our crampons as fast as we could while carrying forty-pound packs. The ice ended in a corner with loose rock that Doug climbed to reach the top of the rock buttress. Mark guessed it would take at least six more hours of easier but exhausting snow and ice climbing to reach the small, relatively flat spot where we wanted to spend the night. It was getting dark as we finally reached our bivouac spot. We still had all the work of leveling a platform, setting up the tent, melting snow for water to drink, cooking, and filling our bottles for the next day. It was 11:30 p.m. by the time we got to bed.

We woke at 5:30 a.m. to brew up and then headed for our second bivouac at a place that previous parties had named the "Second Snow Ridge." The distance wasn't nearly as far or the elevation gain as much as the previous day, so we looked forward to reaching our camping spot earlier in the day with less effort. I took the light pack since it was my turn to lead. At first it wasn't difficult to traverse under a rocky section of the ridge across a series of snow ribs separated by ice runnels and then up again. As I led up toward the Second Snow Ridge, however, the snow became soft and loose and barely supported my weight. Nearing the crest, I backed off trying to climb a ten-foot vertical to overhanging wall of meringue-like snow. After checking different route possibilities, I eventually went more to the right and excavated a trench with my ice tools to cut back the overhanging snow to slightly less than vertical. As I dug over my head, a large block of snow broke loose and slammed into my chest, knocking me off my feet. I swung onto my left arm holding the top of my ice tool whose shaft I had pushed into the snow—fortunately the sudden force of all my weight coming onto the ice tool didn't cause it to rotate out of the soft snow, which would have resulted in a long fall since my last ice screw was more than twenty feet below.

After getting back on my feet, I continued digging and climbing spread-eagled against the sides of the trench until I reached the ridgetop. I traversed the unconsolidated snow ridge back to a rocky outcrop where the wind had carved a small cave in a dollop of snow clinging to the side of it. I thought we could enlarge the snow cave to fit the tent. It was getting dark while Mark and Doug climbed the two-hundred-foot rope length up to me and burrowed out our bivouac site. Wet after groveling in the snow for hours, I was getting hypothermic as the temperature dropped. Mark and Doug finished the digging and set up the tent inside the snow cave while I put on warmer dry clothes and dry gloves and then melted snow for hot drinks. We all got into the tent, and I changed into some dry socks to warm up my feet. By the time we finished cooking and went to sleep, it was 11:30 p.m.

We were packed up by 7:00 a.m., and it was Mark's turn to lead. When he had been here before, the snow had been firm enough for his team to walk on top of this ridge. But we found the snow on the Second Snow Ridge had almost no strength; we just fell through it as if we were trying to walk across a tub of glass marbles. To keep from plunging through and out the bottom of the ridge, Mark inched along by boot-packing the snow into a solid trench. He pulled volumes of snow from the sides of the trench into the bottom and then stomped that into a track solid enough to support his weight. But two hours of work took him just fifty feet. We were only halfway up, and we could see sections of snow ridges on the upper mountain that looked as bad, or possibly worse, than what we had encountered so far.

Mark kept working while Doug and I belayed him from the snow cave, knowing that our progress was too slow and the snow conditions too unconsolidated for us to continue. Mark had a much greater investment of time and effort in this project since it was his third try, so it was harder for him to come to this conclusion. After working for another hour, he came back to where Doug and I were sitting to discuss our options. We only had food and fuel for about two more days, which we could probably stretch for another day. At the rate we were going, though, it might take us another week to climb the mountain. With such bad conditions, I was concerned about safety.

While Mark pounded out a track in the bad snow, our rope team was securely anchored to solid rock in the back of the snow cave. But if we progressed to where we left the cave, we would need to be able to set up anchors in the snow along the ridge to secure our rope team. As far as Mark had gone, he hadn't found any solid snow, ice, or rock where he could place a reliable anchor, and it didn't seem as if that would change ahead. Without good anchors, the roped system we used to protect us if someone fell would be useless. After talking these things over, we all reluctantly came to the conclusion that we should go down.

With a long rappel descent ahead of us, we needed to move quickly and efficiently to reach the glacier at the bottom before dark. As with any series of rappels, we needed to find places for secure anchors and then try to prevent the ropes from getting snagged above us when we retrieved them. Doug and Mark liked the process of building anchors, so they alternated going first. Each time they approached the end of the rope, they looked for a spot in either the rock or the ice to place an anchor. If there was a crack in solid rock nearby, they would hammer in a piton or place a stopper (a metal wedge threaded on a small cable placed in a crack in the rock). If there was a sheet of solid ice, they would build a V-thread.

Rappels are ideally made from double anchors with the load equalized between them using a short piece of small-diameter rope. This redundancy prevents the entire anchor from failing if one of the anchors breaks loose. Unfortunately, on our long descent from halfway up Latok I, we had only enough gear to leave behind single-point anchors. To prevent a single anchor failure from having tragic results, we loosely attached a separate temporary backup anchor to each rappel. The person who went first tested the single anchor by leaning back on the rappel ropes and then bouncing with his full body weight while the temporary backup anchor was in place just in case the single anchor failed. I went last, and because Mark or Doug performed the bounce test each time, I was confident enough to remove the backup anchor before I rappelled down.

Partway down, Doug placed a V-thread in the ice and put in an ice screw as a backup anchor. He didn't drill the V-thread very deep into ice that, instead of being a deep blue-gray color, was a lighter gray. After pulling our ropes from the previous anchor and looping them through the cord tied into the V-thread, Doug clipped in his rappel device. He moved down the ropes a few feet, and as he bounce-tested the anchor, the ice blew out from the V-thread and all our weight suddenly came onto the single ice screw we had as our temporary backup anchor! The screw held, keeping us from plunging thousands of feet to the glacier. In a sudden panic, I yelled, "Oh shit! Fire in another ice screw." As quickly as possible, we placed another backup ice screw.

Doug should have known, and Mark and I should have commented that the color and appearance of the ice indicated tiny air bubbles that would make it weak. We should have spent more time chopping away the aerated surface ice and drilling a deeper, stronger V-thread. I'd never seen or heard of a V-thread failing, and after that close call we paid more attention to the warning signs we had ignored. I appreciated that safety procedures (such as placing a backup anchor) that we had followed hundreds, maybe thousands of times, paid off this time and saved our lives. It was a stark reminder that no matter how much experience any of us had, there was always the need for humility in the ever-changing environment. As one of my engineering colleagues often said when he experienced something new at work: "Every day's a school day."

We rappelled a more direct line straight down a series of ice runnels and rock walls that was different from the way we had come up. It was quicker and would take fewer rappels, but the snowfields above us funneled into this descent route, exposing us to avalanches if it started to snow. When we left camp, high overcast conditions were helpful in keeping it cool and prevented rockfall or small snow slides. But as the day progressed, the cloud layer dropped and snow began to fall as we neared the bottom. The task ahead became more urgent—we needed to get off the mountain before the snow built up and caused avalanches, but we needed to take the time to be careful.

Just as wet snow slides started coming down, the team reached the glacier and walked away from the bottom of the face. Back at base camp, Rasool and Ali had prepared a dinner of dal bhat (a rice and lentil stew), and I crawled into my personal tent still thirsty despite having downed several liters of water and tea. I used a pee bottle at night to avoid having to get up and out

PREVIOUS PAGE, ABOVE: *Hiring porters in Skardu on the 1980 Gasherbrum IV expedition just before the minor riot*

PREVIOUS PAGE, BELOW: *Dave Cheesemond and Catherine Freer carrying loads out from the north side of K2*

THIS PAGE, ABOVE: *Camel train crosses the Shaksgam River on our 1990 K2 expedition.* (Photo by Greg Child)

THIS PAGE, BELOW: *Phil Ershler, Greg Child, Greg Mortimer, and Steve Swenson on the north side of K2 in 1990*

OPPOSITE, ABOVE: *David Breashears hires porters in Kharta in 1994 on the way to Everest's Kangshung Face.*

OPPOSITE, BELOW: *Our bivouac on K7 West in 2004; Chogolisa is in the background.* (Photo by Marko Prezelj)

THIS PAGE, ABOVE: *A figure at the Buddhist Monastery near Leh*

THIS PAGE, BELOW: *T'shering Sherpa, Ang Tashi, Dahn Singh Harkotia, and Lakpa Boding at Saser Kangri II base camp in 2009*

OPPOSITE, ABOVE: *Mark Richey approaches the ice chimney pitch on the 2011 ascent of Saser Kangri II.* (Photo by Freddie Wilkinson)

OPPOSITE, BELOW: *Steve Swenson and Haji Ghulam Rasool at the Nangmah valley base camp in 2015* (Photo by Scott Bennett)

NEXT PAGE, ABOVE: *Looking down the Great Dihedral on Changi Tower at Graham Zimmerman and Steve Swenson* (Photo by Scott Bennett)

NEXT PAGE, BELOW: *After successfully climbing Changi Tower, Scott Bennett, Graham Zimmerman, and Steve Swenson pose with Haji Ghulam Rasool.*

of my tent. In the morning I could tell I was still dehydrated since my urine was the color of apple juice. Big wet snowflakes, together with a cold damp wind, kept me inside either my tent or the mess tent most of the next day.

We had brought a portable shortwave radio for Rasool and Ali to listen to while we were gone and to get news from the BBC. When we tuned into the BBC in the mess tent on the morning of July 8, we learned that a crisis had unfolded in Islamabad surrounding the Red Mosque—a significant place of worship and a community center. A standoff between the army and militants within the mosque had escalated into violence. The fighting was alarming because it had the potential for undoing the shaky truce between the government and the militants, which might unleash a wave of violence across the country.

Later that day, Doug announced he was leaving the expedition now that we had abandoned Latok I. We still had another three weeks to climb before the porters were scheduled to come to get us. I was disappointed that he was leaving, as there were plenty of other spectacular mountains to climb near base camp. We were stronger as a team of three than a team of two. But Doug had personal reasons for leaving, and we had an amicable parting when he hiked out the next day with Ali, who would later return. Mark and I decided to try to climb the Ogre (also known as Baintha Brakk, 7,285 meters, or 23,900 feet), a technical peak that had seen only a few ascents—none from the south side.

A few days later, Doug called us on his sat phone after reaching Skardu. The Red Mosque standoff had ended. The government had launched an assault, and after three days of fighting they cleared the complex. More than a hundred students and militants, including several foreign fighters, had been killed along with about a dozen soldiers. The Karakoram Highway (KKH) had been closed where it borders Khyber Pakhtunkhwa (KPK) because of skirmishes with militants who were protesting what they viewed as an attack on an Islamic institution. The closure of the KKH had caused food and fuel shortages, but after a few days it had reopened and supplies were getting through. Doug had eventually been able to catch a flight from Skardu to Islamabad, so we didn't worry about him traveling the KKH alone. The guesthouse where we stay in Islamabad is secured with a ten-foot concrete wall and a guard at the gate. Doug kept a low profile there before catching his flight back to the United States.

It rained and snowed at base camp for days after Doug left. The weather cleared on July 18, and Mark and I waited for another day, hoping the sun's heat would cause the several feet of new snow to consolidate and slide off the steeper slopes. The next day, we left base camp before dawn, with six days of food and fuel, hoping to take advantage of the freezing temperatures that made for firm snow conditions on the glacier. A small icefall in the glacier guards the approach to the Ogre, and we reached it just as the sun hit and turned the snow into deep, wet slop. We saw wet snow slides in the icefall large enough to sweep someone into a crevasse. Of all the risks we face in climbing, the one that scares me most is the prospect of getting pushed into a hole by a slide and then buried alive by wet snow the consistency of fresh concrete.

It would take several days of good weather for the conditions to stabilize, and the forecast called for only three days of sun. After that, a weak low-pressure system to the north was supposed to draw pulses of monsoonal moisture from the south into the Karakoram. We didn't have time to wait for better snow, so we looked around for something else to climb. Across the glacier there was a safe and fun-looking route on what we called Island Peak because of its position in the middle of the Choktoi Glacier. (We discovered later that two Canadians, Jon Walsh and Jeff Relph, made the first ascent of this peak in 2006, naming it Choktoi Spire.) Heading down off the icefall, we set up camp in the middle of the glacier. The following day we climbed a snow and ice couloir leading to a col on Choktoi Spire. From there we followed its steep rocky north ridge.

Just below the summit it got dark, and Mark used his headlamp to scramble over another tower where he reached the twenty-foot-high monolithic summit block. These last few feet were devoid of any cracks that Mark could use to place a piton, stopper, or cam that would hold him. Without this kind of protection, taking a fall there would almost certainly result in serious injury. Mark found the climbing was too difficult for him to feel safe, so he backed off. Disappointed not to finish the final few feet to the summit, we were satisfied that we had climbed as much of the peak as we safely could using the equipment we had.

When Mark joined me on my small ledge, the wind had died, and it was unusually warm for this elevation at night. With no clouds we had a sweeping view of every constellation in the Eastern Hemisphere, and a thin moon illuminated the great peaks of the Karakoram around us in a luminous, dreamlike glow. Even if we didn't get to the tippy top, this picture was forever imprinted on my mind. With great reluctance I clipped in with my rappel device and started sliding down the ropes toward the glacier somewhere in the darkness far below. After about thirty hours we returned to our tent on the glacier by 10:00 a.m.

We returned to base camp on July 22 and spent a few days with Rasool and Ali packing things up to leave. Asgar and two other Askole men arrived the evening of July 25 to help us prepare loads for the twenty-seven porters who would show up the next morning. As we walked out, Mark and I encouraged the porters to help clean up campsites alongside the Biafo Glacier that had been littered by some trekking groups. With our coaching, they separated the trash into three piles; one for paper to burn, one for compostables to bury, and one for cans and bottles to pack out. Asgar and our Askole porters were realizing the need to be good stewards of these beautiful places; they would present an even more attractive destination for foreign tourists if they were kept clean.

When we reached Skardu on July 29, I worked with some friends to get an appointment with Brigadier General Ikram ul Haq at his army base east of Skardu near Khaplu. Mark and I thought the brigadier general might help us get permission for a future climbing expedition in the Kondus valley. We drove to the army base in two jeeps. A Pakistan International Airways pilot who flew Boeing 777 jets internationally was in one of the jeeps with Mark and me. The pilot was a friend of a friend who knew the brigadier general, and helped arrange the meeting. We were shown into General Ikram ul Haq's office. A courteous man, he indulged us in a two-hour conversation over cold drinks, tea, and hors d'oeuvres. We discussed the Siachen conflict (the theater of operations he commanded for the Pakistan Army). He felt that both Pakistan and India were trapped in a standoff that neither army wanted. Despite a three-year cease-fire, he said both sides suffered numerous casualties and expended large sums of money to maintain forces in a harsh high-altitude environment. He liked the idea of a demilitarized

Siachen Peace Park that was being proposed by individuals and groups on both sides as an honorable way to disengage.

Mark and I briefed General Ikram ul Haq on our twenty-seven-year history of climbing in Pakistan and the various humanitarian and conservation efforts with which we had been involved. We asked about getting permission to climb in the Kondus valley, stressing that we were not journalists or spies—we were only interested in going there to do first ascents of the valley's many unclimbed peaks. The brigadier general politely told us that it was a restricted area and he didn't have the authority to give us permission. We must get permission from the Army General Headquarters (GHQ) in Rawalpindi, he said. If we got permission from GHQ, he would help us in any way that he could. Based on how I got my previous permit, I knew the Brigadier at the army base near Khaplu had enough influence over the climbing permit process to enable us to go there. I figured that he did not want to deal with climbers in his theater of operations, so rather than say no, he referred us to the Army GHQ—a place he knew would be a black hole for our inquiry.

Mark and I drove to Islamabad in a hired van. The towns along the Karakoram Highway seemed full of the normal chaos of crowded shops and honking cars. We didn't see any disturbances or protests. According to our usual security practice, we spent the night in Chilas rather than drive after dark the KKH section mostly populated by Pashtun tribesmen. Before our departure for home, we learned that security concerns were high after a wave of militants' bombings in response to the Red Mosque assault. We met with Col. Manzoor to discuss the Alpine Club of Pakistan/American Alpine Club camp for Pakistani women climbers that had been postponed several times because of the terrorist attacks. The camp was rescheduled for mid-August. After the Red Mosque siege, the peace agreements between militants in the tribal areas and the Pakistan government collapsed, and the Pakistani Taliban began attacking the army again. (We learned later that the ACP decided the camp might become a target for militants and canceled it as a security risk.)

Back home, I thought about the chaotic situation in the Karakoram. It wasn't clear if or when we would be able to return to Pakistan. Militants in the Federally Administrated Tribal Areas (FATA) and parts of Khyber Pakhtunkhwa (KPK) continued to challenge the government by attacking security forces, traditional tribal leaders, and implementing Sharia Law in areas they controlled. They used the collective anger over the Red Mosque incident to bring together otherwise disparate groups into a single movement they called the Teherik-i-Taliban Pakistan (TTP). In November 2007 the Pakistan Army launched an operation against the TTP to take back control of the district of Swat in KPK. In December the former prime minister, Benazir Bhutto, was assassinated in Rawalpindi, just south of Islamabad, after returning from exile to run in the 2008 General Election. The TTP, al-Qaeda, and the Pakistan military establishment all had motives for killing her. The Marriott Hotel in Islamabad was bombed in the fall of 2008, killing 54 people and injuring 266.

Other events caused relations between the United States and Pakistan to deteriorate even further. In January 2011 a CIA contractor named Raymond Davis, operating under the guise of a diplomat, shot and killed two potential Pakistani assailants in the city of Lahore. And in May of that year, a team of US Navy Seals raided Osama bin Laden's northern Pakistan compound and killed him. After these complex events, American climbers found it almost impossible to get visas on time, or to get them at all. Given the political violence and strong anti-American sentiment in Pakistan, I had to see how the situation played out before I planned another expedition there.

CHAPTER 10

THE RISK OF REGRET

SASER KANGRI II SOUTHWEST FACE, 2009
TSOK KANGRI, 2011
SASER KANGRI II SOUTHWEST FACE, 2011

O ur Latok expeditions in 2006 and 2007 had gone really well, so when Mark Richey suggested that we look at some peaks in India for a 2009 trip, I was interested. He thought we should check out peaks in the eastern Karakoram, in the Ladakh region of Kashmir on the Indian side of the Line of Control (LOC) and the Actual Ground Position Line (AGPL). These mountains were just a few miles away as the crow flies from where we had climbed in Pakistan, and many of them were spectacular peaks. But in the eastern Karakoram we would be safe from Pakistan's internal conflicts. The linear swath where the two countries' armies were faced off was what we called a "political wilderness" where only military personnel could go. The extent of the closed areas varied over time depending on how much fighting was going on.

Mark had been to the eastern Karakoram in 2001 on an expedition led by the famous British climber Chris Bonington. The Indian government, through the Indian Mountaineering Foundation (IMF), had started to issue climbing permits for a few peaks in a small area in the southeast corner of the range, and Bonington's expedition went to explore and climb in the Arganglas valley. Mark Richey and his American partner, Mark Wilford, made the first ascent of a peak they called Yamandaka (6,218 meters, or 20,400 feet), which they named after a fierce but benevolent Buddhist god. From the summit they observed a sea of mountains to the north, most of which were unclimbed, in an area that was still closed. After the India-Pakistan cease-fire in 2003, the Indian government opened some new areas of the Karakoram to climbers, including the mountains that Richey and Wilford were looking at.

Indian mountaineer Harish Kapadia—diligent chronicler of the Indian Himalayas and joint leader of the 2001 expedition to the Arganglas—had sent Mark a DVD with pictures of the eastern Karakoram. One of the photos was from the Kardung La and showed the southwest face of a large mountain in the distance that stood well above the surrounding peaks. After some research, Mark and I established that it was Saser Kangri II (7,518 meters, 24,665 feet). Additional research turned up an account in the 1986 *Himalayan Journal* by an Indo-Japanese expedition stating they had climbed the "west summit" of Saser Kangri II in 1985. But our photo of the peak did not match that description. It showed a long east–west summit ridge where the east end seemed to be the high point and the west end did not rise up to create a separate peak. Mark and I came to the conclusion that the Indo-Japanese "west summit" did not really exist. If that were true, Saser Kangri II was the second highest unclimbed peak in the world. (The highest unclimbed mountain is Bhutan's Gangkhar Puensum [7,570 meters, or 24,836 feet], where climbing mountains above 20,000 feet is prohibited.) Because the 1985 expedition had claimed a summit, many thought Saser Kangri II had been climbed. This misinformation had helped keep others away.

Mark and I decided to get a closer look, and we applied to the IMF for a permit to climb Saser Kangri II in 2009. Outside of a close circle of friends, we kept our plans a secret because it could become a race to see who would get there first if the international climbing community became aware of the existence of such a significant unclimbed peak. The IMF made a public list of expeditions each year that had been granted permits, but having our plans made public once we had a permit was not a concern; the IMF was not supposed to grant multiple permits for a peak like Saser Kangri II for any given year. Since Mark had been to the area before, he volunteered to be the leader. He invited his partner from the Yamandaka climb, Mark Wilford, to join us, along with another member of their Arganglas trip, Jim Louther from the UK. I had met Wilford, an experienced and well-respected American climber, but we had never climbed together. I didn't know Jim, but I accepted Mark's recommendation that the four of us would make a good team.

Chewang Motup and his wife, Yangdu, ran an adventure tour company that had provided services to the 2001 Bonington expedition to the Arganglas valley. Mark had been pleased with their services and asked them to help us obtain our permit for Saser Kangri II. Even though the IMF announced the area around Saser Kangri II had been opened to climbers, we knew it was going to be difficult to successfully navigate our way through the bureaucracy and obtain a permit. Fortunately, Motup was very familiar with IMF regulations. He knew the local officials where we would be going because he had grown up in the Nubra valley, not far from Saser Kangri II.

The IMF regulations for the eastern Karakoram stated that all non-Indian teams needed to be a "joint expedition," which meant that our team needed to include an equal number of Indian and American climbers with joint leadership. Although it wasn't explicitly stated, our understanding of the IMF's reason for this was to give Indian climbers a chance to learn from foreign climbers. To meet this requirement, Motup agreed to be the coleader with Mark, and for our Indian team members he recruited several ethnic Sherpas from Darjeeling and others from Ladakh and Kaumon—mountainous areas in India where the locals are accustomed to this environment. The Indian team members had grown up learning how to survive in a rugged alpine landscape, and most had been taught basic to intermediate climbing skills. Motup submitted the application to the IMF in late 2008, and we hoped they would issue us a permit the following spring.

In the meantime, back in Seattle, changes were afoot for me professionally. In March 2009 the CEO of the engineering firm I was part owner of called me and the other Seattle owners into a video conference that included the owners from our other offices across the United States. He announced that the Board of Directors had recommended we sell the company. The share price that had been negotiated with the buyer was announced, and a face-to-face ownership meeting was scheduled for later in the spring to vote on the deal. After leaving the conference, I did a quick calculation based on the number of shares I owned and realized I could retire early if I wanted to. I enjoyed the engineering work, but I also felt that my shelf life as a consultant was nearing its end and the never-ending hustle to win projects and justify my salary was getting old. Given the opportunity to do something different, I decided immediately to "retire."

I called Ann to tell her about the upcoming sale. "So guess what," I said, "I'm going to retire at the end of the year." After a long pause Ann said, "Well that's a big surprise, but it sounds like a good deal for you. If that's what you want to do, I think you should do it."

The IMF eventually issued the expedition team a permit on July 17, 2009—quite close to our August 1 departure date. Once we had the climbing permit, we applied for the special visa that was required for us to enter the eastern Karakoram, which was classified as a high-security area. Jim had no problem getting his visa in the UK, and neither did Mark, who got his from the Indian embassy in Washington, DC. But because we lived out west, Wilford and I had to send our passports to the consulate of India in San Francisco, which balked at issuing us the special visa, even though they had a letter from the IMF instructing them to do so. It didn't help that I had stamped visas in my passport from India's archenemy Pakistan. The consulate requested a letter explaining what I had been doing there. The visa application process dragged on, and I resented all the time it took asking every high-level person I knew in the Indian government for help—time I otherwise would have spent with my family. The consulate finally issued us our visas late in the day on Friday, July 31, and my flight to Delhi left the next morning. I hired a courier to pick up my passport from the consulate in San Francisco, deliver it to Alaska Airlines at SFO, and put it on a late-evening flight to Seattle. Ann drove me to the airport in the morning, and we stopped at air cargo to pick up my passport before I boarded my flight.

At the briefing in Delhi with the IMF we met Biju, a friendly Indian Air Force captain who had been assigned to our expedition as the liaison officer. On August 4 the two Marks, Jim Louther, and I flew with

Biju from Delhi to Leh, the historic capital of the Himalayan Kingdom of Ladakh, which is now a district capital within the Indian state of Jammu and Kashmir. From the air, Leh reminded me of Skardu, which is not so far away on the other side of the LOC in Pakistan. Both towns are irrigated oases located alongside the Indus River, surrounded by dry, rubble-strewn mountains. But beyond topography and flora, the similarities ended. Unlike the Islamabad-Skardu connection on the government-run Pakistan International Airlines, air transportation from Delhi to Leh was easy and reliable. Several privately owned airlines provided service in addition to Air India, the government-owned airline. Leh is connected to the rest of India by two separate paved highways (as opposed to the single narrow, winding, and precipitous road to Skardu). There was an Indian Army and Air Force base near the Leh airport to support the large number of troops stationed in this politically sensitive area, but we saw almost no military presence once we drove into Leh.

Leh is at an altitude of 11,500 feet, so we planned to spend a couple of days there to acclimatize. Motup and Yangdu's summer office in Leh was next to our hotel courtyard, and Motup greeted us there with a huge smile and a firm handshake. In the office we met Yangdu, who stood to greet us and then went back to her computer to continue making arrangements for the many trips they had going at this busy time of year. From what I could see and from earlier correspondence, Motup seemed to be the external face and strategic planner for the company, and Yangdu and her staff took care of all the details. Their skills seemed complementary, and I was happy that we had what looked like a very good team as our local agent. Unlike Skardu, where ancient non-Muslim (Buddhist) rock art has been vandalized, Leh seemed comfortable sharing its space with several religions. Ladakh is primarily Buddhist, and we visited a number of extraordinary sixteenth-century working monasteries located in and around Leh. In the middle of town there was a beautiful mosque with a towering, white minaret from which we could hear the call to prayer several times each day.

To supply their troops on the Siachen Glacier, the Indians had built a road over the Kardung La across the Ladakh Range between Leh and the Nubra valley, where Motup was from. Early on the morning of August 6, Jim and I borrowed mountain bikes from Motup and rode up to what the Indians claimed was the 18,380-foot-high Kardung La (5,602 meters) and the "World's Highest Motorable Road." But our altimeters showed it to be several hundred feet lower. What seemed like a fun and challenging outing to see the countryside turned into a physical ordeal: we weren't acclimatized well enough to climb the 6,000 feet to such a high pass after only two nights in Leh. The jeeps with the rest of our team picked us up at the pass by midday. I was in a jeep with Motup, and I learned that he had grown up in the small village of Tigr, where we were headed. At the northernmost tip of India, the Nubra valley has become isolated from the rest of the world by political and mountainous barriers. To the north is the rugged eastern Karakoram, to the west is the disputed and heavily militarized LOC/AGPL between India and Pakistan, to the south is the rugged Ladakh Range, and to the east is the disputed boundary between India and China, where troops still face off since the 1962 border war.

In September 1972, when Motup was just seven years old, he was sent off to a boarding school. Before that he had a tutor, but his father was an educated civil servant and wanted his son to continue with his studies, so he enrolled Motup in a school in Srinagar. The city was about 330 miles away from Tigr, and in the 1970s traveling there was so arduous that it might as well have been on the other side of the world. This was before the road over the Kardung La was built, and it took Motup several days to walk 70 miles south from the Nubra valley and over the pass to the town of Leh. From there, he traveled by bus 260 miles west to Srinagar, the main urban area in the Kashmir valley. Motup's father would sometimes arrange for him to accompany other locals traveling to Leh—crossing the Kardung La could be dangerous as it was subject to blinding snowstorms any time of year. When Motup was at the boarding school, he came home from school only a couple of times each year. He was terribly homesick, especially at first. Often he wasn't able to find other travelers going between Leh and the Nubra valley, and by age ten Motup was able to make the difficult journey alone.

The only student from such a remote and primitive village, Motup was an outsider at school. But his upbringing had given him a love of the outdoors, and by twelve he became an active participant in the school's outdoor program. One of the teachers, a man from England, taught the young people basic mountaineering skills. Motup's love for adventure in the mountains continued to grow, and as a young teenager he stopped going back to the Nubra valley for his summer vacation and remained at school to trek and climb in the mountains there. Recognizing Motup's talent and skill in the mountains, the school sent him at age thirteen to the

Nehru Institute of Mountaineering (NIM) in Uttarkashi, where he was the youngest student taking an adventure course. After the adventure course ended, he returned to school in Srinagar. In 1982, at seventeen, Motup returned to the NIM for his basic mountaineering course and the next year for his advanced mountaineering course.

Motup did so well that the NIM recommended he be included on an Indian Army team being assembled by the IMF to go to Everest in the fall of 1985. He was considered to be too young for the Everest trip, but he was determined to go, so he traveled on his own to Kathmandu and hiked with some porters he hired to the base camp, thinking he could discretely follow the IMF team up the mountain. Once he got to Everest base camp, however, Motup realized how foolish his plan was, but he knew a few of the climbers there, and they didn't send him back. Eventually they asked him to help carry loads up through the Khumbu Icefall. Motup made a good impression, even though the expedition suffered a great tragedy when several members were trapped in a storm high on the mountain and perished.

The next year, Motup was asked to join another expedition to the Siachen, and in 1988 he started working for an Indian adventure travel company. He started Rimo Expeditions in 1990, the company he still runs. Part of his business regularly brought him to Darjeeling, where he got to know many in the Sherpa community who had migrated there from Nepal in the days of the British Raj. There he met Yangdu, the daughter of Nawang Gombu, a famous climbing Sherpa and the nephew of Tenzing Norgay, who made the first ascent of Mount Everest with Edmund Hillary. Gombu had reached the summit of Everest in 1963 with Jim Whittaker on the first American ascent of the mountain. Both Motup and Yangdu had deep connections within the Indian mountaineering community and ran a well-respected and successful adventure tour company.

After a long jeep ride down the north side of the Kardung La, we reached the Nubra valley and Motup's home village of Tigr. There we met up with the rest of our team. Motup introduced us to Ang Tashi and Lakpa Boding, two Sherpas who had climbed Everest, as well as Tshering Sherpa and the Ladakhi climber Konchok Thinlese, who comprised the Indian members of our climbing team. Motup suggested we bring another Ladakhi climber, Dhan Singh Harkotia, who was less experienced, but he could help carry loads in exchange for us teaching him basic mountaineering skills. We looked forward to working with the Indian climbers to help us get to base camp, do a reconnaissance of the area, and climb some peaks for acclimatization. They could also support our efforts up to the base of Saser Kangri II. But we wouldn't be able to take them with us on the climb itself. Having unfamiliar partners without the expertise to be on such a big, steep, technical mountain wouldn't allow us to develop the synergy we needed to climb alpine style on this difficult undertaking. In addition to the Indian climbers, we had Manbhadur Rai as our cook and Soop Singh as his assistant. In total, with the four of us, our LO Biju, Motup as our coleader, the five Indian climbers, and two cooks, we had a total of twelve expedition members.

From photos, maps, Google Earth images, and the account of the 1985 expedition on this mountain, we decided the best climbing route to the "east" summit of Saser Kangri II was via the southwest face. But there was no record of anyone having been to the south side of Saser Kangri II, so we had to discover a way to get there. Normally the approach to a mountain would go up the valleys and then onto the glacier that led to the base of the peak, but the southwest face of Saser Kangri II sits above the South Shukpa Kunchang Glacier, which eventually drains into the Shyok River. During the warm summer months, the Shyok, like all the major rivers in the Karakoram, becomes swollen with snowmelt. Approaching Saser Kangri II via the Shyok was similar to the treks I had made in 1986 and 1990 along the Shaksgam River on K2's north side. Walking up these types of valleys entailed multiple river crossings each day because the channels zigzagged back and forth between cliffs that towered over either side of the gravel floodplain. The Shyok River was much larger than the Shaksgam, however, so the summertime floodwaters were much deeper and swifter and lasted longer. The Shaksgam floodwater lasted from around mid-June until late August, but Mark's friend Harish had informed us that walking up the Shyok would likely be impassable between April and October. Unless we wanted to hike up the river in April and be trapped by floodwaters for five months, we would have to find a different way.

Jim used a British Army contact to obtain Indian topographic maps of the area even though they had been classified for security reasons. Reviewing satellite imagery available on the internet that Mark and I had looked at, we pieced together a working approach. Our expedition would leave the road that runs up the Nubra valley at the place where the Sakang Lungpa

River flows in from the northeast, and then we would hike up that valley to the glacier with the same name. A few miles above the snout of the Sakang Glacier, an unnamed glacier flowed in from the east that we could follow up to a 20,000-foot pass. A small glacier on the other side of that pass would take us down to the South Shukpa Kunchang Glacier, which led to the base of the southwest face of Saser Kangri II. On paper, it looked like the best approach, but we had no detailed photos that might show cliffs or huge glacial crevasses. These kinds of obstacles could block the way or make it very difficult to move all our equipment and supplies to where we would start our climb. It was exciting to have such a unique opportunity to travel through this "blank on the map" as Himalayan explorers had done a hundred years ago.

On August 8 we drove from Tigr up to the bridge over the Sakang Lungpa River just above its confluence with the Nubra. There we met the thirty porters that Motup had hired to carry our supplies and equipment to base camp. We had forty-five loads, so there were not enough porters to move all the loads to our base camp at the same time. Most of the experienced local porters were busy working for the Indian Army up on the Siachen Glacier, so there was a shortage. The porters we hired looked young and inadequately dressed. We decided to have them accompany us now and then hire fifteen of the strongest porters to make a second trip with the remaining loads.

Just as Motup had told us, the Sakang Lungpa flowed from the mountains in an impassable deep, narrow, rocky gorge, so we needed to follow a rudimentary shepherd's path that climbed 3,000 feet from the road up a steep rocky hillside just south of the river. We thought this might be a hard day for Biju, our LO, so I walked slowly with him up the long, steep hill from the road, encouraging him along and making sure he didn't get lost or hurt. What I didn't expect was how slowly Wilford climbed up that hill. He and I had crossed paths several times in the past, and I had looked forward to climbing with him after hearing and reading about all of his accomplishments over the years. Traveling with him for several days, Wilford had told me about his career as a climbing equipment sales rep and his busy family life with a wife and two young children. He had devoted much of his life to climbing, and I could relate to his stories about the difficulties in trying to balance work, family, and climbing. Had these responsibilities interfered with the physical training he needed to do in preparation for this trip?

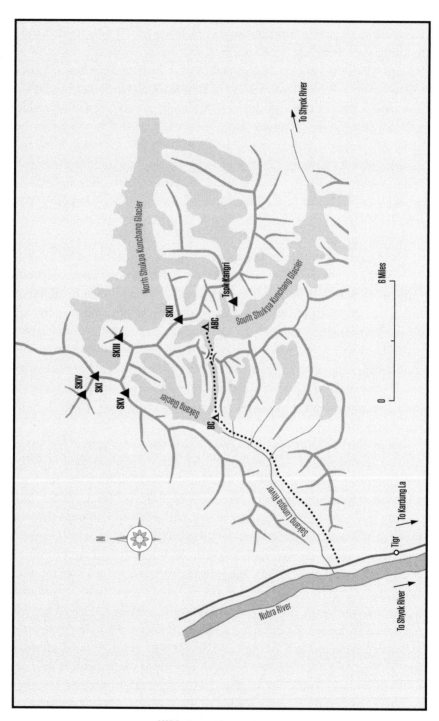

MAP 6: *Saser Kangri Group*

At the top of the long hill above the road, the path traversed along rocky ledges and treacherous slopes, and a slip could mean a several-thousand-foot tumble off a cliff into the river roaring in the gorge below. Fortunately the shepherd's path was littered with goat droppings that enabled us to follow in a scatological Hansel and Gretel manner when the trail disappeared among the rocks. After eight hours of walking on our first day, we reached camp and had a lovely evening with plenty of help with the chores from our Indian team members. The next day, we walked two and a half hours to a large meadow above the snout of the Sakang Glacier. There we made our second camp and established a supply cache. Mark sent our porters back down with instructions for half of them to bring up the remaining loads while we looked for a suitable site above for our base camp. Our expedition had enough supplies at our supply cache to feed the porters when they came back; it would take them three days to ferry everything from there to our base camp.

That afternoon, Mark, Wilford, Jim, and I made a reconnaissance several miles up the east lateral moraine of the Sakang Glacier. We found an unnamed glacier in a valley above us to the east; we thought it led to the pass we could cross over to the South Shukpa Kunchang Glacier. We searched the hillside for a suitable base camp site. Tucked between a rocky peak on one side and the lateral moraine from the unnamed glacier, we found a small meadow at 17,000 feet split by a stream of fresh running water that was a perfect spot for our base camp. Surrounded by large granite boulders, we could also practice our rock climbing. As we walked back to camp at the supply cache, we marked a route for the porters with small cairns.

The next morning was meant to be a rest and acclimatization day before moving up to base camp, but Biju looked ill. We clipped a portable blood oxygen sensor onto his finger; it measured 64 out of what should have been 90 or higher at this altitude. His resting pulse was 120. Those numbers indicated Biju was experiencing serious altitude problems that could develop into a life-threatening ailment like high-altitude pulmonary edema (HAPE) or high-altitude cerebral edema (HACE). He needed to descend to a lower elevation, and after breakfast he left with one of the Sherpas. After descending to the Nubra valley, Biju was fine, but rather than rejoining us later, he made his way back to his air force unit, and we never saw him again. Typically if the LO leaves the expedition, a replacement is not assigned, and this was our case too. On August 11 the expedition moved up to base camp. It took two more days for the porters with the rest of our loads to move everything from the supply cache up to base camp. The Indian team members worked hard to make a comfortable camp where all of us would spend the next six weeks.

On August 12, while the Indian team members finished setting up all our tents and building a latrine, my three Western teammates and I climbed up the rocky moraine that led onto the unnamed glacier. It gave me a thrill to think we were entering territory that, as far as we knew, no one had seen before. The unnamed glacier was about a half mile wide, and we kicked steps in the calf-deep snow that ascended gently for a couple of miles. We rounded a bend and saw a snowy pass about four miles ahead of us at the head of the valley. The four of us cached some equipment there and returned to base camp.

I had gotten to know Jim better and was impressed by his cardio fitness, good humor, and ability to teach the Americans how to play bridge. The stories he told us about his previous adventures—like skiing across Greenland while pulling sledges with all their supplies, and climbing some big, snowy peaks—were impressive. But these trips hadn't provided the kind of experience needed for the steep, technical climbing we would likely find on Saser Kangri II. Between Jim's lack of technical experience and Wilford's fitness issues, did we have the right team for this project?

The next day Mark stayed behind to recover after straining his back the previous day, but Wilford, Jim, and I brought Tashi, Lakpa, Tshering, and Thinlese with us up the unnamed glacier. We followed a circuitous route around several crevasses to reach the pass at 20,000 feet. The four Indian climbers went back to base camp after dumping the supplies they had carried, and the three of us spent the night there to acclimatize. In the morning we anchored a length of rope and rappelled over a short ice cliff onto snow slopes on the other side of the pass. As we walked down to the South Shukpa Kunchang Glacier, I felt huge relief knowing we could at least get to the base of our mountain.

It was a beautiful clear day. Looking up, for the fist time we could see the entire southwest face of Saser Kangri II. The nearly 25,000-foot-high summit stood atop a 6,000-foot wall of rock and ice that was too big to fit within my field of vision; I had to scan up and down and back and forth to see the whole thing. No one spoke as the magnitude of our undertaking sank in and each of us examined the face to make our own determination about its feasibility. My first thought was *What have I gotten myself into?* But when I realized that large areas on this face were not threatened by overhead hazards, and it consisted of solid-looking granite and firm snow and ice, my attitude took a quick turn. I said to myself *This is very cool.*

The southwest face of Saser Kangri II had the potential for some of the best conditions I'd ever seen on a steep technical mountain of this size, and it provided the shortest, most direct way to the summit. When I saw that the west end of the summit ridge reached by the 1985 Indo-Japanese team definitely did not look like the highest point on the peak, I got even more excited. Just as I started to say something, to my astonishment, Jim said, "Maybe we can find an easier way farther west around the corner." Wilford agreed. I was shocked that these guys didn't see it like I did. Jim seemed overwhelmed by the undertaking, and it felt like part of Wilford was somewhere else. Mark knew them better than I did, so I didn't say much. We needed to get his opinion before I weighed in on what I thought we should do. Back at our camp at the pass, Mark had arrived with Motup and Thinlese. His back was feeling better. Jim, Wilford, and I explained to Mark what we had seen on our recon. We decided to go back to the vantage point on the glacier the next day and talk about it together.

In the morning I roped up with Mark on the glacier, deliberately hanging back to let Wilford and Jim get ahead of us. "I think this mountain is amazing," I told Mark, "and the possibilities for a route on the southwest face look good, but the other guys don't seem that psyched." Mark responded, somewhat impatiently, "Well, let me take a look at it." When we arrived, he surveyed the face for several minutes with the binoculars, then offered his assessment. "This looks awesome," he said. "I'm amazed that we found something this cool on such a high peak that is probably still unclimbed!"

With Mark's blessing, the others warmed up to the idea, and we started to break down how we might climb the southwest face. "There is the large snow and ice couloir in the middle of the face," Wilford said. "That would be the logical place to start up, but there are some large ice cliffs high on the left side." I didn't think they would threaten us. "The couloir is wide enough and has a concave shape," I said, "so if we keep to the right-hand edge, anything falling down, unless it is massive, should stay to our left." Mark pointed out that we couldn't follow the couloir all the way. "About halfway up the face," he said, "it necks down into some steep narrow gullies that funnel all the avalanches coming down the upper half of the mountain onto the left side of the big couloir underneath." He thought we could avoid those gullies by moving out of the couloir to the right and connecting a series of ice ramps that would take us up through the rock wall and onto the summit snowfields. I agreed. "That certainly looks safer." The crux sections would be climbing the rock bands that separated the ice ramps. We took some photos and headed back to the col. With the weather looking like it might storm, we headed back to base camp. I was feeling optimistic—there appeared to be a safe-looking line up this beautiful wall, with good solid rock and ice that avoided the "no-go" zones where the face was exposed to hanging ice cliffs that could break off at any time.

The team wasn't acclimatized well enough yet, so after a period of bad weather, Mark, Wilford, Jim, and I climbed back to the pass on August 24 with Tashi, Lakpa, Dhan Singh, and Tshering. The plan was to climb an easy snow peak on the other side of the col and farther up the South Shukpa Kunchang Glacier with our Indian team members, to give them an opportunity to practice their mountaineering skills. We made a camp at 21,300 feet and spent a couple of nights there to complete our acclimatization. But the weather was bad, so we abandoned the practice climb and headed back to base camp. Over the next few weeks the forecasts called for only short windows of good weather—not long enough to climb Saser Kangri II. On September 8 we had a brief period of good weather that enabled us to make a short reconnaissance up the southwest face to evaluate conditions. I liked hanging out with both Marks and Jim, but my earlier feeling that this group would not be able to climb Saser Kangri II had not gone away. Climbing on the mountain would be fun no matter how far we got, and any progress we made would provide useful information for a future attempt.

We finally got a decent forecast and started up on September 19 from our camp on the glacier. Our porters were scheduled to arrive in six days and we were running out of time: this would be our only opportunity to go as high as we could on the southwest face of the mountain. We followed the route we had laid out for ourselves almost a month ago up the right-hand edge of a broad snow and ice gully in the center of the south face we called the Great Couloir. After that we planned to veer out onto the wall on the right. The first day went well, and we stopped early at a large ledge about six hundred feet up that Mark dubbed the Launch Pad. The climbing was among the best I'd had on a big mountain, with ice that was firm but not too hard or brittle and surprisingly solid granite.

On day two we climbed icy slopes and exited the Great Couloir as the sun left the face. With no suitable place nearby where we could chop a ledge out of the ice big enough for our tents, I climbed what we called the Ice Chimney, looking for something better above, but I didn't find anything. We spent a bad night sitting on small ledges chopped out of the ice. Our poor bivouac was made worse by the severe cold. Earlier in August it had been much warmer, but four weeks later, we experienced arctic-like temperatures. We waited for the sun to come around to warm us on our second morning. The immediate goal was to find a better spot to bivouac a bit higher on the mountain, where we could set up our tents and eat and drink properly. Above the Ice Chimney the team climbed a snow and ice ramp to the right and rappelled down to a lower-angle slope, where we spent three hours chopping ledges in the ice that were wide enough for our two tents end to end. We prepared a good meal and plenty of hot liquids, but that night it started snowing. In the morning the weather was still stormy. Mark zipped open the tent he and I shared. Looking at Jim, whose head poked out of the other tent where Wilford sat behind him, Mark asked, "Should we go down?" Jim replied: "If you want to continue going up, I want to send you to a psychiatrist."

The team had accomplished what it could, and we decided to descend. We had completed a reconnaissance of this unexplored area, reaching 22,500 feet on the southwest face of Saser Kangri II. It was a good effort, and I left convinced we had found a safe but challenging way to the summit. I wanted to return later and finish the job. Flying home from India, Mark and I had a layover in Newark and agreed to try and go back to Saser Kangri II the next year.

That fall, after I returned from Saser Kangri II in September of 2009, Jed had left for college in Portland, Oregon; Ann and I became empty nesters, and I prepared to officially leave the engineering firm in January 2010. With fewer responsibilities, I was free to pursue other interests and to drill down on projects I was already committed to. I'd served the first year of a three year stint as president of the American Alpine Club and I looked forward to having more time to spend on efforts to modernize the club. I had also begun to do some writing, and of course I had more time to climb. My most important climbing project was preparing for another expedition to Saser Kangri II.

Mark and I worked on getting a team together for later in 2010. He would act as the leader again, but this time we decided to climb as a threesome to better distribute the weight. It would be similar to our Latok expeditions in 2006 and 2007. Mark suggested we invite Freddie Wilkinson. Nearly half my age and twenty-two years younger than Mark, Freddie had a solid resume of difficult first ascents and new routes on mountains all over the world. Like Mark, he was a dyed-in-the-wool New Englander, and the two of them had done many local climbs together. Their multigenerational friendship was solid. Freddie was unavailable to go to India in 2010, however, and neither Mark nor I could find a third partner we felt comfortable with. Freddie eventually convinced Mark to wait another year, so that we could go together in 2011. We planned to go a month earlier, so we could make summit attempts in August and avoid the bitter cold we had experienced there in September 2009.

The application process was a replay of what happened on our first Saser Kangri II expedition. The Indian Mountaineering Foundation issued the permit for the climb a couple of weeks before we left, and we received our special visas at the last minute. The US contingent on our team was larger this time. When Mark and I planned the trip, we discussed sharing our base camp with another group that could attempt one of the many other unclimbed peaks in the area. Freddie's wife, Janet B. Wilkinson, a skilled climber in her own right, liked the idea, and she assembled a team with two of her climbing partners, Emilie Drinkwater and Kirsten Kremer. I met Janet as she boarded the plane to Delhi with Mark, Freddie, and me on July 2, 2011. By reputation I knew she was a strong rock climber. During the long flight I learned she was originally from Ohio, which explained the Midwestern pragmatism I sensed—a good complement to her technical capabilities.

As we flew eastward, I teased Freddie about his cropped hair that had gone prematurely gray since meeting him about ten years earlier in Alaska. When I pointed out that the old guys (Mark and me) were not gray and still had all of our hair, Freddie laughed. "Yeah, you must know how to stay calm," he said, "because years of scaring myself in the mountains has made me go gray." He displayed a fresh, easygoing confidence with us, something we would benefit from. Before the trip, I had received numerous endorsements from other climbers about Freddie's abilities as an alpinist, a partner, and all-around fun person to hang out with.

At the airport in Delhi, it was easy to spot Emilie's blonde hair above the sea of dark heads. She and her husband ran a climbing school and guide service in upstate New York. (Later, as the trip progressed and the rest of us got grubbier, Emilie always looked like she just stepped out of an outdoor fashion magazine.) Kirsten met us at our hotel the next morning. She had long brown hair, sharp features, and an animated temperament that she displayed while dancing around the room to describe her long journey. Fiercely independent, Kirsten lived in a remote cabin on Alaska's Glenn Highway east of Anchorage, where she worked as a heli-ski guide. Both Mark and I, and Freddie to some degree, had a lot more experience climbing in the Great Ranges than the women. It was a good opportunity for them to learn how the permitting, financing, logistics, and picking climbing objectives worked on a trip like this.

Our flight to Leh was unable to land because of a layer of low clouds so while waiting for the weather to clear, we circled overhead for thirty to forty-five minutes. Looking out my window was like being on a merry-go-round with a panorama of the highest mountains in the Karakoram passing by over and over. Across the Actual Ground Position Line in Pakistan, K2 came into view, followed by Broad Peak, Masherbrum, the Gasherbrums, and Chogolisa. Closer to us in India, the summits of the Rimo peaks and eventually the Saser Kangri group poked out of the clouds. I could see the route we had followed partway up Saser Kangri II in 2009, and the top seemed so close it made me wonder why it was such a big deal.

I enjoyed the mental exercise we went through when planning the expedition. Breaking down the enormous project into smaller tasks entailed deep discussions months before leaving the United States. Mark, Freddie, and I debated different strategies for accomplishing each of these tasks that, linked together, comprised an overall game plan for getting to the summit. Mark's and my experience on the mountain in 2009 guided the development of our 2011 strategy; we adopted successful tactics from before and developed new ones for the things we needed to change. Walking across the tarmac from the plane to the small terminal building, I felt my excitement about the adventure grow. All of the training and preparation, the sum total of our previous Himalayan experience, the synergy the three of us were developing, and our previous involvement with this mountain in particular, gave me a strong feeling we would be successful this time.

In Leh we had a happy reunion with Motup, whom Mark and I hadn't seen in two years. We rested on July 6, and Motup introduced me to a Ladakhi man named Chhering who had served in the Indian Army and participated in Operation Meghdoot, the Indian military action when the army took the Siachen Glacier by force in April 1984. Chhering had been flown by helicopter up onto one of the passes west of the glacier in December of that year in marginal weather. He described the extreme cold and almost unbearable conditions at elevations around 20,000 feet in the winter. The army had not yet established permanent facilities like the heated bunkers they had now. When the weather finally cleared at the end of February, Chhering's unit was face-to-face with an outpost the Pakistan Army had established on a mountain above them that was complete with anti-aircraft artillery. Chhering proudly described how he and a group of fellow soldiers had climbed up a steep rock and ice face at night and destroyed the outpost.

As in 2009, our IMF permit required a joint expedition, and we met the Indian members who would round out our team. Motup and Mark were our coleaders, as before, and I was pleased to see that Konchok Thinlese, Dhan Singh Harkotia, and Tshering Sherpa from the 2009 expedition had joined us again. Pemba Sherpa (whose reputation for carrying heavy loads had earned him the nickname King Kong) and Jangla Tashi Phunchok completed the Indian climbers. Santabir Sherpa was our chief cook, Arjun Rai and Aungchok were cook's helpers, and Mahipal was the kitchen boy. The Indian members were an integral part of the team and, as before, they would help carry all the supplies and equipment from base camp over the pass to advance base camp. When we were climbing on Saser Kangri II above ABC, they would keep us supplied, monitor our progress, and provide assistance in case of an emergency.

On July 7 we drove from Leh over the Kardung La to the Nubra valley. This time we stayed at the small Rimo Hotel owned by Motup's brother in their home village of Tigr. Motup's father was there to greet us, and the resemblance between them was remarkable. His father regaled us with stories each evening about his work several decades earlier manning remote outposts along the Chinese-Indian border when he was a young man. Two days later, we began our three-day trek to base camp. I knew from before that the 3,000-foot climb up the hillside from the road was a good test for the team's overall fitness, especially that of our liaison officer, Raj Kumar, a sergeant in the Indian Army. The weather was cloudy with a few showers that kept it cool, and Raj made it to our first camp, accompanied by Mark, about two hours behind the rest of us.

We took turns accompanying the LO, and on the second day of the trek Emilie and I lagged behind to walk with Raj. It took us six hours to travel the short distance that the others covered in three hours at a comfortable pace. Emilie and I learned more about Raj, his work, and his family. He lived in Agra, near the Taj Mahal, with his wife and daughter, but he didn't spend much time with them because he was stationed in the Kashmir valley in Srinagar. Noncommissioned officers were not allowed to bring their families with them.

The predominantly Muslim Kashmir valley was the focal point of an ongoing insurgency between various Kashmiri Islamic separatists and the Indian government. The conflict had a particularly violent phase between 1989 and 2007, when Pakistan had supported the insurgents with arms, recruits, and training and the Indian Army brutally repressed the entire populace. Under international pressure to help fight the War on Terror after 9/11, Pakistan gradually withdrew much of their support for the insurgents and the level of violence was reduced substantially. But the situation in the Kashmir valley was still tense, and Raj told us that he and his fellow Indian Army soldiers traveled in convoys for protection. As we walked along, Raj moved slowly and felt poorly at altitude. He returned to the Nubra valley a few days later.

On July 12 the team established base camp in the same meadow as we had two years earlier—just as the winter snow was melting. We had timed our arrival for almost one month earlier than before, which was perfect. It was great to finally be there. That afternoon, when I went to the mess tent for tea, the group was playing cards. As the card game became more animated, Kirsten broke out the booze and started dancing with Janet and Emilie. On most expeditions we saved our limited supply of Scotch till after we reached the summit or failed to reach the summit. I took over as the DJ with my iPod and portable speakers, and we danced and sang until dinner was ready. Mark especially enjoyed being social at base camp, where there is a lot of downtime between climbing excursions and waiting for good weather. This large, jolly group kept him entertained. I was free to spend these periods of inactivity in my tent reading and working on some writing projects.

From base camp, Mark, Freddie, and I, with help from our Indian team members—Thinlese, Dhan Singh, Tshering, King Kong, and Tashi—spent a week carrying loads up the unnamed glacier to the pass. By July 23 we had set up ABC on the South Shukpa Kunchang Glacier below Saser Kangri II. This time we'd brought skis with climbing skins, so instead of sinking in the snow with each step, we moved up quickly and easily in the beautiful mountain amphitheater. The next day, Mark, Freddie, and I made our first foray up onto Saser Kangri II to acclimatize and to see if we could get high enough to find better bivouacs than we had in 2009. We got to the base of the route at 6:30 a.m., and Freddie led the eight rope lengths up to the Launch Pad using the rock anchors for belay stations that Mark and I had rappelled from in 2009. It took us about three hours to reach the bivouac ledge, where we found remnants of our old tent platforms. Freddie and I worked to level a larger platform in the rocks and set up the tent, while Mark fired up the stove on the other platform to melt ice for tea.

By afternoon we had to take shelter in our small tent to get out of the sun. The heat caused rocks and small, wet snow slides to fall down the face. Fortunately the Launch Pad was situated on top of a small rib of rock that protruded from the face just enough that the missiles fell to either side of us. There was nothing for us to do but wait till it cooled off and then head down early in the morning when the wall was frozen again. It was too warm to even think about going higher on the wall to acclimatize. We needed to climb shady and colder north-facing routes on other mountains for that. In 2009 we had cooler temperatures in August, and I hoped that was a normal pattern that would make it safe to get back on the southwest face of Saser Kangri II almost a month from now.

At 5:00 a.m., Mark started rappelling, followed by Freddie. I went last after removing our backup anchors. We were off the face before any rock and ice started falling, and we skied back to ABC, where we ate and rested for a few hours in the heat of the day. The camp had a tent for the three of us to sleep in, plus a couple more for the Indian members of our team, but we were the only ones in camp. Later we went looking for objectives to keep us busy for a few weeks until the weather cooled off. Freddie had a hunch that we would find something good to climb on the north sides of several peaks located up a remote, uncharted pocket glacier tributary to the

South Shukpa Kunchang Glacier a short distance down from camp. That afternoon we skied up to have a closer look at these mountains, and the north face of a 21,325-foot peak came into view. It revealed a strip of steep ice that dropped directly from the summit to the glacier. This aspect of the mountain was in the shade most of the day, so we figured it would remain well frozen and safe. It was one of the most compelling ice climbs I'd ever seen in the Karakoram.

That evening, high cirrus clouds moved in, and a large lenticular cloud formed over the summit of Saser Kangri II, indicating deteriorating weather. But with the prospect of an exciting objective to occupy us until conditions were right, we skied down to base camp the next day. We arrived in the early afternoon, and it was a pleasure to lie in the green grass beside the creek. Tashi brought us some Tang, and Santabir—with help from Arjun Rai, Aungchok, and Mahipal—served us a lunch of French fries, garbanzo bean curry, paratha (fried chapatis), and tuna fish. After lunch we had hot water for a shower. This was happiness. We had a great team, fantastic staff, and a couple of world-class mountaineering objectives that we were in a good position to climb. My only concern was a persistent sinus problem. The cold, dry air at high altitude always irritated and inflamed my nasal passages, causing them to produce excessive amounts of mucus. This condition often led to a stubborn sinus infection that wouldn't improve given the stress of living at high altitude. I started a course of antibiotics.

After three days of rest at base camp, the weather improved and we went back to ABC. On July 31 we left the tents at 4:00 a.m. and skied up the pocket glacier Freddie had named the Baby Ruth, after one of his favorite places in the Alaska Range. It got light just as we arrived below the ice face and took off our skis. We plodded up the snow cone and got to the bottom of the steep climbing after the bergschrund crossing that was easier than it looked. Freddie led for three rope lengths up steep ice runnels through the rock, and Mark wanted to lead the next block that brought us to the end of the steepest climbing. My turn to lead took us another five hundred feet up a sixty-degree ice face, then Freddie took over again. We were near the top of the mountain, where all the corniced snow ridges came together. Choosing the easiest route from there to the summit was not easy. Freddie led us through a gap in the corniced ridge left of the summit, hoping we could climb to the top along the ridge or on the other side. The ridge consisted of weak unconsolidated sunbaked snow, which forced us to traverse around the crest onto the south face and up to the summit just as the sun was setting.

As the sun cast its last shadows, it lit up Saser Kangri II and the surrounding peaks with an amber glow that was especially spectacular from our vantage point. Later on, our Ladakhi companions suggested we name the mountain Tsok Kangri (6,580 meters, or 21,588 feet), after a Buddhist practice to help gather merit and wisdom in life. The weather that had been ambiguous most of the day was now windless and clear. Looking north, we saw the summit of Saser Kangri II, and again it seemed that the "west summit" claimed by the 1985 Indo-Japanese expedition was not really a summit. We were pleased to see that the top of the southwest face on Saser Kangri II, hidden to us from below, was a broad low-angle snow slope leading to an easy snow ridge that angled up to the summit. I had felt unusually listless climbing up the last several hundred feet, but now I was content. I was sitting atop Tsok Kangri with my good friends enjoying our magnificent surroundings. But then the coughing began. It's not unusual to develop a cough in this setting, but it produced some awful green-yellow, bloodstained phlegm. The sinus infection I had been concerned about appeared to have gotten worse, despite the antibiotics.

The summit was a narrow, precarious place that dropped off steeply on both sides. I had kicked a small ledge in the snow where I could sit. It was going to be a long, cold descent in the dark, so I put on insulated pants under my harness. We rappelled directly from the summit, with Mark going first, dropping over the cornice onto the north face. After about a dozen rappels and some downclimbing, we reached the glacier at about midnight. I felt a deep fatigue that made it hard to do even simple things like putting on my skis. Gliding by headlamp down the Baby Ruth glacier to the South Shukpa and climbing back up to ABC was unusually difficult for me. I moved slowly, taking shallow breaths through my nose, because a deep breath would send me into a fit of coughing. Clearly something was wrong. This was only a day trip up a 21,000-foot peak. I pledged that I would head back to base camp and possibly the Nubra valley to try and cure myself before we headed back to Saser Kangri II.

Janet, Emilie, and Kirsten were at ABC when we got back on August 1, and they took a rest day with us. The following day it was snowing lightly, and all of us left ABC and skied to base camp. It would be a struggle for me to get better there at 17,000 feet, but fortunately it was only one long day of hiking to reach the Nubra valley at 10,000 feet. Thinlese came with me, and we left base camp a couple of days later while the others headed back up to ABC. My plan was to spend time at the Rimo Hotel, where I could recover more quickly in the thicker air. At the hotel we found Raj Kumar, our liaison officer. He had gone to the army base nearby for a complete physical after leaving base camp nearly two weeks earlier. Other than being treated for a cough, he said he had checked out okay. Since then, he had been trying to find someone to accompany him back to base camp but hadn't had any luck. So he had explored the valley and helped a team of American and Indian doctors who had recently set up health clinics in the area. Raj seemed lonely and bored, so he followed me around while I settled in for a period of convalescence.

After resting for five days, I still felt poorly and experienced periods of dizziness that made it hard to walk without feeling wobbly. Raj took me to a clinic in the village run by the Indian government, where the examining nurse gave me a different antibiotic. I tried to pay for the medicine, but she refused, saying it was provided for free. From what I could see, Indian government-funded health care, education, water supply, sanitation, and transportation infrastructure in the Nubra valley far exceeded what the Pakistan government did for the local people in Baltistan.

That evening, I called Brownie Schoene, a doctor and climbing friend in the United States who specialized in pulmonary and high-altitude medicine. He thought the sinus infection may have gotten into my inner ear and that was causing the dizziness. I was pretty sure I wasn't suffering from high-altitude cerebral edema (HACE), and he agreed to rule it out since I didn't have a headache and my cognitive ability was fine. He advised switching to the antibiotic the nurse at the clinic had given me, but recommended I have a doctor look in my ears. I was discouraged. After six days in the Nubra valley I hadn't improved much. The clock was ticking, and the summit of Saser Kangri II seemed very far away.

The next day, Raj took me to a hospital in the town of Diskit—about a ninety-minute drive down the valley on the other side of the Shyok River. A doctor there examined me thoroughly. He didn't think I had an inner ear infection, but he suggested that I might have a blocked eustachian tube that was causing the dizziness. He prescribed more of the antibiotic I was taking, and I picked up some eucalyptus oil to put into a pot of boiling water that I could use for steam inhalation to clear my head.

The kitchen staff at the hotel in Tigr were all Buddhists, and for religious reasons they would not butcher anything living. But I was getting tired of eating rice and lentils every day and craved a good meat curry. Before leaving Diskit, Raj and I visited the Muslim butcher, who slaughtered several chickens for us, putting the meat into plastic bags so that we could take it back to the Rimo Hotel cooks who were willing to prepare it. My mood improved with the combination of a delicious dinner and the doctor's opinion that nothing major was wrong with me. Within a couple of days I was taking walks up to the monastery behind the hotel, where I sat beneath the apricot trees eating their fruit with the maroon-clad boys and older monks.

On August 12, Kirsten, Emilie, and Janet came down to the Rimo Hotel with Mark and Freddie. They'd had a great week climbing three new peaks while I was convalescing, and now the women were scheduled to go home. After consuming about twenty tall cans of Godfather beer and four plates of French fries, they took showers and we had a great dinner complete with mutton—I had no idea where that came from. After the women departed, Mark, Freddie, and I were ready to finish our climb. But the weather had turned stormy, so Mark and Freddie decided to rest in the Nubra valley a few more days. I was feeling better, eager to escape from Tigr and get back to base camp so I could readjust to the altitude and prepare for our next attempt on Saser Kangri II.

Thinlese had been waiting for me at his home in a small village up the valley from Tigr, and the two of us made a quick eight-hour seven thousand-foot climb back to base camp. The effort felt good after spending so many days recuperating. If only I could stay healthy and we could get some good weather, then maybe, just maybe, we would be able to get to the summit this time. When Thinlese and I reached base camp, we found Tashi, Tshering, King Kong, and Dhan Singh in one of their tents playing cards and gambling away who knows what. They had been waiting there after accompanying the three women plus Mark and Freddie to ABC earlier in the month. Different combinations of Americans and Indian team members had climbed together while I was in town recovering.

Mark and Freddie showed up a few days later, looking a bit rough after partying at the hotel the night before. According to weather forecasts, it looked like a spell of clear, calm weather was due in a few days. So on August 20 we left base camp for another trip to ABC—this time we knew it was for real. As I skied up the unnamed glacier, concerns about my health and safety, the physical pain, the route, and the weather made me anxious. But as happens to me on all big climbs, excitement pushed the dark feelings to the back of my mind. The anticipation of being the first to climb such a beautiful mountain, and sharing it with two great partners, outweighed my fears.

After crossing the pass, we skied down onto the South Shukpa Kunchang Glacier and up to advance base camp. We spent the afternoon packing and preparing ourselves for the climb the next day. Now that the three of us were making an attempt on Saser Kangri II, our Indian team members joined us at ABC in case we needed their help after we descended and to help carry supplies and equipment down to base camp once we were finished. Fully acclimatized and rested, we took only two and a half hours to reclimb the pitches to the Launch Pad, where we had been almost a month earlier. The temperatures had dropped considerably since then, and we didn't feel so vulnerable to falling rock and ice. We relaxed all afternoon in the tent, eating and drinking. We planned to start at 2:00 a.m. to reach the top of the Great Couloir before the sun came around onto the face. Above the Great Couloir it would be cold enough to keep everything frozen during the day. We needed to get above our 2009 high point and establish a good bivouac before nightfall so we could eat, drink, and get some sleep. Achieving those goals would determine whether we had a reasonable shot at the summit.

We were under way by 3:30 a.m. with a short rappel off the Launch Pad onto the ice slope below. It was my block to lead, and I found great conditions with two to eight inches of firm snow over the ice, making it much quicker and easier to climb than the bare, hard ice we had in 2009. The climbing was easy enough for all three of us to move together clipping our ropes to ice screws I placed along the way. We gained altitude quickly, traversing up and out of the Great Couloir not long after sunrise. We reached our 2009 high spot by noon.

Mark took over leading there. This time we kept climbing and, without much trouble, moved through a mixed rock and ice section that we thought would be the crux of the route. Mark and I looked up and off to the side of our climbing route for a lower-angled snow and ice patch to build a tent platform for the night, but Freddie said, "Let's not make the same mistake you guys made before. We need to keep moving up our line of ascent and not waste time traversing off to the side." We would find a bivouac place along the way. Mark and I couldn't argue with the voice of reason coming from our youthful partner so we forged ahead.

It was getting late, and we needed to find a place to stop. It's easy to be lured into believing that climbing ever higher will eventually produce a flatter and easier place to build a tent platform. When we found a lower-angled area on a rock rib, we decided to stop while it was still light and do the best we could to build a platform for our 4.5- by 6-foot three-person tent. We had learned from our 2009 attempt that building decent tent platforms on such a steep face was a challenge. Mark had developed a new piece of gear he called the Ice Hammock that made this easier. A long rectangular piece of reinforced nylon fabric, the Ice Hammock could be stretched lengthwise across the slope and anchored to the mountain with loops of nylon webbing sewn onto each end. It acted like a retaining wall, and we filled the space between it and the slope with snow to create a flat area for our tent.

Freddie and Mark volunteered to do the physical work of building the tent platform, while I hung our stove from the wall and did the time-consuming work of melting snow to serve tea and fill our water bottles. After such a big day, I felt pretty good, although my health problems had not gone away completely. I had mild cold symptoms with associated phlegm, and I was weaker than normal. A corner of the tent hung a bit off the ledge that Freddie and Mark built, but all three of us fit inside the tent fairly comfortably. Our altimeter measured 21,982 feet (6,700 meters), and with a nice place to spend the night, we had accomplished the things that had stopped us in 2009. The weather was clear and calm, and our summit chances looked good.

On the morning of day three, we were already established on a major snow ramp that angled up the right side of the face for several hundred feet. Earlier, while examining the route from ABC, we saw that the ramp ended where it steepened into a vertical rock headwall. Exiting from it seemed possible on the left through a short but steep section of rock we called the Escape Hatch. The only major obstacle separating us from the summit was being able to climb this feature. It was Freddie's turn to lead, and we made quick progress up the ramp to where we kicked out a small stance (a ledge) in the steep snow and ice below the Escape Hatch. Freddie traversed to the rock as Mark and I watched anxiously. With the picks on his ice tools and the points of his crampons, he gingerly hooked and scratched his way up the granite cracks to the top of the difficulties.

While climbing the relatively easy ice pitches up the ramp that morning, my mild cold symptoms got worse, and I coughed up some ugly stuff. I discovered midday that I had not tightened the lid on a full water bottle I'd put inside my pack that morning. Half the contents had leaked, soaking my sleeping bag and clothing. Above the Escape Hatch, I thought we should look for our final bivouac site from where we could climb to the summit the next day. We could leave everything except water, food, and some clothing behind in our high camp and be able to move faster on summit day. Also, if we put the tent somewhere nearby, I could wait there for Mark and Freddie if I was too sick to go with them the next day. I had discussed this option with my teammates before we started up the climb because of my health uncertainties. I was fairly confident of my ability to help the team get to the high camp and not force Mark and Freddie to retreat because I was sick. But whether I was healthy enough to continue above the high camp was a decision I had reserved for the morning of our summit day.

We were still climbing on the steep part of the face. Freddie insisted that we should continue climbing up to the summit snowfield and find an easy flat place for the tent rather than spend hours building a lousy platform where we were. His rationale made sense, but in my weakened condition I wasn't sure I could go that far without resting for the night first. Mark intervened and mentioned to Freddie that what seemed best was not always realistic. Freddie understood, so he and Mark did the work to carve a tent platform out of a patch of snow and ice that clung to the rock under an overhang. I assumed my usual job on this climb of anchoring myself to a rock wall above a stance I had kicked into the snow nearby. I proceeded with the physically easier but time-consuming task of melting snow with the hanging stove to fill water bottles. I dried out my sleeping bag and clothing in the sun before it disappeared over the horizon. After erecting the tent, we all piled in. I sat near the door and continued melting snow and cooking. It was a relatively warm evening and the weather was perfect.

After our dinner of mashed potatoes, crackers, salami, and cheese we got some sleep. We were at about 23,000 feet—only 1,640 feet below the top.

I had a good night, and on the morning of August 24 the good weather was still holding. When it came time for me to decide whether to stay or go, I chose to go. My health wasn't great, but after years of going to these altitudes, I felt I could do it. I knew Mark and Freddie would make it to the top, and I dreaded the thought of sitting in the tent all day by myself given these stellar conditions. The risk of getting into trouble by going seemed less than the risk of regret by staying.

Mark led four rope lengths of steep but moderate climbing from our bivouac to the summit snowfield. There we sat on flat ground for the first time since leaving the Launch Pad three days earlier. We walked, roped together, up onto the summit ridge. Freddy kicked the last steps in the snow to the top and pulled in the rope as Mark joined him. I reached the summit last. Mark gave me an enthusiastic bear hug that forced the air from my lungs and made it even harder for me to get enough oxygen. But he was so thrilled I didn't have the heart to tell him he was hurting me. It was a beautiful summit day—not a cloud in the sky, windless, and relatively warm for nearly 25,000 feet. Looking down the summit ridge to the west, we saw the point below us reached by the Indo-Japanese expedition. It was certain: we had made the first ascent of Saser Kangri II. The entire Karakoram Range was visible, including the mountains in India as well as K2 and all the major summits in Pakistan.

After spending an hour or so on the summit, we walked down to the top of the steep climbing and made several rappels back to our high camp, where we stayed another night. That evening my sinus problems got worse, as I suffered a sleepless night, sitting in the tent doorway coughing and hacking up phlegm into the snow. By morning my condition had everyone concerned about whether I could manage the long, exhausting day it would take to get down.

Despite all the coughing and hacking, I made the thirty rappels from our high camp to the glacier at the bottom. Mark and Freddie traded going first to build rappel anchors, and I went last, retrieving the backup gear at each station. We arrived at our skis on the glacier around 10:00 p.m. Exhausted, I had a hard time keeping my balance while skiing to ABC. I fell several times and was nervous about skiing across the snow bridges over crevasses along the way. Unfortunately our Indian team did not keep a light on at ABC, and we got lost in the darkness on this featureless expanse of snow trying to find the tents. After wasting energy wandering around, we eventually found the camp and our Indian team woke up to give us some tea and food. It was after midnight when we went to sleep.

At 3:00 a.m. I woke up coughing. Now my cough produced a thick, gluey mucus that I couldn't expel. It was sticking in my trachea, and I was choking on it. Every fifteen minutes or so I'd start coughing involuntarily, and the phlegm would plug my airway. Each time this happened, I'd roll over onto all fours and cough and hack to get a partial clearing that allowed just enough air into my lungs to keep me from blacking out. After a couple of these episodes, I started to panic. To save room in the tent, we were sleeping head to toe. I reached over and shook Mark's foot, waking him from his hard-earned sleep. After witnessing one of my coughing and choking sessions, he became alert and woke Freddie. They called Brownie Schoene, the US doctor whom I had consulted about my sinus problems earlier in the trip. By this time, I couldn't talk so Mark and Brownie discussed my situation. I wrote a note for Brownie and passed it to Mark: "Could I choke to death on this thick mucus that is getting lodged in my airway?" Brownie replied, "Yes, you could." I was frightened now and had an even harder time balancing the amount of air my body needed with the reduced amount available at 19,000 feet. I was limited to the meager oxygen I could suck through my airway, which felt like a narrow straw. I tried to slow my metabolism and reduce the amount of oxygen I needed by sitting still and trying to remain calm. For an experienced yogi this might be easy, but for me it took a lot of concentration—the effort was torture. Time seemed to go by so slowly that what seemed like an hour was only five minutes. As the seriousness of my situation became more clear, any discussion about how I might walk from ABC, over the pass, to base camp, and from there to the Nubra valley, was dropped. Mark, Freddie, and Brownie decided to initiate a helicopter rescue.

When the sun came up, I went outside the tent and sat in a snow chair the Indian climbers had made for me. If I started to cough and choke, they lifted me up onto my feet, which seemed to create more room in my lungs. (Mark and Freddie told me later they had sterilized a plastic tube and were prepared to do a tracheotomy on me with a pocket knife if my airway became completely obstructed.) To soothe my throat and help prevent coughing and choking, I drank endless cups of tea. The usual dehydration I suffered on the mountain had caused my cold-like mucus to be sticky and thick. After I'd been rehydrating for several hours, the phlegm liquefied, and suddenly I coughed it all up, to my instant relief.

Breathing better, I was out of immediate danger, but I was still sick and weak, so Mark and Freddie continued working on arrangements to have a helicopter fly me out. Mark had communicated our position and situation to Global Rescue, a United States–based medical evacuation and rescue service we subscribed to. Global Rescue was under contract with the American Alpine Club to provide a small medical rescue benefit to its members, but we had all purchased an expanded benefit that would cover the much higher cost of a medical evacuation in remote parts of the world like this. Mark had spoken to his wife, Teresa, who was in Leh, as well as to Motup. Teresa had come with a friend to India for some sightseeing and to meet us when we hiked out. Global Rescue, Motup, and Teresa worked all day with the Indian government to overcome bureaucratic hurdles before they would send a helicopter to get me. Unlike in Nepal, a private helicopter could not be used because we were in a high-security fly zone (only military aircraft were allowed). It seemed as though a foreigner had never been evacuated from this area before, so there wasn't any approval process.

What Global Rescue, Motup, and Teresa discovered was that the US State Department had to write a letter on behalf of one of its citizens (me) to the Indian Foreign Ministry asking for a rescue. The Foreign Ministry then had to write a letter to the Indian Department of Defense asking them to perform a rescue for a US citizen, as requested by the US government. The Indian Department of Defense had to write a letter to the Indian Air Force asking them to do this and similar instructions from the IAF headquarters had to be sent to their wing in Leh. Somewhere in this process, Global Rescue also had to prove they were responsible for paying the cost of the rescue. Global Rescue, Motup, and Teresa monitored the progress of each step in this complex process to make sure these instructions didn't get stuck somewhere along the way. It was an amazing feat for them to accomplish in one day. Apparently the helicopter pilots in Leh had mobilized their equipment early that morning when they first heard about my situation, but they didn't obtain permission to fly until later that afternoon.

Up at our ABC, we had given up on seeing a helicopter that day, so Freddie and Mark prepared a place for me spend another night in the tent.

Once inside and breathing relatively freely, I dozed off. All of a sudden, it seemed, Freddie, Thinlese, and Tashi dragged me out of the tent and helped me into my boots and puffy jacket. First I heard, then saw, the two small bubble-top helicopters flying toward us at about two hundred feet above the glacier. They swooped down and made a circle around our camp; the rotor wash blew snow everywhere as one landed on the helipad that Freddie had stomped out in the snow. Tashi and King Kong, flanking me, put my arms around their shoulders. I paddled my feet across the snow as they dragged me to the helicopter. I climbed into an empty seat in the back of the small cockpit that had been stripped of any extra weight so they could fly at this altitude. The two pilots sitting in front rotated the chopper 180 degrees as we lifted from the ground and headed down-glacier.

The noise of the engine straining to remain aloft in the thin air was muffled by the set of headphones I wore. The pilots took photos of the spectacular surroundings as we flew down the glacier. The helicopter gained elevation over a pass and flew past the confluence of the Nubra and Shyok rivers. We went up and over the Ladakh Range and down to Leh, where we landed after about a thirty-minute flight. As soon as I stepped out onto the tarmac there was a photo shoot with the pilots, wing commander, army doctor, and district commissioner. They were all involved in helping with the rescue, and I was grateful to them.

After the formalities on the tarmac, Teresa accompanied me in a small ambulance that took us to the hospital. By American standards the hospital was pretty grim. The ER was a chaotic single room packed with eight beds occupied by patients. There was barely enough room to accommodate all their family members as well as hospital staff. They put me in one of the beds, took my vital signs, and the doctor listened to my chest. The doctor talked to Brownie in the United States, and they came up with a treatment plan that included four injections of an antibiotic. Concerned about the hygiene of the injections, I watched them use a syringe and needle that were taken from sterile packages. I verified that the small bottle used for my injection had the name of the antibiotic on it that I was supposed to receive. The nurse who administered it was skilled at finding a good vein.

I was moved from the ER to the ward where I spent the night. In Peru, where Teresa had grown up, it is customary for the family and friends of a hospitalized person to help provide care 24/7, so she wouldn't leave me in the hospital by myself. She got permission from the staff to bring a sleeping bag and pad to spend the night on the floor next to my bed. Just as she was bedding down, however, a rat scurried past her head. Teresa jumped up and into the bed beside me, head to toe. Unfortunately, my coughing kept us both awake for most of the night.

The next day, I convinced the hospital staff to discharge me around noon, so I could recuperate at the hotel where Teresa and her friend were staying. My hotel room was much quieter and more comfortable. I returned to the hospital twice to receive antibiotic injections. I spoke to Ann, who told me she had been notified around 8:00 p.m. Seattle time on August 25 that I was seriously ill on the glacier. (It was 8:00 a.m. the following day in Leh, and I was sitting outside the tent on the glacier drinking tea.) A family friend had come over to stay with Ann, and they had been up all night waiting for news about me. Twelve hours later, she finally received a call letting her know I had been evacuated to the hospital in Leh, and I would be okay. Hearing each other's voices was very emotional for both of us, it was a big relief for everyone in my family too.

Motup's office was next door to the hotel, so I stopped by to thank him and Teresa, who was also there, for all the work they had done, along with Global Rescue, to get me off the glacier. It was a fabulous team effort! The Global Rescue representative called the hotel each day and asked me about my health and whether I wanted to go to Delhi for additional medical attention. I refused. Resting in the hotel garden among the trees loaded with ripe apricots was a great way to recover, and the over 100°F heat in Delhi wasn't appealing. To be honest, I didn't want to miss the reunion when the rest of my expedition returned to Leh. My separation from such a great team had been too abrupt. I wanted to see everyone again before we went our separate ways.

On August 30 the team showed up in Leh, and we had a dinner party for everyone that night at the hotel. Mark, Freddie, and I thanked our Indian team members—Konchok Thinlese, Dhan Singh Harkotia, Tshering Sherpa, Pemba Sherpa, and Jangla Tashi Phunchok—for their work, mostly between base camp and ABC, and for helping me when I got sick. We expressed our appreciation to Santabir, Arjun Rai, Aungchok, and Mahipal, who managed base camp and kept us well fed. I was especially grateful to Mark, Freddie, Teresa, and Motup for all the work they did to save my life. The following spring, Mark, Freddie, and I were invited to Chamonix, France, where we received a Piolet d'Or for our climb of Saser Kangri II.

Several weeks after returning home, my dad emailed an Indian Defense website article he found about my rescue. The story named the helicopter pilots, and the website published comments people had submitted about the article. My father had written expressing my family's appreciation to all the Indian Air Force personnel who were involved in the rescue and asking for their contact information so he could thank them personally. Directly below my father's comment were numerous comments from people in India: "How can one be sure Mr. Howard Swenson, who has posted his comment above, is [the] real guy who is the father of Mr. Steven J. Swenson?" Additional comments included: "With Siachen being so military sensitive strategic location for India with two of India's main enemies sitting at its border . . . it's not good for officers to email any person. . . . Who knows, comment poster might be enemy spy in disguise of Mr. Howard Swenson." At the end of his email my Dad had written: "Just call me 008, because 007 is already taken."

A year later, I spoke at a conference in India attended by prominent Indian mountaineers as well as retired Indian Army leaders who had served in the Siachen Conflict. The audience was particularly interested in my stories and photos about climbing in the Chinese- and Pakistan-administered parts of Kashmir. These were areas they would never be able to visit because they are off-limits to Indian nationals. I discussed my experiences as a climber and touched on the region's politics.

To add a little levity to such a serious subject, I told my father's 008 story to illustrate the extreme level of distrust between adversaries in the area. "In my opinion," I said, "nothing would be gained on the ground by either side from continued conflict in these mountains. Without some kind of diplomatic solution, there will be continued loss of life and severe environmental damage to sensitive landscapes." When I finished speaking and looked around the room, it seemed as if the number of scowling faces was about equal to the number of nodding heads.

Miriam, the widow of Ali
Hussain, a Shia Muslim
cook killed by militants at
Nanga Parbat base camp,
and two of her children

CHAPTER 11

ATTACK

NANGA PARBAT, 2013

On June 22, 2013, Pakistani climber Sher Khan was at Nanga Parbat base camp (14,100 feet) in the Diamir valley on the north side of the mountain. The Diamir valley is on the opposite side of Nanga Parbat from the base camp in the Rupal valley that Doug Chabot, Steve House, Bruce Miller, and I had shared in 2004 when we had attempted to summit the mountain from the south. Sher and two other Pakistani team members made up the My Dream 8,000er–Pakistani Nanga Parbat Expedition 2013 that was climbing the Kinshofer Route up the mountain. They had descended from Camp I to rest.

For climbers who want to reach the summit of all fourteen of the world's 8,000-meter (26,246-foot) peaks, the easiest way to achieve their goal is to climb the easiest routes on all of those peaks. On Nanga Parbat (8,126 meters, or 26,660 feet), the Kinshofer Route is the safest and most accessible route to the summit. As a result, between May and August the Diamir base camp is a busy place, and 2013 was no exception. Including Sher Khan and his team of three, there were eight expeditions and fifty-seven climbers attempting Nanga Parbat at that time. By contrast, when my friends and I had been on the opposite side of Nanga Parbat in 2004, we were the only climbers in the Rupal valley; the routes from that side are harder and not commonly done.

The weather in late June 2013 was good, so most of the climbers were staying in camps higher on the mountain to acclimatize. At base camp Sher Khan and ten other climbers were resting, recovering, or helping partners who were recuperating from health problems they had experienced higher on the mountain. At around 9:30 p.m. Sher Khan was in his tent when he heard a commotion outside. He zipped open the tent door, and in the darkness he saw a group of men with AK-47s dimly lit by a few lanterns. The armed men rousted climbers from their tents, and soon the muzzle of a gun poked inside Sher Khan's tent. He was told "Go, go," followed by "Come out!" The men spoke Urdu and sometimes Pashto. They also spoke Shina, which told him that some of them were from nearby. They wore uniforms used by the Gilgit Scouts, a Pakistan paramilitary force that patrolled the area.

A man put a gun to Sher Khan's head, placed him in a line with the other climbers, and tied his hands with a rope. He understood then that they were being attacked by a dozen or so militants or thieves disguised as Gilgit Scouts. As the men with guns rounded up the rest of the people in camp, they shouted, "Taliban, al-Qaeda, surrender!" One of them told Sher Khan in Urdu to tell the others in English to get their money and satellite phones. One by one, the climbers were escorted to their tents to collect those items. The armed men either smashed the phones with stones or shot them with their Kalashnikovs.

An Ismaili Muslim from the Hunza Region in Gilgit-Baltistan that is farther north from Nanga Parbat, Sher Khan hoped he could save his life by pleading that he was a Pakistani Muslim. When he did, one of the men asked him to prove it by talking about the Muslim morning prayer. Sher Khan knew that Ismailis have a different prayer than Sunnis, so he said nothing. Eventually, he and two Hunza men working as kitchen staff at base camp were separated from the others and told to stay on their knees and not look up. The armed men moved the non-Pakistani climbers and a cook from Hushe away from Sher Khan and his two friends, then they heard shooting—first in bursts from automatic weapons, then single shots.

Sher Khan stole a quick look and witnessed a man walking along a row of bodies, shooting them again one by one. When the shooting stopped, the men chanted the slogans "*Allah Akbar* [God is great]" and "Today these people are revenge for Osama bin Laden."

When the terrorists left, Sher Khan and his Hunza friends waited a while before rushing to the kitchen tent to get a knife and cut the ropes around their wrists. They grabbed a radio and retreated up the mountain toward Camp I. Sher Khan wasn't able to reach any of the other climbers who were at Camp II until 7:30 the next morning. (Karim, one of Sher Khan's teammates, made a regularly scheduled radio call at that time.) Sher Khan broke down, crying as he told his friend what had happened.

At the time of the attack, a Chinese climber, Zhang Jingchuan, had been put in line, tied up with the others. He had dropped to the ground as his companions were being shot. Using his training from four years in the Chinese Army, Zhang had managed to work his wrists free of the ropes. He had jumped up and run into the night, zigzagging to avoid being an easy target. Seeing him escape, the gunmen shot at him. A bullet grazed Zhang's head, and with blood running down his face, he reached the edge of a ravine and jumped, with no idea how far down the bottom was. Zhang fell onto the slope and rolled to the bottom, where he hid. He could hear the attackers talking above, searching for him.

About an hour after the shooting stopped, Zhang crawled back to his tent. He could see a light on the other side of camp, indicating the militants were still there. But he snuck into his tent and grabbed his jacket, boots, and a working satellite phone. He then hiked up the mountain to the safety of Camp I. Zhang was the only climber at base camp, besides Sher Khan, who survived the attack. He called for outside help on the sat phone. A military helicopter arrived at base camp at dawn, but by then the killers had disappeared.

Nina Adjanin was part of the nineteen-member International Nanga Parbat Expedition. She was at Camp II (20,000 feet) that morning, along with several of her teammates and other expedition members. After Karim's conversation with Sher Khan, Karim told Nina and the other climbers the terrible news. They tried desperately to radio their teammates at base camp and panicked when they couldn't get a response. Although Camp II was about six thousand feet higher and two miles from base camp, the camps were in direct line of sight. Nina mounted her camera with its powerful zoom lens on a tripod so they could take a look. Their worst fears were confirmed. When they focused on the site below, they could see a military helicopter at base camp and a row of body bags lying on the meadow near the tents.

The climbers at Camp II immediately left for base camp. Five military policemen were there when they arrived, and the bodies had been taken away. All their tents and equipment were gone. The police suggested that the climbers leave on foot, but they refused because they had no way of knowing where the assailants were. Most likely the killers had walked down the Diamir valley, the same way they had come up. Nina and the other climbers asked the police why they didn't go to the mouth of the valley and capture the killers. The police said they were afraid. Nina and her friends erected several tents, unpacked the sleeping bags they had salvaged from their camps on the mountain, and spent the night at base camp. The next morning, several Pakistan Army helicopters arrived carrying troops to secure the area, and the climbers were flown to a military base in Gilgit. Six hours later, they were loaded onto a military cargo plane and taken to Islamabad.

In the terrorist shootings, eleven people were killed—ten climbers and a base camp worker. The victims were parents, teachers, engineers, guides, businessmen, doctors, and a cook. They were members of international climbing teams from countries including China, Lithuania, Nepal, Pakistan, Slovakia, and Ukraine. If the attack had come during a period of bad weather, it's probable that more than fifty climbers would have been at base camp waiting for better conditions, and the death toll would have been much higher. Initially the Teherik-i-Taliban Pakistan (TTP) and an affiliated group claimed responsibility for the attack, but it's unclear who the attackers were. Those responsible may never be prosecuted. As with other incidents involving tribal militant groups, it's hard to know who is helping whom.

There is a long history of Pashtun tribal antagonism and violence toward foreigners or other religious or tribal groups as well as Pakistani and earlier British governments. Before Partition in 1947, which led to the sovereign states of Pakistan and India, Pashtun tribesmen in northwest India (who also inhabit the valleys around Nanga Parbat) had fought local wars with British troops intermittently for over eighty years. When climbing expeditions from Germany tried to make the first ascent of Nanga Parbat in the 1930s, the local Pashtuns didn't want to work for them as porters, but regional leaders forced them to do so. After Partition, the Pashtun tribes, like many of the other ethnic groups across the country, didn't view having a common religion as a reason to embrace the new government of Pakistan, which they viewed as being made up of outsiders.

When our team traveled to the south side of Nanga Parbat in 2004, we knew that the tribes around the mountain, especially those on the north side, weren't that friendly, so we hired locals to help facilitate our presence. But everyone involved in tourism in this area—the climbers, the trekkers, and the Pakistani-run adventure tour companies—had failed to recognize the danger from Pashtun militants relocating from tribal areas farther west and spreading their fundamentalist message in these valleys north of Nanga Parbat. Foreign tourism in Gilgit-Baltistan was devastated by what happened at Nanga Parbat in 2013, and the economic impact in the region has been severe. Climbing expeditions stopped coming, but those climbers focused on ascending all the fourteen peaks above 8,000 meters (over 26,200 feet) would have to go to Pakistan at some point, because five of the Himalayan giants are located there.

The only previous attack on a foreign climber or trekker in Gilgit-Baltistan occurred in 1998, when Ned Gillette, a well-known American mountain climber, sailor, skier, photographer, and author, was killed by a local man in a botched robbery attempt. Before the 2013 attack, none of the other thousands of foreign adventure tourists traveling in Gilgit-Baltistan had been victims of political violence. For this reason, climbers and trekkers had felt the area was safe since it is well to the north and east of the Afghan border and areas in Balochistan, the Federally Administered Tribal Areas (FATA), or Khyber Pakhtunkhwa (KPK), where most of the militant violence associated with the current war in Afghanistan had been occurring. In an attempt to ease the fears of foreign climbers after the Nanga Parbat attack, the Gilgit-Baltistan Police Department established a fifty-member, high-altitude unit in early 2015. This unit began sending policemen on foreign expeditions to provide security. Although the intent is admirable, it's unclear how such a small force will be able to protect climbers and trekkers throughout such a vast area.

Graham Zimmerman
traversing the Polish Col
toward Changi Tower

CHAPTER 12

PASSING THE TORCH

CHANGI TOWER, 2015
K6 CENTRAL, 2015

decided to go climbing again in the Pakistan Karakoram in 2014. It had been seven years since my last visit, and I wanted to see how Rasool and my other friends were doing, given the economic impact of the Nanga Parbat attack in 2013. I wanted to evaluate how safe it was to travel from Islamabad to Skardu, where security risks were, I hoped, still minimal. Because I had taken ten trips to Pakistan's Karakoram Range over the previous thirty-four years, climbers in the United States and other Western countries regularly asked me about climbing there. Once I made an on-the-ground security assessment, I could pass that information along. Ultimately, I hoped to help bring back some of the tourism to the Pakistan Karakoram and improve the local economy.

On June 8, 2014, a month before I was slated to leave Seattle, ten foreign militants from the al-Qaeda–affiliated Islamic Movement of Uzbekistan

(IMU) attacked Jinnah International Airport in Karachi. Thirty-six people were killed in a shootout, including the ten militants. I had been scheduled to fly to Islamabad, not Karachi, but a successful attack on Pakistan's busiest airport in its largest city indicated that the country's security situation was not good. I made the difficult decision to cancel my trip. Six months later, on December 16, 2014, seven Teherik-i-Taliban Pakistan (TTP) gunmen attacked the Army Public School in Peshawar. As in the Karachi airport attack, the militants were foreigners—from Chechnya, Afghanistan, Egypt, and Morocco. They opened fire on school staff and children, killing 145 people—132 of them schoolchildren. The Pakistan Army launched a rescue operation, killing the seven terrorists and rescuing nearly a thousand students and staffers. Pakistan's prime minister, Nawaz Sharif, made a statement to the Afghan government criticizing the use of their territory by militants to attack Pakistan. "Wipe out the Taliban, or we will," Sharif said, later stating that there was "no such thing as good Taliban and bad Taliban." Only time will tell if Pakistan's civilian government has the power to enforce this policy across all the security and intelligence services.

The aftermath of the Karachi airport and Peshawar school attacks was different from that of previous terrorist operations. The public overwhelmingly condemned the attacks, and the upper-class military and civil service community in Pakistan were outraged by the murder of innocent children at a school where they themselves sent their children. For the first time it seemed like Pakistan was launching a comprehensive, area-wide operation against all the main perpetrators of attacks that endangered the Pakistani public and, by extension, tourists.

The comprehensive military operation in the tribal areas significantly improved security, and terror attacks were reduced to their lowest level since 2008. I decided in January 2015 to try to organize an expedition to the Pakistan Karakoram for that summer. I knew enough about this range to narrow down my research process. I had been to the K6 massif, which consists of three separate peaks—all above 7,000 meters (22,966 feet). K6 Main (7,282 meters, or 23,891 feet) was first climbed by Austrians in 1970. K6 West (7,040 meters, or 23,097 feet) had been climbed by a Canadian team in 2013. But K6 Central (7,100 meters, or 23,294 feet) was still unclimbed, so I investigated this peak to explore possible routes.

The K6 massif separates the Charakusa and Nangmah valleys, and I had seen it from the Charakusa side when I was there in 2004. I had looked at it again in 2005, when I was in this valley with Raphael Slawinski, who went on to do the first ascent of K6 West with his partner, Ian Welsted, from that same side in 2013. But all my photos of K6 Central from the Charakusa valley showed it to be a very steep technical wall threatened from above by hanging ice cliffs that could send huge avalanches down any potential climbing routes. I had not been to the Nangmah valley on the south side of the K6 massif, where the Austrians had gone when they made their successful ascent of K6 Main in 1970.

Reviewing maps, photos, and satellite imagery from Google Earth, I saw that a rock and ice buttress extended down from the summit on the south face of K6 Central. The crest of the buttress looked like it protruded enough to be protected from avalanches falling from ice cliffs on either side. The only photos I could obtain had been taken from a peak in the lower Nangmah valley, and they didn't show the bottom third of the face. That part was hidden behind a long ridge in the foreground coming off K6 that separated the East Nangmah Glacier from the upper Lachit Glacier. From what I could tell, it seemed worthwhile to launch an expedition that followed the 1970 Austrian approach to K6 Main over a pass in this ridge they called the Austrian Col to the upper Lachit Glacier and look at it from there. I wrote to my friend Nazir Sabir and his tour company in Islamabad, asking for help getting a climbing permit for K6 Central in July and August.

I continued my research to find a smaller peak in the area we could use for acclimatization—and in case the route we had chosen on K6 Central was not feasible. I found a photo in an article on the 1970 Austrian account showing a beautiful granite tower with the caption "Changi (6500m) from the east—a fine peak south-east of K6." Further research turned up an unsuccessful Polish attempt in 2010 on this same peak, which they called Changi Tower. I was pleased to find such a compelling, unclimbed granite tower just across the Lachit Glacier from the south face of K6 Central. But the discovery confused me. My research had turned up a different peak in this area, sometimes called Changi Tower, which had already been climbed! Digging deeper into international climbing journals, I eventually discovered there was a 5,820-meter peak (about 19,000 feet) in the upper Nangmah valley named Changui Tower that had been climbed, and it was regularly confused with the taller, unclimbed Changi Tower. To add to this misconception, some accounts had misspelled Changui Tower as Changi Tower. A spelling similarity and an error, plus its remote location hidden behind the ridge separating the Nangmah from the Lachit Glacier, must have kept the actual Changi Tower off the radar for most climbers looking for first ascents.

My next step was to assemble a team, and because my usual expedition partners weren't available, I used the opportunity to mentor some talented younger climbers who hadn't been to Pakistan before. They would benefit from my permitting and expedition-planning experience, and I could rely on their youthful enthusiasm and strength to get us up the peaks. I had been rock climbing a few times with Graham Zimmerman, a twenty-nine-year-old alpinist from Washington State. He trained hard and seemed to have an unflappable positive attitude. In 2014 he had been nominated for a Piolet d'Or for his ascent of Mount Laurens (3,060 meters, or 10,042 feet) in Alaska. Plus, he had planned a trip to Pakistan a couple of years earlier that had fallen through.

I sent Graham an invitation, along with some photos and information, to which he responded immediately. "Steve, I'm really excited to be asked," he said. "I'd put any plans for the Karakoram on the back burner given our previous permitting and visa issues plus concerns about security." With my experience, he hoped to get beyond those limitations. Graham was on board. "These look like great objectives, and I'm super psyched!" I asked him to suggest a third team member that he knew well and could trust. Graham suggested Scott Bennett, also twenty-nine, originally from Michigan but living in Boulder, Colorado. Graham had planned the previous expedition to Pakistan with Scott, and assured me that Scott was just the kind of person we wanted on a trip like this.

I had climbed a couple of smaller peaks in the Fitzroy Group in Argentine Patagonia with Scott and another friend a year earlier. Physically strong and technically talented, Scott got along well with others. At the end of a long walk on the first day of that trip, Scott, our other friend, and I had been the first to arrive at the place where climbers usually bivouac. In a vast, uneven boulder field tucked beneath a large rock, we set up our small tent on the only flat spot. The next day, we made an ascent of a relatively easy peak and returned to our tent under the rock, planning to spend another night and climb the following day. We arrived to find an Argentine climber dismantling our tent, so he and his partner could take our bivy spot. Just as I got ramped up to tell this guy off, Scott interceded and negotiated a way for us all to move around a bit so everyone could use the camping spot. I told Graham I thought Scott would be a great addition. Scott was as excited as Graham to be part of the team, and we waited all spring for our permit application to be approved.

My main concern was our age difference. I'd recently turned sixty-one, and I'd be spending a couple of months in Pakistan trying to keep up with two under-thirty-year-olds. We talked over the logistics of climbing Changi Tower and K6 Central. The routes we wanted to climb were a long distance from base camp over enormous rugged landscapes, so establishing an advance base camp close to the actual climbing route would work best. Changi Tower and K6 Central were still unclimbed, largely because it was difficult to reach them. After reading the account of the 2010 Polish Changi Tower expedition, I concluded that the Poles had run out of steam low on the peak because they hadn't established a well-stocked ABC where they could rest and recover and make multiple attempts if the first one failed. I proposed to Graham and Scott that we establish an ABC on the other side of the Austrian Col, at the head of the Lachit Glacier, from which we would launch our alpine-style attempts.

The budget I put together included the cost of equipment, supplies, and some local help to establish an ABC. Unfortunately, even with grants from the Mugs Stump Award, the Everest Foundation, and the New Zealand Alpine Club (Graham has dual citizenship), and me allocating my share of the grants to the two young guys, both Graham and Scott found it difficult to afford the trip. I made a few calls and discovered that some unused money had recently become available for an American Alpine Club Spitzer Climbing Grant. With approval by this committee, an AAC grant was awarded to Graham and Scott which allowed us to proceed.

By June we still hadn't received our permit. Scott and Graham were nervous, but Nazir and his staff reassured me that the permit would be issued and that the particular agencies were always late giving approvals. The permit was indeed issued on June 18, and the Pakistani consulate in Los Angeles expedited the process to issue our visas just a couple of days before our July 2 departure.

A blast of muggy heat greeted me like an old friend as I exited the plane in Islamabad. Sultan and Sarwar from Nazir Sabir Expeditions greeted us, and we followed them, pushing carts loaded with our duffel bags through a maze of twenty-foot-high concrete blast walls. The barrier around the airport was new, a stark reminder of how much the country's security situation had changed. We arrived at the Chancery guesthouse around 3:00 a.m. and got a few hours of sleep before starting our day's work.

Before leaving the United States, the key security precaution I had insisted on was flying from Islamabad to Skardu. My partners and I had made a pact with each other—and a promise to our friends and family—that we would not take the road. Sections of the Karakoram Highway run through areas adjacent to tribal areas populated by Pashtun Sunnis near the north side of Nanga Parbat where climbers were attacked two years earlier. If the weather and backlog didn't allow us to fly from Islamabad within a reasonable amount of time, we would return home rather than risk the drive. Sultan, the tour company's main man for everything logistics, had gotten us confirmed seats to Skardu on Sunday, July 5, the day after our arrival. With Sultan and Sarwar's help on our one day in Islamabad, we changed money, bought food, purchased medications and first-aid supplies, and made a deposit with a helicopter rescue service in case we needed an emergency evacuation. My old friend Colonel Manzoor Hussein was still president of the Alpine Club of Pakistan, so before going out for dinner together, we did the required expedition briefing with the ACP at our hotel along with Nazir, Sultan, and Sarwar. Colonel Manzoor reviewed the regulations and formally assigned our liaison officer, Air Force Major Abbas, to the expedition. Cheerful and respectful, Abbas was from a town four hundred miles south of Islamabad and had never seen snow.

Pakistan International Airways had started flying Airbus A320 jets to Skardu on the weekends. During the rest of the week PIA flew smaller turboprop planes, so it was much easier to get confirmed seats on the weekend. The plane took off and climbed above the clouds heading north from Islamabad. Fortunately the weather was good. We were able to see Nanga Parbat and not long after that we circled down to land. Reaching Skardu so quickly was amazing. There were no other trekkers or climbers on the flight. Nazir had told us in Islamabad that their business was less than half of what it was before the Nanga Parbat attack.

Rakmat from Nazir Sabir Expeditions met us in Skardu and arranged our transportation to the Snowland Palace Hotel, where we had stored a cache of equipment. Doug Chabot, Mark Richey, and I—with help from a few other climbers—had accumulated these supplies over the past decade. My old friend Rasool was waiting for us, and we greeted each other with a brotherly hug. It had been eight years since we had last seen each other, and I noticed that Rasool had aged considerably. He had slowed down a bit, but he still had the same lively personality and wit. Rasool brought his son-in law, Nadeem, as the assistant cook. Nadeem, a diligent and hard worker, had worked for me on our family trek into the Charakusa valley in 2005. Rasool wanted to keep future employment opportunities in the family, so his succession plan was to train Nadeem to be our cook. The only problem with Rasool's plan was that Nadeem spoke almost no English, which would be a basic requirement if he were to work for us alone. We went through our cache, to determine the condition of the tents and other equipment that we'd need.

Graham and Scott were excited to be in Skardu, and they interacted well with my Pakistani friends and the locals. Abbas seemed to play by the rules, but he also liked to joke around with us and had a warm, open personality. My strategy with him was to build trust. He had already received a lot of input from Nazir, Colonel Manzoor, Rasool, and Rakmat about my experience, and he deferred to my decisions as the expedition leader.

We planned to hire two porters with climbing experience to carry loads at least partway to our ABC. To save money, Nadeem could serve as one of these porters, then revert to his assistant cook role. Rasool suggested we hire Ibrahim, an experienced porter who had come with them from Hushe. In the basement of our hotel, where we organized everything, we distributed clothing and equipment to Rasool, Nadeem, and Ibrahim to use at or above base camp. Our plan was to send Ibrahim back to Hushe after establishing our ABC and then have him return to base camp at the end of the expedition to help bring everything down.

We spent the next two days provisioning and packing our equipment and supplies into fifty-pound porter loads. We had brought the usual food from home for climbing, but at base camp we would eat local food, so Rasool and Nadeem bought everything we would need to feed six people for almost two months. The last time I had been in Pakistan, we had to provide a kit for the liaison officer with all of his equipment for the expedition. This time, Sultan told us we needed to give the man $1,500 to buy his own kit. I didn't like this arrangement, because I knew Abbas had no experience living at a 14,000-foot base camp. He probably wouldn't buy all the gear he needed so he could pocket what he didn't spend. In that case, he'd be cold and wet, and we'd have to give him some of our gear.

It was the Muslim holy month of Ramadan, when fasting is obligatory for all adults unless they are elderly, ill, or traveling. Between sunup and sundown, Muslim followers refrain from eating and drinking anything, even water. Ramadan takes place according to the Islamic calendar, so it falls at different times each year according to the Western calendar. In 2015 the holy month was June 18 to July 18. It is a physical hardship for followers when Ramadan falls during months with the highest temperatures and longest days. Back in Seattle I had read that there was a heat wave in Karachi, and more than a thousand people had died. The temperature when we arrived in Islamabad was 109°F, which was normal for July. I guessed that people were not dying from the heat but because they were not drinking any water for sixteen hours each day.

Everything slows down during Ramadan. We needed to hire local people in Skardu to do hard physical labor. Rasool was a religious man and had been to Mecca twice, but he and Nadeem were pragmatic followers and considered themselves "travelers" on a difficult journey, which allowed them to eat and drink while working. They would resume fasting on days when we rode by jeep to Hushe, for example, because they would be sitting most of the day. Abbas didn't have to do any work, so he was fasting. He stayed up late at night and took food and water until 3:30 a.m. when the sun rose, then he slept every day until noon or 2:00 p.m. He was minimally active until 7:30 p.m., when the sun went down and he broke fast with iftar, the evening meal.

After the Nanga Parbat killings in 2013, the Gilgit–Baltistan provincial government increased security for expeditions. The province assigned a policeman to each expedition, so we had a guard with an assault rifle who hung around our hotel. He was very friendly to us, spoke good English, and wore a badge that said, POLICE IS YOUR FRIEND. The attempts to keep track of us and protect us meant that we had to fill out a lot more paperwork to register with various government security agencies. I wished they had similar registration requirements for keeping track of militants.

On July 8 we loaded three jeeps with passengers and porter loads for the eight-hour drive to Hushe. Abbas told me to wake him up when it was time to go. That was fine, but he had to carry his own bags down to the jeeps. He looked at me like I couldn't be serious. "Abbas," I told him, "good leadership isn't just ordering people around. You can inspire people to follow you by helping alongside them." He told me he was sorry if he had said anything to offend me. "No worries," I said, "just look for opportunities to help out and be part of the team."

Before heading out of town, I called Ann. Rasool spoke with her as well, asking about Lars and Jed. He told her not to worry about me because he would be helping us. As we drove along the Indus River with the smaller peaks towering above, Graham and Scott were pretty excited. It was all new to them, and it was fun for me to be around that kind of enthusiasm. We had to stop at police checkpoints at the bridge over the Indus River, in the town of Khaplu, and as we headed up the road into the Hushe valley. At each stop a different policeman got in the jeep to ride with us. I appreciated that they were making an effort, but it seemed unnecessary to me in this part of Baltistan.

The warm, sunny weather we experienced flying into Skardu continued, melting the snow at higher elevations. The increased flow had washed out the road in several places between Khaplu and Hushe, but by the time we got to the washouts, local road crews had regraded the stream crossings enough for our jeeps to ford across. In 2005, when I was last in Hushe, we had camped in a field, but since then a Spanish NGO had built a guesthouse. It had tiled bathrooms, plumbing that worked, paneled bedrooms with carpeting, and a nice dining hall. My room had a beautiful view of terraced fields with Masherbrum (7,821 meters, or 25,659 feet) as a backdrop. We spent the night there, and all my old friends came by for dinner—some of whom I had hired for my first Pakistan expedition thirty-five years earlier.

Early the next morning, we drove a short distance back down the road to the village of Kande (at 9,500 feet, or 2,896 meters) to begin our trek up the Nangmah valley to base camp. Counting out forty-four loads, Graham and Scott had their first experience managing the process of hiring porters. Scott recorded the name and number of each load that was assigned by Graham to the twenty-three porters we hired from Hushe and the twenty-one porters from Kande. (I had explained that to keep the peace, we needed to hire workers from each of the two nearby villages.) One of our porters was Rasool's son, Fida Ali, who was now twenty-two years old. Along with his pregnant wife and two-year-old daughter, Fida Ali lived in Rasool's house.

Graham, Scott, Abbas, Rasool, Nadeem, Ibrahim, and me (plus our forty-four porters) set out around 10:00 a.m., but it was already hot, and Ramadan was not over yet. Although I didn't want to interfere with Abbas's religious beliefs, I said, "It will be very difficult for you to make it to camp if you are fasting. Do you think you might be eligible for a dispensation as a 'traveler'?" He thought he would be, so I walked with him and set a slow, steady pace punctuated with frequent stops to drink and eat. The team and our porters arrived at camp at about 2:00 p.m. in a forested meadow with waterfalls pouring over big granite walls that surrounded us. Abbas was tired and admitted that taking my suggestion had enabled him to finish the hike.

Our plan was to reach base camp the next day. Just before we went to bed, Rasool told us that the Kande porters said the place where we wanted to locate our base camp in the upper Nangmah valley was five stages rather than the four stages we had agreed on. (These low-altitude porters were paid a certain amount per stage—the distance between specific locations that were several hours apart.) On popular treks to places like K2 base camp, the names and locations of each stage were well documented. But on less-popular trekking routes like those in the Nangmah valley, stages were ill-defined and provided an opportunity for porters to haggle for more money after the trip was under way.

The team left camp at 6:30 a.m. under cloudy skies. Graham and Scott went ahead to locate our base camp as far up the valley as possible for us to still have access to running water. We needed flat places for our tents and protection from natural hazards like rocks rolling down the hill on us. Only the Austrians and the Poles had established base camps this far up the valley, so none of the local porters with us knew where to go. I had been in this situation before and knew the porters would stop lower than where we wanted to be and claim it was the base camp. To go farther we would have to pay them for another stage. It was critical that we place our base camp as far up the valley as possible, to minimize the distance we would have to carry loads from there to Changi Tower and K6 Central. I was willing to renegotiate what we paid the porters to accomplish this, as long as their demands were reasonable.

I hiked last with Abbas, who was elated at seeing mountains and glaciers for the first time in his life. At around 10:00 or 11:00 a.m., as I was giving the major a geology lesson, we caught up with the porters, who, as expected, claimed they had reached base camp. I looked at the map we had been given by the Polish expedition, and it showed we needed to be several hundred feet farther up the grassy hillside and another mile or so farther north. When I asked the porters to keep going, they insisted this base camp was four stages, and if they went to the K6 base camp, where I was insisting, it would be five stages. Rather than set a precedent, I offered to pay them for four stages plus a 500-rupee tip. Apparently that was enough, because they all cheered, grabbed their loads, and charged up the slope.

It had been raining off and on for the past couple of hours, and as our motley crew wove its way up along intermittent grazing paths, it started to come down hard. The head Kande porter said he knew the location of the upper K6 base camp, so I stayed behind to coax Abbas up the hill. Apparently, the head Kande porter didn't really know where he was going because about one and a half hours later Abbas and I caught up to everyone perched on the hillside with Graham and Scott, not sure where to put base camp. The porters were soaked; we needed to find a place quickly so they could hurry back down to Kande after we paid them and before they became hypothermic.

I ran up to a terraced area with several large boulders and found it had good running water, so I called all the porters to me. They dropped their loads and, because they had done a good job getting us here in miserable conditions, I offered them a bit more money. They cheered again as Graham and Scott found an overhanging boulder out of the rain where they could set up shop to disperse porter payments. With help from Fida Ali, Graham and Scott called out each porter's name, counted out and handed him a stack of rupees, shook his hand, and thanked him. The mob that crowded around them soon thinned and then disappeared as each man clutched his small treasure and hurried off down the hillside.

Rasool, Nadeem, and Ibrahim set up the mess tent and the kitchen tent and covered all the porter loads with tarps. After some tea and biscuits in the mess tent, Graham, Scott, and I constructed a platform in the hillside and set up a tent for the three of us to share for the night. We built another platform for Abbas's tent. The three Hushe guys could sleep in the kitchen tent for the night, and we would finish setting up base camp the next day. Rasool and Nadeem served us a simple dinner of rice and lentil stew. We had happily achieved another key milestone: positioning our base camp right where we wanted it, on the hillside near the West Nangmah Glacier at about 14,000 feet.

It rained all night, and we got up to a soggy morning. But by noon the rain stopped, and Graham, Scott, and I found places on the hillside to construct platforms and erect our individual tents. When the sun came out later, we dried and sorted gear and food that needed to go to our advance base camp. K6 emerged from the clouds for the first time, lit up by the setting sun. Scott yelled, "Holy shit! That is awesome!" Graham said, "The summit of K6 Central is way up there!" As I headed to my tent after dinner, Abbas sat outside giving Nadeem and Ibrahim English lessons.

On the morning of July 12 it rained again, and Graham, Scott, and I headed out for a reconnaissance to find the easiest, most direct route between base camp and the East Nangmah Glacier and then beyond that to the Austrian Col. We had some information about where the Austrian and Polish expeditions had gone, but conditions change over time. Maps from that first expedition forty-five years ago showed the East and West Nangmah Glaciers flowing into each other, with the snout a couple miles farther down the valley. Climate change over the decades had caused the glaciers to recede to above their former confluence. Now we walked past the snout of the West Nangmah Glacier to get to the left lateral moraine of the East Nangmah Glacier near its snout. The soil and rock we walked on was glacial debris recently left behind by these receding glaciers, and much of it was loose and shifted underfoot. After climbing a thousand feet up this moraine, it leveled out, and we traversed out onto the East Nangmah Glacier.

We looked up to where the two previous expeditions had crossed over the Austrian Col to the upper Lachit Glacier on the other side. The snow slopes up to the col seemed thin over the underlying rock, and in places the route was threatened by ice cliffs that hung overhead. The Polish map showed an alternate route to the Lachit Glacier over what was called the Hidden Col (5,444 meters, or 17,860 feet), a quarter mile north of the Austrian Col (5,502 meters, or 18,051 feet). The Hidden Col was lower, less exposed to overhead hazard, and looked to be steep but straightforward snow climbing in current conditions. Rain soaked, we turned around and marked our way back to base camp with rock cairns. Graham, a geologist, also set GPS coordinates. (As one of the assorted things he did to support himself, Graham performed geological surveys around the world—he had excellent navigation skills.) We accomplished our goal for the day by finding a good way up onto the East Nangmah Glacier. The Hidden Col was, in fact, a better way to cross over to the Lachit Glacier than the Austrian Col.

The next day we dried our gear and clothing, and I spent the afternoon resting in my tent. As I headed to the mess tent for dinner that evening, I looked down the grassy hillside and saw a man walking toward me with an automatic rifle. I panicked and started to run away to warn the others, thinking we were about to be attacked. But after my initial scare, I realized it was Nawaz, the policeman from Kande, who had told me four days earlier that he had been assigned to stay with us at our base camp to guard us. I thought it was an unnecessary expense to provide food and tent space for another person, and I had suggested he stay in Kande and guard the entrance to the Nangmah valley instead. After greeting Nawaz, we walked to the kitchen tent, where he told Rasool that he thought he might lose his job if he didn't stay with us. Apparently it had taken him fourteen hours to walk there from Kande while fasting for Ramadan. If Nawaz was concerned about his job, I told him, he should stay with us.

On July 14 we left base camp at 4:00 a.m., just as it got light, with the intent of carrying loads up to the Hidden Col. We brought Nadeem and Ibrahim to help, now that we knew the route. Scott scurried across the boulder field and pulled Graham along with him while I tried to go at my own steady pace and not fall too far behind. Trying to keep up with those two for the next couple of months would leave me exhausted and useless. Nadeem and Ibrahim could have easily kept up with them, but they followed behind me out of respect and to make sure I was okay. The five of us followed our cairns up the moraine. To safeguard against a potentially deadly crevasse fall, we roped up to each other before traversing out onto the East Nangmah Glacier. Graham and Scott went ahead and did all the step kicking in ankle- to calf-deep snow, while I followed with Nadeem and Ibrahim. By the time we arrived at the couloir leading up to the Hidden Col, it was just coming into the sun.

Our plan was to do all our climbs from the Lachit Glacier on the other side of the Hidden Col alpine style, without any fixed ropes or camps. We needed to make several trips to move our supplies and equipment the three miles from base camp over the Hidden Col to our advance base camp. On this trip we placed several fixed ropes to make that job quicker and safer. Partway up the couloir, the solar radiation became increasingly intense; we were concerned that the heat could trigger small, wet snow slides from the rock walls on either side that might fall on us. We tried to work quickly, even though we were not yet acclimatized. By noon, all five of us had reached the col. Nadeem and Ibrahim had some climbing experience, but I coached them on how to use the fixed lines going up and rappelling back down. We crossed back over the glacier and reached base camp at around 4:00 p.m. Everyone was tired, not just me. Carrying loads up to the Hidden Col was another milestone to celebrate. Graham made some recovery drinks, we ate some cheese and crackers, and we enjoyed a big dinner before bed.

I didn't sleep well. Now that we had been to the top of the Hidden Col, I realized we needed to adjust our strategy. Thinking about logistics kept me awake. My original plan to carry loads all the way to ABC and return to base camp in a day had become unrealistic and unsafe. We had a lot to carry and it was too far to allow us to time our carries to avoid the steep climbing up the couloir to the Hidden Col in the sun, which would expose us to rockfall and avalanches. Changi Tower and K6 Central were different types of climbs and required different equipment. Changi Tower would be a technical rock and ice climb: for the rock we needed double sets of mechanical camming devices, pitons, cabled aluminum wedges, large diameter ropes, and rope ascenders plus a large number of carabiners and slings. For the ice we needed a few ice screws. K6 Central would be a high-altitude, mostly snow and ice climb. For that, we needed more ice screws, much less rock gear, and ropes that were smaller in diameter.

After breakfast, I ran some ideas by the team that involved placing a cache camp on the base camp side of the col. It would be safer for the two Pakistanis to shuttle loads between base camp and the base of the couloir where we could put an extra tent for storage. Graham, Scott, and I could then focus our efforts on carrying loads up the couloir on the west side of the col in the early morning, when it was shady, and then down the other side to ABC. The couloir below the east side of the col would be in the sun in the morning, but we could minimize our exposure to heat-generated rockfall or wet snow slides because it was much faster going down. Scott, Graham, and I agreed on the details of this plan.

After finishing breakfast, Scott and Graham talked about what their families, especially their parents, thought about their climbing. Both of them had become involved in the outdoors with their families when they were young, and their parents were generally supportive and proud of what they were doing. But both their families had similar concerns about safety, security, and career paths. It was interesting for me to participate in a conversation like this because I could understand both sides of the generational relationships. My sons were close in age to Scott and Graham, so I knew the parental perspective. And I'd faced my own challenges trying to explain to friends and family why climbing was so important to me and a worthwhile pursuit. Having the benefit of a few more years to think about these things, I told them: Be yourself! The attitudes of the people who love you will evolve, and it's okay to set boundaries with those who can only see things from their own perspective. It was a privilege to be here with such thoughtful young climbers. Scott was a genius—he had undergraduate degrees in economics and history and was very well informed about a variety of subjects. His work as an arborist was simply a means to support his climbing habit. For his part, Graham was a professional climbing athlete in addition to working as a geologist. I hadn't seen him in a bad mood yet—he was enthusiastic about whatever we were doing, and engaged easily with everyone, from the porters to the liaison officer.

To make sure we reached the Hidden Col in the shade, Graham, Scott, Ibrahim, Nadeem, and I left base camp at 3:00 a.m. on July 16. We carried heavy loads to below the col and left some of what we brought in the small tent we'd set up on the glacier for our new cache camp. The five of us took lighter loads up to the col, and Scott accompanied Ibrahim and Nadeem to make sure they rappelled safely down to the glacier before walking back to base camp on their own. Graham and I repacked at the col and rappelled down the opposite side, carrying heavy packs and each dragging a full duffel bag down to the snow slopes at the bottom. About two hundred yards east of us, a rocky ridge protruded from and separated the snow slopes we were on from the main Lachit Glacier. There was a saddle a half mile farther down this rocky ridge that we recognized from Polish expedition photos. Graham and I continued to carry and drag our loads down the snow slope, and Scott soon joined us carrying another load. We reached a slope at the base of the saddle in the rocky ridge and left most of our loads there. After climbing a couple hundred feet to the rocks with our tent, stoves, and some food, we set up ABC at 17,430 feet. Another milestone achieved!

From ABC we got our first view of the entire 5,000-foot-high south face of K6 Central (7,100 meters, or 23,293 feet) that towered above us. After studying it for about an hour, I concluded there wasn't a route on it that was free from significant overhead hazards. From photos of the upper part of this face, we had thought a rocky buttress extending down from the summit would provide a safe zone from the ice cliffs on either side. But now that we saw the lower part of the face for ourselves, we discovered this protective buttress stopped about 1,500 feet from the glacier at the bottom. From our vantage point it looked like we would be forced to climb up slopes threatened from above until we reached the shelter of this buttress—a game of Russian roulette that I was unwilling to play. Scott and Graham talked about potential lines on the face that minimized the risk, but I decided not to voice my opinion yet. There was plenty of time to observe K6 Central and talk about it later. Our first objective was Changi Tower, two miles east of us on the other side of the Lachit Glacier.

As we turned our attention to Changi Tower (6,500 meters, or 21,325 feet), it looked bigger and more challenging than I had anticipated. The steep rocky part of the tower dominated the skyline across from us, rising about two thousand feet above the south end of the Polish Col, an icy 19,400-foot-high pass in the ridge. It was midafternoon by then, and the sun projected a harsh flat light on the tower's west face, making it difficult to pick out the cracks, ice runnels, ledges, and other features we would link together to map out a feasible route. Although the tower was the main attraction, there was a lot of climbing just to reach it. Below the Polish Col, an 800-foot ice face extended down to a small glacial cirque. The cirque sat at the top of a broken-up, dangerous-looking glacial icefall that tumbled more than a thousand feet down over a steep section in the underlying rock and formed a tottering mass of ice towers and gaping crevasses.

While dozing that afternoon in the tent, I realized my work to establish our ABC was winding down. What should my role be now that we were getting into position to start these climbs? Scott and Graham were stronger, more skilled, and faster climbers than I was. As was the case on all these expeditions to the great ranges, it was less important to share the leading than it was to assign everyone the jobs for which they were best suited.

Although it would be fun for me to do some of the leading on Changi Tower, it would be more efficient if Graham and Scott did all of it. I would follow in support, carrying as much food, fuel, and bivouac equipment as I could. I decided to propose this when the time came.

As I was occupied with these thoughts, the afternoon slipped away, and the slope we climbed up that morning to get to ABC had gone into the shade. The three of us dropped down and brought the loads we had left behind up to our camp. As the sun set, we sat on the rocks outside our tent, mesmerized by the size and beauty of the mountain amphitheater surrounding us.

The next day we climbed up to the Hidden Col. We saw Ibrahim and Nadeem arrive below us on the glacier; they were dropping final loads for ABC on the other side at cache camp. Scott rappelled first and reached the storage tent before Graham and me. The weather was changing for the worse, and we intended to keep going to base camp, but Scott filled his pack with supplies and headed back up to the col, telling Graham and me that we could wait for him at the tent. He must have known that his taunt would force us to carry loads to the col as well.

Climbing back up, I felt that as I acclimatized, my breathing became steadier and my heart beat a bit slower. But after several days of chasing Scott and Graham around, I experienced a deeper fatigue that was hard to recover from—a symptom of being older. Accepting that it was harder, or not possible, for me to do things that I could do when I was younger wasn't easy. I wondered if this would be my last expedition to these huge, serious mountains. Heading down, I was glad that we made an additional carry because now all the supplies and equipment we needed for Changi Tower were either at ABC or sitting at the top of the Hidden Col. Back at base camp, those earlier doubts faded. After a couple days' rest, I could imagine myself on the summits of Changi Tower and K6 Central.

With our load-carrying job to ABC complete, we paid Ibrahim and sent him back to Hushe. We could use his help again at the end of the expedition to bring everything down, but he might not be available then if he found other work in the meantime. The next day, July 18, it started to rain hard in the afternoon. That evening, in our soggy little outpost, we celebrated Eid al-Fitr, the end of the Muslim holy month of Ramadan, with Rasool, Nadeem, and Abbas. Muslims celebrate Eid like Christians celebrate Christmas, with family meals and gifts. Rasool and Nadeem made a big dinner with a cabbage, carrot, and cucumber salad; chicken and rice curry; and mangos for dessert. After dinner we tried to use our satellite phone so Rasool could call Hushe, but the phones in his village seemed to work only intermittently, and we couldn't get through.

After two more days of rain, the forecast called for possible clearing, which was good enough for us to head back to ABC on July 21. So far, we had spent only one night at ABC at 17,430 feet (5,313 meters), which was insufficient acclimatization for our ascent of 21,325-foot (6,500-meter) Changi Tower. The goal was to spend more time at higher elevation. For efficiency's sake, we decided to acclimatize by finding a route through the broken-up icefall below Changi Tower and spend a night at the Polish Col.

It had been unusually warm so far this season. In seasons past, our base camp at 14,000 feet (4,271 meters) would be close to the elevation where it would still snow in the summertime. But when the clouds lifted, we saw the snow line was around 18,000 feet (5,486 meters). Everywhere below this level it had been raining—and that included the Hidden Col and our route up to it. The winter snow that blanketed the entire East Nangmah Glacier when we first arrived had melted back to old bare ice on the lower part. When we got above the line where the winter snow hadn't melted, we sank up to our crotches in the rain-soaked, sloppy mess. What we thought would be a three- to four-hour trip from base camp to ABC took almost seven hours.

We rose to a foggy moist morning at 3:00 a.m. and left ABC around 4:30 a.m., when it got light. With enough food and gear for two days, we planned to spend the night as high as we could get—hopefully as far as the Polish Col. We got lost in the fog right away, as the cloud ceiling dropped. I suggested we stop and wait for the clouds to lift, to see where we were going. After about an hour it cleared enough to see we had gone the wrong way, but from our vantage point we took turns pointing out ways that we might go up through the jumbled maze in the icefall across from us. From a distance it seemed easy to plot our route around the ice towers and crevasses, but after we got there and climbed up into the icefall, we found ourselves in a complex labyrinth full of dead ends blocked by huge crevasses and ice walls.

At first we found a way up the left side of the icefall, but a forty-foot-high wall of ice forced us over onto the right side, where we made good upward progress in a groove between ice towers on either side. We came to a fork where it looked like an ice wall above would block the way, so we traversed left and continued up, only to find the way dead-ended by this same barrier that extended across the width of the entire icefall.

Just as we began to think there were no good options for getting past this obstacle, we spotted a small avalanche slope back on the right side above the fork where we had gone left instead of up. Snow from above funneled down this slide path and filled the crevasses in the icefall, creating what looked like an easy way around the ice wall. In good weather it would be safe to climb up this slope and traverse into the small glacial cirque above the icefall. By now it was early afternoon, and the heat caused small pieces of ice to fall off the towers and walls around us. It was time to get out of this creaking mass of ice debris, so we traversed over to a rocky outcrop on the edge of the icefall and set up our bivy tent for the night. We could check out the slide path on the other side early the next morning when everything was frozen.

In the morning we traversed back to the fork and continued up the groove we had been following the day before. We reached the slide path, which made it surprisingly easy to climb up and traverse into the basin below Changi Tower. Once we reached this small glacial cirque, we were high enough to look off to the southwest, where all the weather came from, and noticed a dark mass of clouds moving in our direction. Although we wanted to climb farther and spend the night acclimatizing on the Polish Col, we could become trapped if it started snowing heavily; the slide path we had just ascended would be running with avalanches. We waited for about an hour watching the weather, and seeing no real improvement, we left some supplies and equipment there in our tent and descended back to ABC.

Soon after we arrived at ABC, a huge avalanche broke off the serac high on the right side of the buttress we had been looking at on the south face of K6 Central. As we expected, the crest of the buttress protruded enough from the wall that the avalanche did not go over it but was deflected to the right side. When the avalanche fell to where the buttress ended, however, it completely swept across the lower third of the entire face. The billowy mass of snow and ice continued toward us, and by the time it reached ABC, the big pieces of ice had dropped out, but the wind blast gave us a good dusting of snow. I saw it coming and got under the tent vestibule, followed shortly by Graham and a bit later by Scott, who didn't realize how long he would be getting sprayed. After it was over, any doubts I had about the safety of this route were confirmed, but Graham and Scott didn't seem convinced of that quite yet. They thought only a small part of the route was exposed. I decided to postpone a discussion on the south face of K6 Central until after we were done with Changi Tower.

The morning of July 24 revealed a high overcast with no precipitation, so we made another acclimatization trip up through the icefall. This time instead of taking two days to reach the glacial cirque below Changi Tower from ABC, it took two hours, following our previous path and using the GPS coordinates Graham had set. We brought more food and climbing gear that we stashed in the tent. We did a quick turnaround because the storm that had been brewing for the past twenty-four hours looked like it wasn't going to hold off for another day—in fact, it was forecast to last at least a week. Back at ABC, Graham, Scott, and I packed up a few things we might want and headed over the Hidden Col, down the sloppy glacier, and across numerous streams full of snowmelt to base camp.

Rasool and Nadeem welcomed us and put together a meal of cheese chapatis and rehydrated powdered soup mix that was fortified with fresh vegetables and a few eggs that they called "super soup." The sun went behind Changui Tower (not to be confused with Changi Tower that we were trying to climb over on the Lachit glacier above ABC), whose granite walls rose up out of the hillside behind base camp. I was tired after several days of hard work, so I took a nap. I woke up feeling much better, and we had a late dinner of more soup and potato salad. Rasool and I talked late into the evening about our mutual friends back in America.

We had entered a period of warm, unstable weather characterized by dramatic afternoon thundershowers with heavy rain and hail. In my experience this pattern was unusual for the Karakoram. On July 28 the weather forecast was just good enough for us to head back to ABC with thoughts of climbing Changi Tower. After we got there, it started to rain hard so we discussed our options. "Maybe we can try the south face of K6 Central if it gets colder," Graham said. I had to tell them what I'd been thinking. "I'm not going to go up on this route," I said, "because I think the bottom part is too exposed to avalanches from the ice cliffs above."

Turning toward me, Graham looked relieved now that the subject was broached. "After the big avalanche the other day," he said, "Scott and I have been talking about it, and it does seem too dangerous." Scott nodded in agreement. We didn't have to make a decision today, I told them.

We could keep watching K6 Central from different angles and focus on climbing Changi Tower. That climb was much safer looking, and we were well positioned to get onto the tower with the resources and strength to be successful. I was pleased we all were in agreement. Soon the rain turned to hail and back to rain, then it snowed all night. In the morning we went back to base camp.

It looked like we were going to be waiting for at least four or five days before the weather would improve, so Graham, Scott, and I settled into our individual base camp tents to rest and work on various reading and writing projects. One afternoon, Rasool came to my tent to ask what we wanted for dinner. I invited him inside so we could visit. Sitting across from each other while the rain tapped on the tent fly was a perfect time to talk. I was working on a section in my book that was primarily about him. In his usual modest way, Rasool said, "Thank you very much, Steve sahib, thank you very much. You are a famous man, and cook for Steve Swenson is a famous man." I thanked him for all the work he had done for us and told him he deserves all the recognition he gets for being a big part of our expeditions and any successes we've had. We reminisced, and Rasool thanked me for giving him opportunities like going with us to China to K2's north side and for sending him to Kathmandu to have cataract surgery.

Bedruma—Rasool's wife, partner, and confidante since they were both teenagers—had passed away in 2010. "I am so sorry that Bedruma died," I told him. "When you called me from Skardu to tell me, I wished I could be there with you. She was a great woman, and I know you still think about her all the time." Rasool started to cry and thanked me again. I knew he had remarried, and he and his new wife, Amina, had two young children. "I'm glad you have Amina for a partner to keep you company and to share the great joy of Sughra and Rosi," I said, "but I know you still miss Bedruma." We looked at each other for a minute or two in silent recognition of all we had been through together. Rasool said, "You are more than a friend—a brother—like family." As he reached over to open the tent zipper, he wiped his tears away. "I'm cooking now," he said.

One morning Rasool told me more about how the local tourist economy had been affected after the Nanga Parbat attack in 2013. Because the number of tourists had dropped so much, the villagers couldn't rely on those jobs any longer. They see their children needing an education that gives them the skills to get jobs beyond the village, in larger cities or towns like Khaplu, Skardu, or farther. The village leaders opened a private school in Hushe that has an accelerated learning program, and those who can afford the tuition send their children there. Those students are better prepared to pass exams that allow them to continue their schooling. But if the village suffers from a reduction in tourism, parents who no longer have the money for private school send their children to the government primary and middle schools, which are not as rigorous and leave those students at a competitive disadvantage. Rasool reminded me that the people in his village comply with the Islamic system of *zakat* (tithing) to help the poor.

It was early August, and we had spent more time in base camp and less time at ABC than planned. We were running out of some food items. When I asked about it, Rasool snapped to attention. With his right hand placed over his heart, he joked by saying, "Rasool's still alive; this is my responsibility." We laughed because there was no doubt that the only thing that would prevent him from taking care of us was death. That evening he had us call his daughter in Hushe on the satellite phone. After numerous tries we managed to get through, and Rasool left a list of items for Fida Ali to bring up to base camp with the help of another porter a few days later. Abbas went back to Hushe with Fida Ali and we didn't see him again until we arrived back in Skardu at the end of our expedition.

Finally, on August 5, the forecast we had been waiting for arrived—drier weather the next day that might last for six days. We headed to ABC, plowing through the usual unsupportive snow on the East Nangmah Glacier. But the real surprise was how much the snowpack, or lack of it, had changed in the couloir leading to the Hidden Col. All the warm weather and rain had melted the snow and ice, exposing the underlying loose rock in places. This made the couloir much more dangerous from rockfall. The risk was apparent as we climbed quickly through the debris from a large recent avalanche, which had left the couloir covered in dirt, rock, snow, and bare ice. It was late by the time we got to ABC, so we decided to rest the following day and start climbing the day after that.

That night I was hit with a severe bout of diarrhea that forced me to charge out of the tent several times to avoid shitting myself. The next day my diarrhea worsened, and every hour I ran for the latrine we had dug in the snow. Early the next morning, when the alarm went off at 2:00 a.m.

for us to start our climb, I told Graham and Scott that I was too sick to go. "You guys should go without me," I said, "because this weather will not last and I'd hate to see all of us miss the summit because we waited an extra day." Graham and Scott didn't want to go without me, and because the forecast was for good weather for another four days, they decided there was enough time to wait and see if I felt better in twenty-four hours. I tried to spend the day drinking and eating to keep up my strength, even though I didn't have much of an appetite. By evening I was much better but still felt like someone had punched me in the gut. As we bedded down, I said I was ready to go, but I wasn't feeling 100 percent.

The morning of August 8 we left our advance base camp at about 2:00 a.m., heading down the glacier in the darkness past new lakes and streams flowing over the ice to the start of our route through the icefall. It had been fifteen days since we were last there, and it had changed dramatically. Even though the ice features around us looked completely different, Graham was able to navigate by headlamp using his GPS to take us straight to the entrance slot that marked the start of our route. We pieced together the route through the ice towers, crevasses, and ice walls. At daybreak we emerged onto the glacier basin below the Polish Col, where we had left our tent with some equipment and supplies. We sorted our gear into a lighter lead pack and two heavier packs for the followers.

After crossing the basin, we climbed unroped up the forty-five- to fifty-degree ice slope and reached the Polish Col (at 19,400 feet, or 5,913 meters) at 10:30 a.m. It was part of the ridgeline that separated the Lachit Glacier we had just crossed from the Kondus Glacier on the other side. Beyond the Kondus Glacier we saw the Saltoro Ridge that marked the Actual Ground Position Line separating the Pakistan Army on this side from the Indian Army that was on the Siachen Glacier on the other side. From the south end of the Polish Col we roped up, and Graham, the designated leader for the day, started climbing up the initial ice face on the north side of Changi Tower.

We climbed about six hundred feet up through some mixed ice and rock, and by 2:00 p.m. we reached a hundred-foot-high, forty-five-degree snow- and icefield that looked to be the lowest-angled slope on the tower. A nearly vertical rock wall reared up above us, and looking toward the summit, it appeared that the rest of our route would consist of much steeper rock climbing, broken up by a few ice runnels and ice slopes. Even though we still had several hours of daylight, I thought this would be the best, and maybe only, place to build a tent platform for the night. Graham and Scott advocated to keep going, but I was concerned that higher up the terrain was so steep that we wouldn't find a place for the tent (I did not want to be forced to bivouac on small ledges hacked out of the ice just big enough for a couple of butt cheeks).

Ideally we wanted to position ourselves on the mountain as high as we could by the end of the day. But we didn't want to do that at the expense of spending the night exposed to the cold and wind, making it difficult to rehydrate, eat, and sleep. Choosing the right place to bivouac would be critical to our success, but without knowing anything about what we might find above, we couldn't know for sure where that should be.

We compromised, and while Graham and Scott climbed up the rock band above us for another few hundred feet, I stayed behind and began constructing a platform. I anchored the ice hammock we brought with us and filled it in with ice and snow that I chopped from the slope in the same way Mark Richey and Freddie Wilkinson had built our platforms on Saser Kangri II. After reaching their high point, Graham and Scott tied our two ropes, one above the other, to rock anchors and rappelled back to me. They helped finish the work to set up and anchor the tent that, despite our best efforts, protruded from the platform by six inches. The three of us squeezed inside by lying head to toe. We hoped that having a warm, dry place to get well hydrated and fed, plus a decent sleep for the night, would give us the strength to keep going strong the next day. Our original plan was to carry our bivouac gear with us for another day and try to find one more place to spend the night on the wall before climbing to the summit the day after that.

While lying in our sleeping bags, Scott offered a new idea. He said, "Why don't we leave the tent and everything behind except our climbing gear and try to reach the summit from here in a single push." I wasn't sold. "After all this work to get this far," I said, "it would be a shame to find ourselves short of the summit as it's getting dark and be forced to descend because we don't want to risk an open bivouac without overnight gear." Scott had been thinking about our options. "From what I can see above us," he countered, "the tower is so steep that we won't find another place to build a tent platform like this one." He knew that carrying all our heavy bivouac gear would slow us down and force us to spend a miserable open bivouac.

It was hard to argue with that logic, so we compromised again and decided to try to reach the summit the next day, leaving all our overnight gear behind except the stove and plenty of fuel and one sleeping bag to drape over us—just enough to survive without injury if we ended up in an open bivouac, having a very cold, sleepless night.

On August 9, we rose in the dark at 4:00 a.m., and after brewing up we were on our way by 6:00 a.m. We used our rope ascenders to climb up the two ropes Graham and Scott had fixed the day before. Scott started out leading for the day, and I felt like we had unleashed a tiger. I had rarely seen anyone climb so quickly up steep technical ground at this altitude. We had a system where Scott led a rope length and built an anchor and fixed the rope between him and Graham. Once it was fixed, Graham climbed up the rope using his ascenders and removed all the gear Scott had placed to protect himself when leading. Graham then fixed the second rope that went to me, and I removed the anchor at my station before climbing up the rope. I tried to reach Graham in time to give him the gear from the anchor, so he could bring up all the gear to Scott before he led again.

After a couple of rope lengths, I had my system adjusted the way I wanted it and was able to keep up with Graham. By noon we had climbed about six hundred feet above our camp. "In my experience," Graham told me, the next time I reached him, "when Scott is on a roll like this, we should just keep him in front." Scott clicked off one technical rope length after another without appearing to tire. I had been concerned that we wouldn't be able to move over such difficult terrain and get to the top before dark. But at the rate we were going, I was optimistic that we would. Up to this point we had been climbing the north face of the tower. Based on what we had scoped out from the Lachit Glacier, we needed to traverse right on a ramp system onto the northwest face to the base of a giant left-facing corner system that I called the Great Dihedral. From the glacier it looked like climbing this prominent feature on the upper part of the tower would take us within a couple hundred feet of the summit. Until we turned the corner and looked up into it, though, we wouldn't know if the Great Dihedral was choked with ice, full of overhangs, stacked with dangerous loose blocks, or filled with other obstacles making it too difficult and time-consuming to climb in order to reach the summit that day.

Graham and I watched Scott traverse around a corner and into the base of the Great Dihedral. We'd hoped he might let out some kind of hoot and holler that the route ahead looked doable. But he said nothing and moved past the base of the main corner system and started up a complex set of flakes and edges on the right-hand wall. Then he set up an anchor in a place that looked to me like it led nowhere and pulled up all the remaining rope between him and Graham and tied it off. As Graham climbed up the rope, Scott continued climbing but this time with a forty-foot loop of rope hanging down between him and the anchor. It was a dangerous maneuver, with the potential for a huge fall before the rope would catch him if he came off. But if he was careful and remained in control, short fixing like this could save us a lot of time.

Graham got to the anchor, pulled in the slack, and put Scott on a real belay. He was halfway through the next pitch that took us back left into the dihedral above an overhanging thin crack topped with a large icicle. Scott had avoided the icicle with his detour onto the right wall. Graham and I managed to climb the ropes across these traversing pitches, and once we were all into the dihedral, Scott led on two mixed rock and ice pitches. The final rope length in this giant corner system was free of ice, so Scott took off his crampons and double boots and changed into snug rock-climbing shoes before launching into what looked like difficult crack and face climbing. At the top of the dihedral, Scott finally let out a yelp of delight. He found he could avoid an overhanging eight-inch-wide crack that was topped with ice by traversing on good face holds on solid granite up and left to a belay around the corner.

It looked like we had two more rope lengths of mixed ice and rock climbing to reach the summit, so Scott changed back into boots and crampons. As the sun was setting, Scott rushed up a small corner above us that was full of loose unconsolidated snow he had to bat away with his ice tools. Graham and I ducked under an overhang to keep from getting pummeled by all the snow Scott knocked down. On the final pitch Scott traversed out to the right along the top of a rock wall that was capped by more steep unconsolidated snow. Again he was forced to excavate the unstable snow-pack, this time away from the edge of the rock wall. He climbed along a narrow strip of granite between the snow and where it dropped away for thousands of feet to the glacier below.

Protection was scarce in the rock, and twenty feet after leaving his last piece of gear, Scott plunged his ice tools into the snow to pull himself from the rock onto a weak snow layer that led to the final summit block. But his tools sliced through the snow like a hot knife in butter, forcing him to step high, with just one leg, onto a thin band of seemingly firmer snow. If it collapsed under his weight, he would be sent tumbling forty or fifty feet down the wall below. He stood up gently, and it held. After kicking steps up a short slope of firmer snow, Scott reached the final rocky summit block and scratched his way up with tools and crampons to reach the top in the fading light. Graham climbed up to Scott as it got dark, and I followed using my headlamp in the pitch black.

The true summit was a few feet higher than where Scott had anchored himself, so each of us took turns climbing up a short delicate snow slope to tag the summit. It afforded no views now that is was dark. Too tenuous a spot to have much of a celebration, Graham took over setting up the rappels as we started down by headlamp. As we dropped into the Great Dihedral, Graham found rock anchors on the left wall that kept us out of the main corner—a good thing since it was full of rock flakes and horns that would have snagged our ropes when we pulled them down. After turning the corner onto the north face, our ropes got stuck on several V-thread ice anchors, forcing one of us to climb back up and free them. After that we clipped our rappel ropes through a carabiner we left attached to each anchor so they would pull easier. We reached our tent at 3:00 a.m. without any more problems and were happy to pile inside—tired but pleased that we had squeaked in the first ascent of one of the highest unclimbed granite towers in the Karakoram.

The three of us slept in late. We didn't get the camp dismantled and packed up until around 2:00 p.m. Five rappels brought us to the Polish Col, and we made another seven rappels from the col to the glacier basin. It was 6:00 p.m. by the time we walked over to where we had cached some food and fuel for the climb down. There were only one and a half hours of daylight left, and Scott and Graham wanted to continue our descent through the icefall to ABC. The weather was good, so I felt there was no need to rush. I asked my partners if continuing our descent this late in the day was a good idea. Scott thought it was fine, and Graham agreed. I was tired and wanted to spend the night where we were. Graham acquiesced and then Scott as well. Now that we weren't hanging off the side of the mountain, we didn't have to be anchored in all the time or worry about dropping anything. We littered the flat glacier around the tent with all our gear and sat outside eating, drinking, and watching the sunset light up the peaks along the western horizon.

Graham, Scott, and I started down through the icefall by 6:00 a.m. on August 11—everyone was grateful we hadn't tried to do it in the dark. We got to ABC around noon and came up with a plan for the next job: moving everything back over the Hidden Col. We took an inventory of everything at ABC and determined each of us would need to carry three loads. Scott and Graham were in a big hurry and wanted to get all this work done the next day. I didn't like all this rushing around on dangerous terrain and suggested we should do this job in two days, especially since we needed several rest days before any attempts on K6. It would be hard to get all this work done tomorrow before the sun came around on the west side of the Hidden Col and the rocks started falling down the couloir.

The day before, Graham and Scott had agreed to delay our descent through the icefall until that morning. I didn't want to keep overriding their decisions, so I went along with their desire to move everything over the Hidden Col in the next twenty-four hours. "We will get caught by the sun on the west side of the Hidden Col for sure if we try to do all this work tomorrow," I said, "so why don't each of us carry two loads to the top of the col this afternoon when the east side is in the shade and then carry one more in the morning when we leave?" I asked Graham what time he thought we'd need to have all the loads at the col the next morning so we'd have enough time to bring everything down onto the East Nangmah Glacier before the sun hit. Graham responded: 6:00 a.m. sharp. The sun would hit it at around 11:00 a.m., so that meant we would have five hours to get everything down the west side. I agreed that this seemed like enough time.

Graham and Scott took a nap in the tent at ABC until 5:00 p.m. I thought, *Good. It will be too late to carry two loads to the col today, and we'll have to slow down and spend another day getting this job done.* But after waking up, they shouldered their packs and headed for the col, so I did the same. By the time we got four loads at the col and two loads to some rocks just below the col, it was well after dark. We went back to ABC for the night, already behind our schedule.

The team got a late start the next morning and didn't get everything to the col until 8:00 a.m. We only had three hours to move everything down the other side before the sun hit. Before I went back down the east side to ferry the last load up to the col, Scott told me he and Graham would get all the loads down the west side to the East Nangmah Glacier except for the last two, which I should bring. While bringing down the last two loads, I would need to clean up the anchors and rappel down while stripping and carrying down the fixed lines. Because Scott had all the rock gear, he would build rappel anchors for me. They had to be placed no more than 60 meters (196 feet) apart because that was the length of rope I would be rappelling with while taking down all the fixed line.

By the time I came back up the east side with the last load, no one was at the col. I removed extra rock gear from the anchor and started rappelling the west side using the two sixty-meter fixed lines doubled up that I stripped from the east side of the col. It was hard to manage all the weight I was carrying (my packs coupled with the increasing number of fixed lines I removed as I went down). I reached a new rappel anchor that presumably Scott had installed about 160 feet below the col and pulled the first rappel. Below me the couloir was even more melted out than when we had been here a few days ago, exposing larger sections of loose rock and dirt.

I started the next rappel with just one of my packs, since I couldn't see where the next rappel anchor was. It was a good idea to not be so heavily laden because when I reached the end of my sixty-meter ropes I could see that I was about forty feet short of the next anchor. This was upsetting. I needed to build another rappel anchor to get down, but Scott had all the rock gear. Fortunately, I had taken a large aluminum stopper from the anchor at the col and was able to make a rappel anchor by pounding it into a crack I dug out of the dirt with my ice hammer. I backed up the nut with an extra seven-millimeter cord looped around a rock horn.

I went back up and retrieved my second pack, rappelled to my new anchor, pulled the ropes down though all the loose rock, stripped and coiled more fixed rope, and rappelled to the next anchor that I was able to reach. All this extra work took a long time. The sun had come around, warming everything. Fortunately, it was overcast, which made it cooler, but the clouds were starting to burn off. I needed to hurry. By this time, Graham and Scott had finished carrying all the other loads down onto the glacier.

Graham came back up to help me and took one of my packs. The hour it took for both of us to strip and carry the remaining fixed rope down the lower part of the couloir that was most exposed to rockfall seemed like it took forever.

I was pretty upset by the time I got to the glacier. Getting a late start, placing rappel anchors for me that were too far apart, underestimating the time it took to remove and carry down the fixed rope, and descending a melted-out, rockfall-prone couloir in the sun made the entire job more dangerous than it needed to be. I didn't want to say, *I told you,* so I said, "All this rushing around the last couple of days seems to be the cause of some bad decision making—and for what? Fortunately no one got hurt. You guys have a lot of years of climbing left, and the odds are against you if you keep doing things like that."

Scott was apologetic over the rappel anchor that was too far from the previous one. Graham, who by his nature wants everyone to love each other all the time, tried to smooth things over. "I think we're all tired and hungry," he said. "We'll feel better when we get back to base camp and get some food and rest." My feelings didn't have anything to do with food and rest, I told them. I thought it was a dumb move, but after expressing that, I let it go. I could relax knowing this mistake was an anomaly. With just this one problem, the three of us had completed a spectacular first ascent of Changi Tower.

We carried and dragged everything from the base of the couloir to Cache Camp, where I suggested that, since it was late, we were tired, and the snow conditions would likely be poor, we should take light packs to base camp. We could make day trips from base camp to bring all our gear down later. After what had just happened, Scott and Graham didn't disagree, and we made our way down to base camp in the sloppy snow of the melting and ever-changing glacier. We had a nice reception and celebration with Rasool, Nadeem, and Abbas. After a delicious chicken curry dinner with fresh vegetables, I fell into a deep, dreamless postclimb sleep.

The K6 phase of our expedition was about to begin, and I had a decision to make. Before the Changi Tower climb, my sinuses had begun acting up again. I'd wake up in the morning with a head full of thick yellow snot, so I started a course of amoxicillin. After my twenty-four-hour bout of diarrhea, I'd felt okay on Changi Tower, but the sinus problems persisted. I wouldn't recover from that climb as quickly as my younger partners.

Graham and Scott had been looking at a different route on K6 Central for the past couple of weeks after all three of us came to the conclusion that the south face was too dangerous. They had pieced together a new route that went to the top of K6 West (7,040 meters, or 23,097 feet) from the Nangmah valley and then traversed over to the K6 Central summit (7,100 meters, or 23,293 feet). I was afraid that racing up this route with Scott and Graham might cause a repeat of the health crisis I had on Saser Kangri II in 2011 (which resulted in my being evacuated by helicopter off the glacier). I didn't want to subject myself, my partners, or my family and friends to that again. Given my health, I didn't have the confidence in myself that I needed to attempt K6. Perhaps climbing Changi Tower was enough for me on this trip.

I woke up early, thinking that the three of us would have a discussion at breakfast about our strategy for K6. In years past I had participated in many such discussions that my partners and I had tried to keep informal with an almost hippie-like idealism—as if a more structured businesslike decision-making process would have stifled our creativity and independence. Eventually my life as a professional engineer helped me realize how critical these strategy discussions were to the team's safety and success. We could communicate in a way that established respect rather than control. Despite our need to act as individuals, working as a team was as important as any of the technical climbing skills we possessed. I spent several hours that morning thinking about how I wanted the strategy conversation to go. In the same way I would have prepared for a work meeting, I drafted a list of points I wanted to cover:

1. Acknowledge the team's success on Changi Tower, including what a big deal it was, and how well we had planned and then worked together to achieve that success.

2. Slow things down. The problems we could have had if we had descended the icefall in the dark and the dangerous way we moved everything back over the Hidden Col were consequences of getting ahead of ourselves. After climbing Changi Tower, the team would naturally experience a deep, insidious fatigue that comes from doing hard work at altitude; this fatigue would resurface partway up K6 if my young partners didn't take time to rest.

3. Tell them that I had decided not to attempt K6 Central. I didn't think I could recover quickly enough from Changi Tower. My health

wouldn't be good enough, and if they had a short weather window to make their ascent, I might slow them down enough to miss the summit.

4. Work with them on strategy and logistics for their climb of K6 Central.

The conversation that morning in the mess tent went well. I told Scott I'd only seen the kind of brilliant climbing he displayed on Changi Tower a few times in my life. When I shared my plans to stay behind on K6, Scott said, "I don't think you'd slow us down." Graham agreed. "Yeah, I think you should go with us," he said, "and we think you'd be an asset, so don't stay behind because of us." I thought they were probably sincere, but my lack of confidence made me feel they were just being polite. "I appreciate your encouragement," I said "but I don't think I'll change my mind." They had the strength and ability to do it on their own, probably more efficiently without me. I emphasized the need for them to rest for several days before starting up, and then we reviewed their proposed route photos. I made some suggestions on bivy sites and reminded them to stop if it got too hot. By lunchtime clouds rolled in bringing rain, and we spent the rest of the day in our tents eating and resting.

The next day, Graham and Scott began to prepare for their climb of K6 Central. It was hard to watch. I'd never been a base camp bystander before, and even though I knew it was the right role for me at this time, I felt some remorse. Intellectually, I knew there was so much for me to be thankful for—and I was! Not many climbers have the opportunity to get up peaks like Changi Tower, especially at my age. But dropping out of the K6 Central climb made me feel as if the slippery slope that brings life to its inevitable conclusion had just gotten steeper. However, remembering that I'm part of something bigger than myself, I felt great pleasure from being actively engaged in a team effort that involved handing this climb off to the youth brigade.

On August 15, Graham, Scott, Nadeem, and I went back up to cache camp to move all the gear that Scott and Graham would need for K6 Central to another cache on the other side of the East Nangmah Glacier. They would walk by this new K6 cache on the way to their climb later. It would save them a lot of work to have most of their food, fuel, and equipment up there rather than having to carry it all the way up from base camp. After getting to cache camp, it took a while for Graham and Scott to sort out their hardware and food before we carried it across the glacier to K6 cache. We headed back down to base camp for a lunch of rice and lentil stew, while Graham and Scott told Nadeem and me how much they appreciated the work we were doing to help them. The forecast was for better weather in a couple of days—good timing for Graham and Scott since it gave them more time to rest.

I worked with Rasool to make a satellite phone call to Hushe. We asked Ibrahim to return and help carry the remaining supplies and equipment down from cache camp with Nadeem and me while Scott and Graham climbed K6 Central. We also needed help with base camp chores because our water supply had dried up (Nadeem was carrying water from a quarter mile away). Nadeem was also working with Rasool to get things packed up to leave before our porters arrived in about ten days. Ibrahim wasn't available, but Rasool's brother-in-law Hadim Hussein was willing to come up and arrived the next day.

It was still raining the morning of August 17, and Scott was suffering from an intestinal bug similar to what I had at our advance base camp. But with every day that the weather remained inclement before the fore-casted improvement, this good weather window was shrinking. The one thing the meteorologist seemed to consistently predict was the arrival of a major storm on August 21. With the hope that Scott's gut would feel better and the weather would improve, Graham and Scott left for K6 Central at midnight.

Nadeem, Hadim, and I went up the next day to move down all the remaining supplies and equipment from cache camp. About six loads eventually needed to be brought back to base camp, and our first step was to bring it all across the glacier to K6 cache. The East Nangmah Glacier between cache camp and K6 cache was full of crevasses, so I accompanied the two Pakistanis to make sure everyone was safe. Roped together, we moved everything in two trips. Between base camp and K6 cache, there were no crevasses or other travel hazards that required climbing equipment, so once we relocated everything, Nadeem and Hadim could move everything down safely to base camp from there on their own.

At 10:00 a.m. when we first got to K6 cache, we saw Scott and Graham high on a snow face above the glacier. By 2:00 p.m., when we finished ferrying everything across from cache camp, we saw them up in a rock band above the snow face. A couple hours later, back at base camp, we saw they had erected their bivouac tent. I exchanged some texts with Scott and

Graham on the sat phone. They were camped at 19,000 feet and would start out in the morning at 2:00 a.m.

Because I was the only climber at base camp with Rasool, Nadeem, and Hadim, I ate in the kitchen with them instead of alone in the mess tent. Hanging out with them, watching them cook and interact with each other, was a new experience. It was interesting to watch Rasool's ongoing process teaching Nadeem to cook. Rasool told me later the reason Nadeem can't speak English is that his father died when he was ten, and his mother remarried a man in Hushe who wouldn't accept her children, so they had been raised by grandparents. Nadeem had to work to earn money to help support his siblings so they could go to school. His brothers and sisters learned English in school, but he never had that opportunity.

I spent Wednesday, August 19, drying the ropes and tents we'd brought down from K6 cache, packing loads, and doing calculations with Rasool to figure out that we would need twenty-seven porters to carry everything down to Kande when we left base camp on August 24. I called Sultan to have him book our flight from Skardu to Islamabad. I looked periodically in the telescope for Graham and Scott, but most of the day they were out of view, so we didn't know if they were okay. It's a lot different and quite nerve-racking to be left behind, watching and waiting. Rasool told me he spent many sleepless nights worrying and praying for us over the years when we were up on one of our climbs. Experiencing this for the first time gave me a greater appreciation for how much Rasool, Ann, and others had worried about me over the years.

Later that evening, we saw Graham and Scott emerge from behind a rock tower and climb up steep snow to the ridge crest below the summit of K6 West (7,040 meters, or 23,097 feet). They texted that night saying they were at about 21,500 feet. Because the weather forecast still called for a major storm on Friday, they were planning to only go to the K6 West summit the next day, Thursday, then back to their high camp. That would give them Friday to descend—hopefully before the storm arrived. It was too bad they didn't have a couple more days of good weather to make the technically easy traverse from K6 West to the summit of K6 Central, which remained unclimbed.

On Thursday morning I called Ann, and she told me Greg Child had sent an email reminding us that today, August 20, 2015, was the twenty-fifth anniversary of our ascent of the north ridge of K2. I called him on the satellite phone and left a message that I was thinking about what we were doing together a quarter of a century ago. Later, in Skardu, I sent emails to Phil Ershler and Greg Mortimer reminiscing about the ascent. It seemed fitting on this day for me to watch Scott and Graham reach the summit of K6 West at around 1:00 p.m. and then return to their bivy by late afternoon. I received a text from them saying they were going to rest at their high camp and start rappelling after dark when it was cooler.

When I got up Friday morning, Rasool said he had watched Graham and Scott traverse the top of the lower ice face they climbed on their first day and rappel out of sight at around 7:30 a.m. That meant they were nearly down onto the glacier. A couple hours later they texted saying they were at the K6 cache. I asked Rasool to make some grilled cheese chapatis and a liter of Tang, and have Nadeem and Hadim bring them up to Graham and Scott and then carry their packs the rest of the way back to base camp. They all arrived at base camp around 1:00 p.m., and Rasool gave wildflower bouquets to the three of us. I figured he gave one to me because I'm the expedition leader, even though I didn't climb K6 West.

Graham and Scott told me the story of their ascent as we ate soup and French fries. From their first bivy, where we had viewed them at the top of the first ice face, they traversed and climbed up a series of mixed rock and ice ledges and short vertical steps to another pure ice face they climbed to their second bivy. On their third day they plowed across and up through deep snow to the K6 West summit and then back to their bivy. They had finished the descent on their fourth day. I filled them in on our departure schedule from base camp, and they took naps in the afternoon as they hadn't had much sleep.

As predicted, that night it rained hard, then turned to snow. I imagined Graham and Scott were glad they didn't get trapped on the mountain by this big storm. We spent the next couple of days packing while trying to keep things dry in the wet weather. On Monday, August 24, several of our porters arrived while the rest spent the night in a shepherd's house in the valley. They would all be at base camp the next morning, and we would distribute loads for the walk to Kande. Graham, Scott, and I had dinner in the kitchen tent so the porters could sleep in our mess tent. We sat on the floor, which was lined with a tarp and foam sleeping pads. On our last night in the mountains together, Rasool asked for everyone's attention. After all these years, I knew how much he liked to make little speeches at times like this. When everyone had quieted down, he said, "I am so happy with this expedition. This expedition is 100 percent. Many expeditions are 90 percent, but I am so very happy—this expedition was 100 percent." I felt the same way: the camaraderie, our climbing success, and a safe trip left us feeling pretty good about what we had accomplished.

Rasool's son Fida Ali and twenty-six other porters gathered at base camp by 6:00 a.m. It was the usual chaos to pack up the tents, kitchen, and personal equipment still in use. Scott took over the process of documenting each porter's name and load as assigned by Graham and Rasool. By 9:00 a.m. the porters left base camp, and Graham, Scott, Rasool, Nadeem, Hadim, and I made one more sweep of the area to pick up any remaining bits of trash before heading down the hillside. Once we reached the valley bottom and hiked along the river for about an hour, we stopped in a large meadow for lunch. One of the porters had sprained his ankle, so Graham, who is an EMT, taped it up. Nadeem, Fida Ali, and Hadim divided the porter's load among theirs, and Scott loaned the porter his ski poles so he could limp along. The bridge we had used across the Hushe River at Kande on the hike in was washed out, so we had to walk a couple of miles upstream to a different bridge, where our jeeps met us on the other side to take us to Hushe.

Back in the guesthouse we sat in the dining hall eating lunch. An old man brought in a small boy—maybe seven or eight years old—with an injured left arm that was bandaged from mid-forearm to above his elbow. The part of his hand that was visible below the bandage was swollen and blue. Above the elbow his arm was twisted at an odd angle, indicating his humerus was broken. The man, who looked to be the boy's grandfather, told us he had fallen off the roof of a building. They were looking for help. Graham knew what to do. He pushed his chair around and volunteered to take a look at it. Sitting the boy on a chair facing him, Graham bent over so they were at eye level with each other. He very gently took off the dirty bandage so he could examine the arm. The boy looked frightened and must have been in considerable pain. The slight jostling to remove the bandage must have made it hurt even more, but the boy sat upright without a whimper.

Graham pointed back and forth between his and the boy's eyes. He asked the headmaster of one of the local schools who happened to be in the dining hall to ask the boy to look at him instead of getting more agitated by looking at his own arm. Graham asked the grandfather and the headmaster to tell the boy how brave he was. He asked the headmaster to translate a story about how Graham had broken his arm when he was a boy. Scott ran and got our first-aid kit, and Graham got the boy's arm splinted up, wrapped, and into a sling. The bone needed to be set, so they told the grandfather to bring the boy back in the morning and we would take him with us to the hospital in Skardu.

After witnessing their spontaneous desire to help, I guessed that for Graham and Scott, coming to the aid of a small, frightened boy who had just broken his arm was as much a part of the experience as climbing Changi Tower or K6 West. As they had for me, the mountains had drawn Graham and Scott here, but the people would be an increasingly stronger force to bring them back.

SOURCES

Ali, Tariq. *The Duel: Pakistan on the Flight Path of American Power.* New York: Scribner, 2008.

Coll, Steven. *Ghost Wars: The Secret History of the CIA, Afghanistan, and Bin Laden, from the Soviet Invasion to September 10, 2001.* New York: Penguin Books 2005.

Davis, Wade. *Into the Silence: The Great War, Mallory, and the Conquest of Everest.* New York: Vintage Books, 2011.

French, Patrick. *Liberty or Death: India's Journey to Independence and Division.* New York: Penguin, 2011.

Gall, Carlotta. *The Wrong Enemy: America in Afghanistan, 2001–2014.* Boston: Houghton Mifflin, 2014.

Gul, Imtiaz. *The Most Dangerous Place: Pakistan's Lawless Frontier.* New York: Viking, 2010.

Haqqani, Husain. *Magnificent Delusions: Pakistan, the United States, and an Epic History of Misunderstanding.* New York: Public Affairs Publishing, 2013.

Hopkirk, Peter. *The Great Game: On Secret Service in High Asia.* New York: Kodansha International, 1992.

Jones, Owen Bennett. *Pakistan: Eye of the Storm*, 3rd edition. New Haven, CT: Yale University Press, 2009.

McDonald, Myra. *Heights of Madness: One Woman's Journey in Pursuit of a Secret War.* New Dehli: Rupa & Company, 2007.

Neale, Jonathan. *Tigers of the Snow: How One Fateful Climb Made the Sherpas Mountaineering Legends* New York: Thomas Dunne Books, 2002.

Peer, Basharat. *Curfewed Night: One Kashmiri Journalist's Frontline Account of Life, Love, and War in His Homeland.* New York: Scribner, 2010.

Rashid, Ahmed. *Descent into Chaos: The United States and the Failure of Nation Building in Pakistan, Afghanistan, and Central Asia.* New York: Viking, 2008.

———. *Pakistan on the Brink: The Future of America Pakistan and Afghanistan.* New York: Penguin, 2012.

Riedel, Bruce. *Deadly Embrace: Pakistan, America, and the Future of the Global Jihad.* Washington, DC: Brookings Institution Press, 2011.

Schaffer, Howard B. *The Limits of Influence: America's Role in Kashmir.* New York: Viking, 2009.

Shipton, Eric. *Blank on the Map.* London: Hodder and Stoughton, 1938.

Weaver, Mary Anne. *Pakistan: Deep Inside the World's Most Frightening State.* New York: Farrar, Straus and Giroux, 2010.

Wirsing, Robert G. *India, Pakistan, and the Kashmir Dispute.* New York: St. Martin's Press, 1994.

ACKNOWLEDGMENTS

While writing this book and engaging in these adventures, I've leaned on many people. So many, in fact, that it would be impossible for me to acknowledge everyone individually. If I forgot to include you in these acknowledgments, my apologies.

I owe my wife, Ann, and sons, Lars and Jed, my deepest gratitude for their love and support. They are the light of my life. I'm grateful for my siblings, Paul, Mary, Joe, and Anne Marie who are always there for me and for each other. I was fortunate to have parents, Howard and Pat, who instilled in their children a strong sense of community and the belief that the small contributions we make as individuals add up to something much bigger than ourselves. Trying to emulate those values has made these climbing experiences all the richer.

This book would not have been possible without the support and encouragement of Mountaineers Books and editor in chief, Kate Rogers. Mountaineers Books is one of the very few publishers willing to entertain book ideas in this genre and by a first-time author like me. Without them, many stories about our beautiful planet and our relationship with it would never be heard. I also owe tremendous gratitude to the editorial skills of Mary Metz, Giselle Smith, Ellen Wheat, and Amy Smith Bell. This book was definitely a team effort!

I want to thank the Mountain and Wilderness Writing program at the Banff Center and its faculty, Tony Whittome and Marni Jackson. Participating in this program as a new author in 2010 helped me establish a solid foundation for this project and ongoing opportunities and encouragement. Katie Ives at *Alpinist* magazine has a great capacity to dive in with enthusiasm and help climbing authors tell their stories. What I learned from her was of great help to me in writing this book. David Roberts, acclaimed adventure writer, read some of my early work, and with his usual honesty told me why it was a mess. I took his opinion to heart and, I hope, improved my writing as a result. Thanks to Ann Dalton, Bernadette McDonald, Chris Potts, Craig McKibben, Doug Chabot, Graham Zimmerman, Mark Richey, Steve House, and Tom Hornbein for their encouragement and for commenting on earlier versions or parts of this book.

Thanks to Cory Richards, Doug Chabot, Freddie Wilkinson, Mark Richey, Marko Prezelj, and Scott Bennett for their photo contributions.

Greg Child deserves his own paragraph of thanks as he not only read and commented on earlier drafts, he also provided photos and wrote the foreword to this book.

During my career as a civil engineer, I had more than my share of time away from the office. I especially want to thank Alan Bushley, Franchot Fenske, John Buckley, and Russ Stepp at R.W. Beck for supporting both my engineering and "climbing" careers; without your understanding none of the adventures in this book would have been possible. I'd also like to thank my many colleagues who kept our business and projects running during my extended absences.

I continue to have an ever greater appreciation for the friendships and the partnerships of those with whom I've gone to the mountains and crags, and with whom I've run and trained with over the years. I've enjoyed the company of so many wonderful people, in so many fascinating places, that I can't possibly name everyone here. Please know that I'm incredibly grateful to each of you for being part of my community.

On the expeditions detailed throughout this book, our local help in China, India, Nepal, and Pakistan was critical to any success we had. To Rasool and the others that I mentioned in the book—and those I did not—please accept my sincere appreciation for all your work and dedication not only in helping us achieve our climbing objectives but also for contributing to our safety and well-being.

Finally I owe a special debt of gratitude to Mark and Teresa Richey, Freddie Wilkinson, Chewang Motup, Brownie Schoene, Thinlese, Dhan Singh, Pemba, Tashi and the pilots of the Indian Air Force 114th Helicopter Unit in Leh for the rescue efforts that saved my life in the Eastern Karakoram in 2011.

INDEX

Abruzzi Ridge, **22**, 80–81, 83

Abruzzi Glacier, **22**, 38, **142**, 147

Actual Ground Position Line (AGPL), 13, 14, **17**, 78, 147, 155–56, 231, 236, 247, 293

Acute Mountain Sickness (AMS), 43

Afghan Taliban, 151, 156, 160, 161, 176–77, 201–02

Aghil Pass, **16**, **22**, 64–65, 74, 83, 91, 109

Ali Khan, 207, 208, 210, 216, 218, 220, 224–25, 227

Alpine Club of Pakistan (ACP), 218, 228, 276

al-Qaeda, 156, 176, 201–02, 229, 266, 271

Ang Tashi, 237, 242, 244

Anwar, 89, 92, 94–95, 103, 107–08

Askole, **16**, **22**, 35–36, 50, 77, 146, **206**, 207, 218, 227

Austrian Col, **170**, 273, 275, 282–83

Baintha Lukpar Glacier, 205, **206**, 207, 216

Balti, 9, **18**, 29, 31, 33, 35, 37, 44, 45, 50, **110**, 115, 150–51, 160–61, 168, 220

Baltistan, **16**, 62, 152, 156–57, 160, 175, 202–03, 253, 266, 269, 278–79

Baltoro Glacier, **16**, 20, **22**, 36–38, 44, 65, 77–78, 146–47, 150, 206

Bennett, Scott, 274–75, 277, 279–87, 289–91, 293–307

Bhutto, Benazir, 145, 229

Biafo Glacier, **16**, 205, **206**, 227

Bibler, Todd, 20, 24–25, 38, 40–41

Blanchard, Barry, 123–28

Bowman, Tom, 49, 51–53, 55–56

Braldu River, **16**, 30, 33, 43–44, 50, 77, 146, **206**, 219

Breashears, David, 122–28

Broad Peak, 14, **17**, 19, **22**, 37, 49, 52, 55, 80, 247

Buhler, Carlos, 49, 51–55

Chabot, Doug, **154**, 159, 161–66, 169, 173–74, 179, 181–82, 185–96, 198, **200**, 204–05, 207–25, 265, 277, 309–10

Changi Tower, 8, **170**, **270**, 273–75, 280, 284, 286–91, 293, 300–02, 307

Changui Tower, **170** 273–74, 290

Charakusa valley, 8, 158, 162, 164, 168, **170**, 180, 195, 203, 205, 273, 277

Cheesmond, Dave, 61–63, 66–69, 71, 73–75, 80, 84, 106, 122

Child, Greg, 7, 10, 55, 57–60, 75–77, 80, **82**, 83, 86–87, 90–91, 93, 95–96, 98–103, 106–109, 116, 304, 310

Chinese Mountaineering Association (CMA), 62–63, 84–87, 89, 94–95, 97, 124

Chogolisa, **22**, 149, 165, 172, 247

Choktoi Glacier, **206**, 217, 220, 226

Choktoi Spire, 8, **206**, 226

Chomolonzo, 125–26

Closs, Lyle, 86, 89, 94, 96–100, 102–103, 107–08

Concordia, **18**, 20, **22**, 37–38, 44, 97, 147

Cronn, Gregg, 61–63, 66–71, 73

Dalton, Ann, 5, 58–59, 61, 69, 80, 85–86, 106, 111, 123, 143–44, 152, 157, 160, 167, 176, 202–04, 208, 234, 245, 262, 279, 304, 309, 317

Dalton, John (Jed), 111, 143–44, 157, 167, 202–04, 208, 245, 279, 309, 317

DeKlerk, Andy, 145, 147–48, 150

Deosai Plain **16**, **178**, 182, **184**

Dhan Singh Harkotia, 237, 244, 248, 250, 254, 262, 310

Diamir valley, 181, 183, **184**, 186–87, 198, 265, 268

Dickey, Tom, 112, 116–17

Drinkwater, Emilie, 246–47, 249, 252, 254

Dumordu River, 43, **206**, 219
East Nangmah Glacier, **170**, 273–74, 282–83, 288, 292, 298, 299, 302–03
East Rongbuk Glacier, 130, 140
Eric Shipton, 63, 65, 83, 109, 308
Ershler, Phil, 76, 80, 83, 86–87, 90–92, 94–103, 105, 107–08, 196, 305
Federally Administered Tribal Areas (FATA), 177, 228, 269
Fida Ali, 119, 148, 150–51, 160, 203, 280–81, 292, 306
Fida Hussein, 87, 89, 95, 100, 103, 107–08, 175, 182–84, 186, 194, 196
Fowler, Charlie, 112, 116–17
Fredrickson, Don, 20, 23–25, 33, 40–41
Freer, Catherine, 61–62, 66–69, 71–75, 80, 84, 88, 106
Gasherbrum I, 14, **17**, 19, **22**, 37–38, 84, 109, 116, 148, 165, 172
Gasherbrum II, 14, **17**, **22**, 37–38, 44, 97, 147–48, 172
Gasherbrum III, **22**, 37–38, 40–41
Gasherbrum IV, 7, **17**, 14, 19–21, **22,** 26, 30, 36–43, **46**, 49–55, 57, 59–60, 75, 77, 97, 111–13, 116, 118, 145, 147–49, 158, 160, 172, 217, 219
Gilgit, **16**, 29, 62, 152, 157, 266, 268–69, 278
Great Game, 62, 308
Gunn, Carolyn, 77, 86
HACE, 38, 43, 70, 132, 241, 253
HAPE, 38, 43, 55, 72, 97, 100, 132, 137–38, 140, 189, 241
Hidden Col, **170**, 282–85, 287–88, 290, 292, 298, 301
Hill, Sandy, 121–29
Hollenbaugh, Jeff, 159, 161–62, 164, 166, 168–69, 171–73, 175, 179–80, 182
House, Steve, 144–45, 147–50, 158–69, 173–75, 179–83, 185–86, 191–98, 205, 265, 309
Hunza, **16**, 29, 218, 266–67

Hushe, **17, 22**, 29, 34, 113–14, 118, 146, 148, 150–51, 158, 160–61, 168, **170**, 174–75, 185, 203, 266, 277–79, 281, 287–88, 292, 303–04, 306
Indian Mountaineering Foundation (IMF), 232–34, 237, 246, 248
Indus River, **16**, 25, 28, 180, 235, 279
Inter-Services Intelligence (ISI), 21, 56, 112, 156, 176
Jangla Tashi Phunchok, 248, 250–51, 254, 260–62, 310
K2, 4, **7**, 9–10, 13–14, **16**, 19, **22**, 29, 32–33, 37, 48, 59–67, 69, 74–77, 79–81, **82**, 83–99, 101–03, 105–09, 111–12, 145, 165, 172, 175, 180, 196, 217, 219, 238, 247, 258, 280, 291, 304
K6 Central, 8, **170**, 272–75, 282, 284, 286–87, 289–91, 298, 300–04
K6 Main, **17**, **170**, 272–73, 282
K6 West, 162, **170**, 272–73, 301, 304–05, 307
K7 Main, **17**, 159, 162, 167–69, **170**, 173, 179, 182
K7 West, 8, 169, **170,** 171–74
Kaji, 125–26
Kande, **170**, 279–81, 283, 304–06
Kangshung Face, 7, 48, 59, 61–62, 67, **120**, 121–22, 124, 128, 133, 135
Kapadia, Harish, 232, 238
Kapura Peak, 8, **154**, 162, 164, 166–67, **170**
Karachi, 272, 278
Karakoram Highway (KKH), 86–87, 112, 146, 151, 183, **184**, 202, 204, 225, 228, 276
Kardung La, **17**, 232, 235–37, **240**, 248
Kargil, **17**, 146
Kashgar, **16**, 62–63, 89
Kashmir valley, 112, 236, 249
Kennedy, Michael, 49–50, 52–53, 55, 217
Kerns, Matt, 20, 24–25, 29, 33, 38, 40–41, 43–44, 49, 51–56
Khaplu, **17**, 174–75, 227–28, 279, 292

Khyber Pakhtunkhwa (KPK), 13, 151, 176–77, 225, 228–29, 269

Kinshofer Route, 181, **184**, 188, 265

Konchok Thinlese, 237, 242–43, 248, 250, 253–54, 260, 262. 310

Kondus valley, 8, 155, 158, 160, 227–28

Kondus Glacier, **170**, 293

Kremer, Kirsten, 246–47, 249, 252, 254

Kuestler, Peter, 86, 89–94, 96–100, 102–03, 107–08

Kunlun Mountains, 63, 90

Lachit Glacier, **170**, 273–75, 282–83, 285–86, 290, 293, 295

Ladakh, 231, 233, 235–36, 261

Lakpa Boding, 237, 242, 244

Latok I, 8, **16**, 50, 204–05, **206**, 209, 217–18, 220, 223, 225

Latok II, 8, **200**, **206**, 208–11, 213, 216–18

Latok III, 205, **206**, 207, 209

Lee, Gary, 49–53, 55

Leh, **17**, 235–36, 247–48, 260–62, 310

Lewis, Jack, 49, 51–53, 55–56

Line of Control (LOC), 13, 14, **17**, 21, 25, 77, 112, 146, 156, 231, 235–36

Louther, Jim, 233–35, 237–38, 241–45

Lowe, Alex, 66–73, 75, 83, 96, 105, 111–12, 115–18, **120**, 121–22, 124–29, 146–47, 152–53, 159, 185

Lowe, George, 61–62, 66–73, 100, 112, 122, 217

Macartney-Snape, Tim, 77, 80

Mace, Charlie, 145, 147–48, 150

Manzoor Hussein, Col., 218, 228, 276–77

Masherbrum, **16**, **22**, 37, **46**, 84, 113, 158, 165, 172, 185, 247, 279

Mazeno Ridge, 8, 181–82, **184**, 186–88, 194–95, 198–99, 204, 209, 214

McKibben, Craig, 20, 23–26, 28, 33, 40–43, 49, 309

Miller, Bruce, 159–64, 166–69, 173–74, 179–84, 186, 193–98, 265, 312

Mortimer, Greg, 86, 89–91, 94, 96–102, 106–109, 305

Motup, Chewang, 233, 235–39, 243, 248, 260, 262, 310

Mount Everest, 7, 13, 38, 48–49, 59–62, 66–67, 75–77, 86, **120**, 121–31, 133–35, 137–41, 143–44, 159, 237, 275, 308

Muhammad Taki, 33, 43–44, 49

Mujahideen, 28, 56–57, 112

Mustagh Tower, **22**, 37

Nadeem, 277–78, 280–85, 287, 290, 300, 302–06

Nanga Parbat, 8, 13, 14, **16**, 28, 73, 168, 173–77, **178**, 179–183, **184**, 185, 191, 194–95, 197–99, 204, **264**, 265–69

Nangmah valley, 8, **170**, 273–74, 279–80, 283, 301

Nawang Chuchuk, 125, 127

Nayser Brakk, 8, **154**, 162, 164, **170**

Nazir Sabir, 29, 160, 217–18, 273, 275–77

Nelson, Jim, **18**, 20, 24–25, 33, 38, 40–41, 43–45, 49

NJ9842, **17**, 77

Nubra valley, **17**, 233, 235–38, **240**, 241, 248–49, 252–54, 259

Ogre, **16**, 76, **206**, 226

Operation Meghdoot, 77, 248

Owens, Lance, 59, 62–63, 66–69, 71, 73, 84, 88, 106

Paiyu, **22**, 29, 36–37, 146–47, 152

Pakistan Taliban, 176–77, 228, 268, 272

Pashtun, 13, 157, 159, 183, 201, 204, 228, 268–69, 276

Peak 6880, 80

Pemba Sherpa (aka King Kong), 248, 250, 254, 261–62, 310

Perry, Mike, 130, 136, 139–40

Peshawar, 51, 55–56, 272

Pinzo, 125–26

Polish Col, **170**, **270**, 286, 288–89, 293, 297

Prezelj, Marko, 159, 161–64, 166–69, 171–73, 179–80, 310

Quinn, Choc, 66–69, 71, 73

Rakhiot Glacier, 181, **184**

Rasool, 79, 87, 89, 93–95, 100, 103, 107–08, 112–15, 117–19, 144–48, 150–52, 158, 160–61, 167–68, 174–76, 182–83, 202–04, 207–08, 210, 216, 218–20, 224–25, 271, 277–83, 287–88, 290–92, 300, 303–06

Red Mosque, 225, 228

Rheinberger, Mike, 130–33, 136–41

Richey, Mark, 204–05, 207–12, 214–228, 234, 238, 241–52, 254–60, 262, 277, 294, 309, 310

Rupal valley, 181–83, **184**, 185–88, 265–66

Sakang Glacier, 239, **240,** 241

Sakang Lungpa River, 239, **240**

Saltoro Ridge, 78, 293

Saltoro Kangri, **17**

Sarpo Laggo Glacier, **22**, 92

Sarwar, 89–92, 94–95, 103, 107–08, 276

Saser Kangri II, 8, 231–33, 238–39, **240**, 242–48, 250–55, 258, 262, 294, 301

Schell Route, 181–82, **184**, 188, 189–91, 193–94, 199

Schertz, Charlie, **18**, 20, 24–25, 28, 31, 33, 38, 40, 43–44

Schoene, Brownie, 253, 259, 261, 310

Scott, Doug, 75–77, 79–80, 182

Scott, Michael, 76–77, 80

Shaksgam River, **16**, **22**, 60, 64–65, 87–89, 91–93, 238

Sharif, Nawaz, 145, 151, 272

Sher Khan, 265–67

Sherpas, 31, 59, 67, 76, 97–98, 122–23, 125–31, 137, 141, 159, 233, 237, 241, 308

Shyok River, **17**, 238, **240**, 253, 261

Siachen Glacier, **17**, **22**, 77–78, 146, 227, 235, 237, 239, 248, 263, 293

Simonson, Eric, 128–33, 135–36, 138–41

Skardu, **16**, 25–26, 28–30, 32–33, 44, 50, 55, 112–14, 118–19, 146, 160–61, 168, 174, 179–80, 182, 185, 202–04, **206**, 207, 218–19, 225, 227, 235, 271, 276–79, 291–92, 304–05, 307

Skyang Kangri, **22**, 80

Slawinski, Raphael, 273

South Charakusa Glacier, 164, **170**

South Gasherbrum Glacier, 38–39, 97, 116, 147–48

South Shukpa Kunchang Glacier, 238–39, **240**, 241–42, 244, 250–51, 255

Srinagar, 236–37, 249

Staehli, Dave, 131–32, 137–38

Stump, Mugs, 50, 52–53, 55, 275

Sughet Jangal, **22**, 65–66, 69, 71, 73–74, 94, 97–98, 108

Suruquat River, 64, 91

Swenson, Lars, 10, 48–49, 53, 57–59, 61, 69, 77, 106, 111, 143–44, 157, 162, 167, 279, 309

Taliban, 151, 156, 160, 161, 176–77, 201–02, 228, 266, 268, 272

Teherik-i-Taliban (TTP), 228–29, 268, 272

Tensing, 125–26

Tigr, **17**, 236–37, 239, **240**, 248, 254

Trango Tower, **22**, 37, 146, 152

Tshering Sherpa, 237, 242, 244, 248, 250, 254, 262

Tsok Kangri, **230**, **240**, 252

Uli Biaho Tower, **22**, 37

Urumchi, 62, 85, 89

Van Steen, Alex, 131–32, 136

Welsted, Ian, 273

Werner, Margaret, 86, 89, 94, 96, 98, 103, 107–08

West Gasherbrum Glacier, 51

West Nangmah Glacier, **170**, 282

Whetu, Mark, 130, 132, 137–40

Wilford, Mark, 232–34, 239, 241–45

Wilkinson, Freddie, **230**, 246–47, 250–251, 254, 256–62, 294, 310

Wilkinson, Janet B., 246, 249, 252, 254
Xinjiang, **16**, 62, 83, 85, 87–89
Yarkand River, 64, 92
Yecheng, 63, 90
Ying, Mr., 62, 84
Younghusband, Sir Francis, 65, 83
Zakat, 161, 292

Zhang Jingchuan, 267
Zia, General Muhammad Zia-ul-Haq,
    55–56, 145
Zimmerman, Graham, **270**, 274–75,
    277, 279–87, 289–91, 293–307, 309
Zug Shaksgam River, 64

ABOUT THE AUTHOR

Steve Swenson and has been climbing for almost half a century. With nearly twenty expeditions to mountains in South Asia, Steve has made ascents of the North Ridge of K2 and a solo ascent of the North Ridge of Everest—both without supplementary oxygen. He and his teammates were awarded the prestigious Piolet d'Or for their first ascent of Saser Kangri II (7,518 meters) in 2012; it was the second-highest unclimbed mountain in the world at the time. Before his recent retirement, Steve worked for thirty-five years as a consultant to municipalities and counties on engineering, design, project management, utility finance, and policy-making projects related to water and sanitation. A past president of the American Alpine Club, Steve has written articles for *Climbing*, *Rock and Ice*, and *Alpinist* magazines as well as the *American Alpine Journal*; he also contributed to *Rock, Paper, Fire*, an anthology of mountain and wilderness writing. Steve, who has two grown sons, Lars and Jed, lives with his wife, Ann Dalton, in Seattle. He is donating his royalties from *Karakoram* to The Mountaineers. For more about *Karakoram*, see www.karakorambook.com.

OTHER TITLES YOU MIGHT ENJOY FROM MOUNTAINEERS BOOKS

The Bond: Survival on Denali and Mount Huntington
by Simon McCartney

"The account of this perilous escape [on Denali] is one of the supreme endurance epics in mountain literature. *The Bond* is the outright classic of mountaineering literature. Nothing else I've read within the genre comes close to its outstanding quality."—Jim Perrin

Sherpa: The Memoir of Ang Tharkay
by Ang Tharkay with Basil Norton

The leading Sherpa of his time, Ang Tharkay was "a sort of Jeeves, Admirable Crichton, and Napoleon rolled into one" according to his traveling companion Bill Tilman.

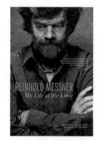

Reinhold Messner: My Life at the Limit
Interviewed by Thomas Hüetlin

A compelling autobiography by the man who made the first solo ascent of Everest, a feat about which Conrad Anker said, "It was like landing on the moon. After that, everything else sort of pales in comparison."

Over the Edge: The True Story of the Kidnap and Escape of Four Climbers in Central Asia
by Greg Child

"The gripping drama of four young American climbers taken hostage in Krygyzstan . . . an amazing story, amazingly told, by one of the best adventure writers of our time."—David Roberts

My Old Man and the Mountain: A Memoir
by Leif Whittaker

"Whittaker writes much as he climbs mountains, with courage, grace, and a dash of humility. It's a great read."
—Daniel James Brown

Everest: The West Ridge
by Tom Hornbein

"Not only did Hornbein play a crucial role in one of the most extraordinary accomplishments in the history of mountaineering, his account of the feat is one of the finest things ever written about this peculiar, hazardous, and uncommonly engaging pursuit."—Jon Krakauer

www.mountaineersbooks.org